Lessons in Cultural Change: The Utility Industry Experience

Edited by
Philip R. Theibert

1994
Public Utilities Reports, Inc.
Arlington, Virginia

First Printing, September 1994
Library of Congress Catalog Card No. 94-68220
ISBN 0-910325-52-9

Printed in the United States of America

Table of Contents

Part Six:
Strategic Approaches to Cultural Change

Part Seven:
Outside Views

Preface

If there is a truism in life, it is this: It is difficult for people to change. Even when a change would improve their health, people cling to old habits. Consider this simple statistic: Ninety-five percent of the millions of Americans who diet each year regain almost all of the pounds they lose.

People's unwillingness to permanently change, even when their health is threatened, has frightening implications for corporations in general and the utility industry in particular. This resistance to change, even when one's life is at stake, proves how difficult it is to convince employees to change work habits and attitudes so that a corporation can compete in a rapidly evolving utility industry.

The challenge to introduce Cultural Change to an organization involves a complex equation influenced by many factors. Your corporation must have the right company structure, the right training programs, visionary leaders, the right compensation system to support the new corporate culture, a strong communication program (so workers, "get the message"), and the right strategic plans to ensure your company is looking at the proper market mix.

The list of factors a company must consider when instituting a cultural change seems endless. And every step in the equation must be done right if you want employees to change their work habits, their way of thinking, and their approach to your industry.

If even one item in the equation does not adequately support the new corporate culture, a company can waste literally millions of dollars and still be stuck with unmotivated workers, who refuse to accept the reality of competition and the desperate need for a new company culture—a company culture that will position their utility for the future.

The challenge of change notwithstanding, installing a new company culture can be done successfully. And the best way to ensure success is to learn from the pros who have been on the firing line, who have made mistakes, recovered, and gone on to successfully anchor company cultures in their organizations.

This book makes no attempt to be esoteric. Rather it presents the experts in the areas that most affect cultural change, ranging from corporate vision to strategic planning to compensation to communication. Again, these experts were chosen because they have "war stories" to tell, because their experience can put you that much further up the learning curve.

Listen to them. They know what they are talking about.

Having said that, let me offer my heart-felt thanks to every author who contributed a chapter to this book. All of them lead packed lives that range from running billion-dollar utilities to operating nationally-respected consulting firms.

I am extremely gratified that they found time to write these chapters. I am sure many chapters were written at home, way past midnight . . . But once again, I thank every author who contributed, knowing full well the time and effort they spent to make this book such a fine collection of writings.

I also thank Susan Johnson of Public Utilities Reports, Inc., who has supported this book every step. It started with a simple phone call, but her enthusiasm and strong work ethic ensured the publication of this work. Needless to say, Susan does not work alone, and a further debt of gratitude is owed to the project manager, Katie Jay, and to all of the other PUR staff members who helped this book come to life.

Finally, but most importantly, I would not have been able to complete this project without the support, encouragement, and understanding of my wife, Kathleen, and my two children, Claire and Tebby, who continually help me keep things in perspective.

Philip R. Theibert

Part One:
CEO's Overview of Cultural Change

Chapter One

The APS Story: When Culture and Vision Make Magic

Mark DeMichele

When I think of utility culture change, and the culture change strategy in which Arizona Public Service has immersed itself over the past few years, several adjectives come to mind— exciting, exhilarating, productive and painful. But the process is best described by one simple word— necessary.

Our company recognized early that we needed to change our culture to succeed in a faster-paced, more competitive environment. So we have made tremendous investments, both in time and resources, to unleash a new vision, launch a new strategic plan and create the kind of high performing culture needed to transform our company and recreate our future.

After three years, we're beginning to see significant change. But it has not been easy, and we are far from finished. Because there are no quick fixes. It took many decades to shape our old culture, and it can't be reshaped overnight.

In light of our experiences, there are two learnings I want to share with utilities. The first is that culture change is a continuing process, which requires significant commitment—starting at the top of an organization. The second goes more toward the process of culture change. I believe that utilities that set out simply to "change" their old cultures will fail. To succeed with culture change, utilities must have the courage to break from the past and create something entirely new. For lasting culture change—the kind of change that will redefine and re-energize your company—you must start with a clean sheet of paper. And once you create your new culture, you can't just stop. You must anchor the culture within your organization.

Finally, I believe utilities must find the courage to create both a bold new vision and the high-performing culture needed to achieve such a vision. As Robert Dilenschneider, author of the book, *A Briefing for Leaders*, writes: "When culture and vision are well matched magic can happen." It's happened at APS, and we have many lessons to share.

Lesson 1: Begin with a Clean Sheet of Paper

APS didn't just set out to change its corporate culture. Our culture change began as part of a much larger goal—to create an entirely new company; the utility of the year 2000. To do that, we needed to put history behind us and focus on the future.

The process began in 1990, but the stage was set even earlier. For years, our rates had been spiraling upward, while we built the nation's largest nuclear power plant. By 1988—the year I became CEO—our rates were among the highest in the nation, and our relations with key publics were among the worst. At the same time, we were beginning to see new market threats and opportunities. But we were far from ready to compete.

One of the first things I did as CEO was promise a belt-tightening like no one had ever seen. I was going to make APS more efficient, more productive and more competitive. And I went about doing that by wielding the proverbial ax. Needless to say, it didn't work.

Why? Because we cut costs—a.k.a. downsized—in the traditional way. We weren't particularly strategic. Following a layoff in 1988, which removed 1,200 positions, we offered an early retirement in 1989. We had fewer employees, but they were doing the same jobs, in the same ways, and facing the same roadblocks.

Employees still didn't understand, on a gut level, how intense competition would become. They weren't positioned or organized to compete. And perhaps, most significant, they weren't particularly inspired. And who can blame them? Those remaining after the layoffs were being asked to do more with less—and getting little in return. They questioned our management—and our proclamations of change.

Moreover, conditions at APS were continuing to deteriorate. Our three nuclear plants were not operating because of equipment and management problems. We were in the throes of a unionization attempt affecting about one-third of our workforce. Our holding company's stock, which a year earlier had sold for $32 dollars and paid an annual dividend of $2.72 per share, was now trading at $5 dollars—one third of book value. And our parent company, Pinnacle West, was suffering from a $1.2 billion loss from a failed diversification effort.

One would think that we'd seen the worst. We hadn't. In 1989, we were hit with a hostile takeover—offering $21 a share, plus proposing future rate levels 60 percent lower than a rate request we had pending.

At the time, many people thought that the takeover attempt was the final nail in our coffin. In reality, our future had just begun. Instead of an ending, that takeover attempt marked a whole new beginning. Instead of dying, we were reborn.

In 1990, we took a different approach. Instead of reworking APS from old models, we started with a clean sheet of paper. Employee teams—working with consultants—took a look at everything we did, how we did it, and who was most qualified to do it.

It took the teams more than a year. Meanwhile, I spent almost six months traveling to every corner of our company—meeting with employees and presenting a case for action. I explained why we had to change, what we were doing, and how employees would be treated if their jobs were eliminated.

When that was done, we rewrote job descriptions for every position, and then declared every position vacant, including mine. Everyone had to reapply for their job, and we hired only the best people to fill those positions. If that meant going outside our industry, so be it. As a result, 1,150 additional positions were eliminated.

By the end of 1990, we had eliminated more than 30 percent of our non-nuclear work force, and reduced annual payroll costs by $100 million. But far more important than what we cut was how we cut. APS had always looked for order takers— people who could do the job. When we restaffed, we looked for doers, but we also looked for dreamers—people who would take risks and try new things. We also changed the organizational structure so people would begin relating in entirely new ways. We moved people so that people could start moving. We broke down bureaucratic barriers. In the end, very little of the old APS remained. We were not only leaner, we were more efficient. By destroying the past, we'd made room for the future. And we weren't about to turn back.

Lesson 2: Create a New Vision

Having broken our ties to the old APS, our company was at a critical juncture. Without the comfort and security of our past, many employees felt lost and alone. We needed a new vision—one that would turn employee despair about the future into hope. We needed a vision to do more than guide our company. We needed to inspire our team.

What makes a vision inspiring? *Fortune* magazine said it best: A challenge so big or audacious that it can seem scary even to the person who conceived it. Our new vision clearly fit that description.

In 1991, APS launched our vision of being one of the Top 5 investor owned utilities in the country. Given the situation I just described, you can imagine the reaction—people laughed. They thought it was a joke. My officers didn't even support it. But I persisted. And it began to take hold.

Many people ask if we could have launched our new vision without having destroyed the old APS. They ask whether we could have spared employees from the agony of having to reapply for their jobs. I don't believe we could have.

In times of crisis, people have a tendency to revert to what has always worked—to retreat to and glorify the past. But in the 1990s, one thing had become clear: the old ways no longer worked. What once made us big—the ways that APS had always gotten things done— no longer made sense. It was time to think in entirely new terms.

So in 1991, we took a basic step back to a strategic planning model, which was founded on the principle that you must decide where you want to be, then build a plan to get there. As Yogi Berra said, "If you don't know where you are going, you will wind up somewhere else."

The first stage of planning was already done. We had a vision of where we wanted to be, and we'd begun to identify the gaps between where we were and where we headed. Now we needed to attack those gaps—beginning with the old APS culture.

Lesson 3: Replace the Old Order

Like most utilities, the old APS had a rate driven, cost plus mentality. Employees didn't understand competition because they'd never really had to compete. Moreover, many had chosen utility careers for precisely that reason—instead of seeking the thrill of competition, employees sought the comfort of regulation.

Employees weren't the ones to create this culture. In a highly regulated environment, control was key. For years, utilities hired order takers instead of risk takers. We rewarded stability instead of ability. But with our new vision, control had become a limitation. The same qualities that built the old APS could easily destroy the new.

Realizing that undoing years of conditioning would not be easy, APS launched a major intervention training program, called FOCUS—a five day session for managers and supervisors, and a three day session for all front-line employees.

Initially, many employees resisted FOCUS. For three years, they'd been through agonizing layoffs and unprecedented cost cutting. They couldn't understand how our company could afford a major training effort. Plus, we were taking employees away from their jobs for days at a time. But I was convinced that, without intervention, we'd quickly revert to the past. So we continued.

5

There's another reason that people resisted FOCUS. One of its major goals was to make employees question every assumption they held about our industry and our company. We forced employees to rethink how they viewed their jobs, their commitment to APS and their future. We wanted them to begin thinking outside the traditional utility box.

In retrospect, that effort—while uncomfortable—was probably the best thing we did. By the end of 1993, all 7,000 of our employees had completed FOCUS. Despite their reservations, FOCUS had accomplished what it set out to do. Instead of fearing a new and uncertain future, employees began flourishing on change. They were beginning to welcome the inevitable changes in our industry.

When they got permission to challenge traditions and rewrite old rules, employees began thinking in entirely new ways. They began to realize that our future wasn't written in stone; that it wasn't controlled by others, but was ours to create. And for the first time, we began seeing beyond the boundaries of regulation to the opportunities of competition.

Lesson 4: Sustain the Vision

A primary goal of FOCUS was to ensure that every employee was aware of the new APS vision, mission and goals. By the end of the program, they weren't just aware—they were inspired. What once seemed impossible had now become a driving force.

While less intensive programs may also have created buy-in for our new vision, FOCUS went beyond creating support. It gave our vision a life. Everything we did began revolving around our vision. As a result, a new, highly focused APS culture began to emerge.

In early 1992, APS began the transition from a centrally-controlled, rule-bound, procedure-based, internally-focused company—to a distributed, innovative, results oriented, flexible and customer responsive company. By aligning our vision and our culture, magic did begin to happen.

So how did we make the magic work? With our vision as our goal and our culture as our driver, we began creating and implementing a new strategic plan. We knew that employees were empowered and inspired, so we needed a plan that would ensure they moved their magic in the right direction.

Our new plan bears little, if any, resemblance to the kind of planning done by the old APS. In the past, planning was based primarily on financial and growth forecasts. We looked at how things were and adapted our plans accordingly. With a bolder vision and a changing industry, that approach could no longer work. Instead of looking at how things were and where we fit, we needed to look at how things might be, where we wanted to fit and what was needed to position us where we wanted to be.

I admit that some of our goals did appear unreachable. Initially, many people called me "impatient and unreasonable." They were right. But I believe in unreasonable goals. In the words of George Bernard Shaw, "The reasonable man adapts himself to the world. But the unreasonable man persists in trying to adapt the world to himself. Therefore, all progress depends on the unreasonable man."

Because of FOCUS, and the willingness of employees to think in new terms, our new plan—while maybe unreasonable—was no longer considered impossible. But our new culture also demanded that we do more than roll-out a new strategy. To sustain our vision, employees needed to be integrally involved in the planning process.

Today, every department has a strategic plan and mission to support the corporate strategic plan, while every employee has an individual performance plan to support their department. Employees understand APS' strategic plan because they use the exact same language in the plans they create for their departments and for themselves. I believe that has been a key element of our success. Every individual in our company is moving in the same direction. As a result, we are constantly building our momentum. We're moving faster than ever to achieve our goals.

Still, plans alone aren't enough. We wanted to ensure that employees focused not just on plans, but on results. Among our efforts, we held work-out sessions that enabled employee teams to by-pass the chain of command, and make recommendations directly to me and other executives. We had to make on-the-spot decisions. And there could only be three answers—yes, no or we need more information. If the recommendation was accepted, we assigned an executive sponsor to ensure it was implemented. Instead of excuses, we saw action.

Meanwhile, other teams looked for ideas to help APS achieve its ambitious new goals. We began comparing APS against the best of the best—both inside and outside our industry. We looked at companies like Duke Power, Intel, Boeing and Federal Express, then benchmarked ourselves against the best. And if we reached our goals, we raised the benchmark.

Lesson 5: Move the Organization

When we completed FOCUS and implemented our new strategic plan, expectations for APS' future were at an all time high. Our "Top 5 Vision" began driving every decision. Our new vision became an obsession. And employees were demanding more of themselves and their co-workers than ever before.

On the one hand, we knew this was exactly the kind of environment needed to achieve our aggressive new goals. But we also faced substantial risk. What would happen if we failed to meet our goals? Could we sustain a high performing culture without high performing results? How could we sustain the momentum that we'd worked so hard to build?

To help ensure results, we implemented several new programs that would provide employees very personal feedback. For example, all plans—corporate, department and individual—contain Critical Success Indicators, so we can measure our progress.

We also began offering a gainsharing incentive, which was part of an overall cost management program. If employees could help cut our annual operations and maintenance (O & M) budget, we promised to share with them the savings.

In the first year of gainsharing, we saved $44 million in fuel and O & M against our budgets. The pay-outs to employees ranged between $1,500 and $3500 per employee. As you can imagine, cost management became very personal. So we've continued that program, and we're continuing to cut our annual budgets.

Lesson 6: Celebrate Success

When creating a high-performing culture and a powerful vision, results and recognition become very important. People need to know that they are constantly moving forward. They want to push themselves further than they ever thought they could go. They want to go even beyond continuous improvement. At APS, that has already begun to happen.

Our first major breakthrough came early in our culture change effort, when we received the 1993 Edison Award for our efforts to transform from a traditional rate-driven utility to a competitive, strategically guided, customer-driven utility that encourages innovation and achievement. As Edward F. Mitchell, chairman and CEO of Potomac Electric Power Company and then chairman of EEI said when presenting the award: "APS' efforts to use its new company vision and strategic plan to create a more productive and responsive utility is a model for the industry. The results of APS' concerted efforts are undeniable. APS is now one of the most innovative, results-oriented, and community-linked utilities in the nation, as proven by high performance and satisfaction ratings across the board."

Believe me, those words were music to our ears. In our first full year since beginning FOCUS and launching our new vision, things were beginning to change, and fast. We achieved the highest customer satisfaction ratings in our history, cut our costs of producing a kilowatt-hour by ten percent, and became ranked as Arizona's premier corporate citizen. Plus, there many more results company wide. We had become leaders in many categories, and our vision no longer looked impossible.

Lesson 7: Raise Your Expectations

There's a quote on the back cover of a inspirational book produced by *Fortune* magazine: "Be realistic—demand the impossible." Since winning the Edison Award, APS has continued to follow that advice.

Throughout our culture change effort, our rallying cry has been "good, best, better." And the better we get, the better our new team wants to become. At APS, there is no such thing as "good enough" because we are constantly striving to become better.

Early in our change strategy, we talked a lot about continuous improvement. Somewhere along the way, however, continuous improvement could no longer describe our efforts. Because instead of making incremental improvements, we were taking quantum leaps. We were always raising the bar on performance.

Incidentally, APS' senior management isn't alone in raising the bar on performance. Employees at all levels are setting stretch goals. Now that they've learned how good they are, they're eager to learn how good they can become. And they're constantly exceeding expectations.

Clearly, our FOCUS program worked in its goal to encourage employees to think more strategically and operate as a high-performing, flexible, self-directed and vision-inspired team. And that's exactly why we decided FOCUS itself wasn't good enough. We could do more.

Lesson 8: Take the Quantum Leap

In late 1993, we launched a new round of FOCUS called "Breakthrough FOCUS." Its purpose was to help take our team to an even higher level—to begin achieving the kind of breakthroughs our new competitive environment demands. We'd already begun creating a learning organization. With Breakthrough FOCUS, we were determined to learn, and accomplish, far more. We wanted employees to take a quantum leap into the future.

Unlike the first FOCUS, Breakthrough FOCUS concentrates on working with the formal and informal leaders of our organization—people who have exceptional vision, energy and creativity, as well as the ability to inspire the same qualities in their co-workers. We're exposing them to exciting new ideas, including bringing in some of the leading business and performance leaders in the nation to talk with Breakthrough Leaders about how to excel in an uncertain world. And we've challenged Breakthrough Leaders to help create strategies for dealing with very complex competitive and business challenges.

In APS' current high performing culture, finding breakthrough thinkers has been no problem. Since FOCUS, all employees are able to think in highly creative and strategic ways. But Breakthrough FOCUS forced us to look even deeper for employees who displayed the following kinds of characteristics:

➠ Communicate, clarify, support, reinforce and model our mission;

➠ Spend most of their time with employees, focusing their performance and results;

➠ Do not allow organizational or personal boundaries to get in the way and strategically empower others to act within the framework of our vision and targets;

➠ Make strategic decisions quickly, openly and based on our values, mission, Critical Success Indicators, and strategic priorities;

➠ Demonstrate enormous energy and have the ability to energize others;

➠ Acknowledge mistakes and make the necessary adjustments;

➠ Demand results from themselves and others and eliminate habitual behaviors that get in our way;

➠ Value a high level of business competency;

➠ Embrace and relish the concept of continuous strategic change; and

➠ Model the behaviors and commitment to the cultural diversity strategy.

Today, APS' Breakthrough Leaders are working harder than ever to help direct, empower and inspire the APS team. They are helping anchor our new culture. As a result, I believe APS is truly on the verge of achieving breakthrough results.

Lesson 9: Create a Sense of Urgency

Although there are many aspects to APS' new culture, the one that stands out above all is our sense of urgency. When you walk inside APS today, you can feel a high level of energy and excitement. And it's that excitement that is anchoring our high performing culture, while keeping our team focused on the future and continually achieving results.

Of course, culture change is a tool, not an end. At APS, we are using our new culture to help push through the organizational and procedural changes still needed to help bring down our costs and position APS to compete and succeed.

For example, we were one of the first utilities to begin reengineering our company. Again, we weren't looking for incremental change, but rather radical and rapid improvements in how we do business, deliver services and create value for our customers.

We began reengineering more than a year ago. And the results to date have exceeded our initial expectations. Employees are finding additional ways to break down barriers, cut through organizational boundaries and apply new technology so that we can do things better and faster for our customers. Had we not created a new, high performing culture to help us reengineer, I'm doubtful we would have achieved the same results.

As a result of reengineering, we recently announced that we would cut another 690 jobs this summer. From a human perspective, that's very difficult— especially on top of cuts already made. But, from a business and procedural perspective, APS is going to be far more effective and efficient.

For example, we've been looking at ways to reengineer our Transmission and Distribution processes. One thing we examined was designing and hooking up systems for new commercial customers. Under the old process, a project would be handed-off up to 30 times. Besides the delay, there was confusion. Sometimes, the wrong materials would be delivered to a site. We'd have what seemed like a fleet of vehicles arriving at a job site.

In the reengineered, new process, we will have a project leader, who is accountable for the whole job—from beginning to end. So it's not being passed from person to person. As a result, we can get the process down from 12 weeks to as little as three days.

To achieve those kinds of efficiencies, we need multi-skilled workers and new technology. For example, we used to have estimators go to a site, do a line drawing and take it to engineering. Later, a surveyor would go back to the exact same site. Now, one multi-skilled person will go out, do their drawing on a notepad computer, feed it into our CAD system, and produce working drawings the same day.

There are many examples of these kinds of efficiencies at APS. As we look further down the road this year, we'll see computers in every line truck, so we can transmit work orders direct to the line truck—instead of handing out a stack of papers each morning. But since I've been asked to discuss culture change—not reengineering—I'll spare you the details.

Suffice it to say, our culture change strategy helped prepare employees to take on the reengineering challenge. In fact, with a high-performing team that's driven to achieve, you have no choice but to eliminate inefficiency and delay. Employees won't tolerate non-performance from either other people or old processes. Nor does a high-performing, strategically-directed team change for the sake of change. They change to achieve results. As a result, we didn't

13

reengineer a process unless we could improve speed, service, safety or cost.

Lesson 10: Flourish on Change

This last lesson is probably the most important piece of advice that I can share with other utilities. When you create a high-performing culture, one that thinks in new, creative and strategic ways, change becomes a driver. People aren't afraid to take risks or make quantum leaps. As a result, your company will be better positioned than ever to change and compete. More important, it can reposition itself when conditions change.

At APS, we have not only destroyed the old utility order, we have created a new, competitive order. We are seeing results and making good on our promises. In fact, we are exceeding the expectations we set for ourselves and promised to others.

The clearest example of how we've changed—and how our new culture helped us change—relates to rates.

Like many utilities, APS had long been known as a rate case machine. Everything we did revolved around rates—raising rates, justifying rates or preparing for rate hearings. In the 15 years before we began the culture change effort just described, our electric rates had increased 338 percent, or 8.5 percent per year. Our focus had always been on rates, not performance. Cost management wasn't even in our vocabulary.

In 1991, we began dismantling the rate machine when we backed away from a 21 percent rate increase request. Instead, we entered into a agreement with our regulatory commission. We would accept a 5.4 increase, get our operations under control and reduce costs, and not go back for a rate increase until 1993. If we failed to meet a cost reduction target, the commission could do a full-blown investigation of our management and operations. If we succeeded, the commission would agree to hear our request for an increase.

When we entered that agreement, regulators were skeptical, at best. We proved them wrong. Not only did we get our costs and operations under control, we decided not to file for an increase in 1993. Instead, we started working on a filing to lower our rates. In May 1994, the commission approved that filing. For the first time in our history, APS decreased its rates. More than that, we agreed—enthusiastically—to continue cutting costs and holding down rates.

Today, we aren't the same APS, and we never will be. We are going to continue to change and challenge ourselves so we can compete successfully in an exciting new world. And we are going to continue to anchor the culture that we've created. Because with the right culture, and the right vision, we really can create magic. And that's the most valuable lesson utilities can learn.

Chapter Two

PECO Energy—A New Culture for New Challenges

Joseph F. Paquette, Jr.

America's electric utilities are experiencing profound changes, unlike anything the industry has undergone since its earliest days. Customers are demanding competitive rates and high-quality service. Investors want a greater return on their investment in light of the greater risk facing the industry. Employees are concerned about their jobs and wages.

The challenge utility executives face is how to develop the new culture needed to meet these demands.

At PECO Energy Company we have taken a variety of actions, both reactive and proactive, to build the high performance work culture this new environment requires.

PECO Energy provides electric and natural gas service to over 1.5 million customers in five counties in southeastern Pennsylvania and two counties in northeastern Maryland. One of the nation's largest utilities, it has an annual revenue of approximately $4 billion and assets of $18 billion. For most of its 113-year history PECO Energy enjoyed a reputation as a technological leader that supplied high quality service but not necessarily at a competitive price.

Three events, occurring over the last five years, forced PECO Energy to change the way we do business.

In March 1987 the Nuclear Regulatory Commission ordered the Peach Bottom Atomic Power Station in York County, Pa. shut down because operators were "inattentive to duty." Then in April 1990 the Pennsylvania Public Utility Commission denied over $300 million of the Company's requested rate increase, which we sought because of the completion of the Limerick Unit Two nuclear power plant.

16

Then in 1992 Congress passed the National Energy Policy Act which brought the realization that wholesale competition was a reality and that retail competition may be on the horizon.

These milestones brought into increasingly sharp focus the need to make dramatic changes if the Company was to survive and prosper.

With passage of the National Energy Policy Act, both the structure of the industry and the underlying federal policies governing the generation and sale of electricity were altered. While not mandating retail wheeling, the act shifted the debate on the issue of retail wheeling to the state level, as the industry has seen with the recent decision by California to allow complete open access by 2002.

To confront the challenges involved in restarting Peach Bottom, a series of actions was begun to change the culture within PECO Energy's nuclear operations. The nuclear group was reorganized. New management was put into place. New training procedures were put into place. Supervisors were promoted based upon performance, not seniority—a major change in the culture that dominated the Company for most of its history.

This effort took several years, and required a variety of changes over that time. The adverse Limerick rate case order, however, demanded immediate, and sometimes radical, steps to control costs.

In response to the rate case decision, the dividend was cut, wages were frozen, officers' salaries and directors' fees were cut, an early retirement plan was offered to employees, and the Company's operations were reorganized. This strategy clearly said that we were becoming a different Company.

The initial action in 1990 was the vote by the Board of Directors to reduce the annual dividend from $2.20 to $1.20 per share. This sent a message to both Wall Street and our employees that the Company was responding to a serious crisis. Since then, the Company's financial position has improved and the annual dividend has been raised to $1.52 per share.

Wages were also frozen for one year. While this was upsetting to our employees, it helped everyone understand that the Company was going through a critical period that required sacrifice. A process of reevaluating every job in the Company to determine if the pay range was comparable to other utilities was also begun then.

While these actions helped alleviate the immediate crisis, they were not a cure. Clearly we had to reduce operations and maintenance costs and we know that some processes used to serve customers needed changing.

To reduce costs PECO Energy in 1990 offered an early retirement plan to all employees who were 50 years old or older and had five years of service. The package, available to 2,608 eligible employees, was accepted by 1,909, at a cost of $249 million, or 70 cents per share. The reduction saves the Company about $75 million annually. In March 1994 the Company announced that another early retirement package, and also a voluntary separation package, would be offered to employees.

The loss of a large number of employees in a short period can put a strain on any organization. But it also forced PECO Energy to build a new organization, one focused on customer satisfaction.

In 1991 PECO Energy decentralized the administration of its electric and gas distribution and customer service function into seven geographic divisions. The vice presidents of each division have direct responsibility and accountability for the quality and reliability of service to the customers in their area. The reorganization marked the first time in fifty years that the Company took steps to significantly change the way the organization was structured.

In 1992 we again focused attention on our nuclear operations. Like every utility with nuclear plants, PECO Energy's nuclear staff increased significantly during the 1980s, partly in response to the increased emphasis on safety that the industry adopted following the Three Mile Island accident in 1979.

Our goal was to find ways to reduce expenses within the nuclear group without compromising safety. As we examined nuclear staffing it became clear that many positions were redundant, and could be eliminated without affecting the public's health and safety. As a result over 600 positions were eliminated, or about 18 percent, with an annual savings of $31 million, while all operational and safety indicators improved.

The Company also began implementation of its job rate range reevaluations. The study disclosed that, for many positions, PECO Energy employees were paid above the market level. As a result, the salaries of about 40 percent of the Company's employees were effectively "frozen" until the market catches up with their frozen salary.

While the decisions to cut the dividend, offer early retirements, reevaluate jobs, and reduce staff were difficult, they were also necessary. However, management realized that more was required if we were to develop a new culture within PECO Energy, and compete in the changing utility environment.

The real pressure for competition is not coming from regulators, but rather from customers, especially the large industrial users with access to independent power producers. Nearly every utility in the nation is feeling this pressure, but for PECO Energy the risks are greater. Because of the large capital investment made in nuclear power in the 1980s, the Company's rates are among the highest in the nation.

To remain competitive with high rates requires a concerted effort to retain customers, which makes it necessary for every employee to focus on customer service. This requires an overhaul in the processes used to serve customers. For most of its history the electric utility industry was a technology-driven business. This new environment demands that we be a customer-driven business.

To achieve this, PECO Energy began a Quality Management process in 1991. This process emphasizes changing behaviors through positive reenforcement and building strong teams.

Every employee is being trained in the QM process, from the CEO and the entire senior management team to front-line employees. The goal is for everyone to show how they are using quality management tools in their daily jobs and to graphically demonstrate where improvements are being made.

Another important aspect of our efforts to foster change involves the use of reengineering. Initially there was some reluctance to describe what we were doing as "reengineering." There was concern that employees would see it as another management fad — a "program of the day" approach to management.

But as the term began working its way into the popular lexicon, managers and front-line employees grew more comfortable describing what we were doing as "reengineering." We started in those processes involving direct contact with customers, such as handling requests for service and information.

The project involved 50 employees from the seven operating divisions, as well as customer and marketing services, gas operations, production, and information systems who worked on developing new processes aimed at improving customer satisfaction.

The reengineering process had three primary goals: 1) increased customer satisfaction; 2) improved regulatory performance; and 3) decreased cost of serving customers. The initial studies looked at three fundamental customer needs: 1) requests for information; 2) requests for physical work; 3) providing accurate billing and convenient payment methods.

Quality management gives us the tools necessary to improve performance. Reengineering makes certain we are doing the work needed to meet the customer's needs. Together they are changing the way we do business daily.

In order for quality management and reengineering to work, we also had to examine the way our business was organized and ask if it was meeting the customers' needs. After careful examination, we decided that a new structure was necessary. In March 1994 PECO Energy reorganized into five business units.

They are: Consumer Energy Services Group, which distributes energy products and service to retail customers; Gas Services Group, responsible for all natural gas operations; Power Generation Group, responsible for the operation of the fossil-fired and hydroelectric plants; Nuclear Generation Group, responsible for operating the Limerick Generating Station in Montgomery County, Pa. and the Peach Bottom Atomic Power Station in York County, Pa., and Bulk Power Enterprises, which markets and sells energy products to wholesale customers outside PECO Energy's service territory.

During the past few years the pace of change within PECO Energy and the entire electric and gas utility industry has been rapid and in some ways disconcerting to many employees. Changing a culture cannot take place overnight. In order for executives to *lead* in this new environment, they must help employees understand why they should *follow*.

This can be done through an aggressive communications effort. To help reduce some of the inevitable anxiety change produces, PECO Energy's management has an ambitious communications program. All senior officers meet regularly with small groups of employees, discussing what is happening within the Company and the industry and what PECO Energy must do to meet the new competitive challenges. While these meetings provide management an opportunity to explain the corporate strategy, the real value comes in the listening. We learn a great deal when we take the time to listen to the concerns of our employees.

These actions, taken together, are creating a new culture at PECO Energy. But simply creating a new culture is not enough. People must understand how you changed and why. To communicate our new approach to business to a wide audience, the decision was made to change the corporate name from Philadelphia Electric Company to PECO Energy Company. The name change, which took effect January 1, 1994, more clearly reflects our business. But

just as important, it helps our customers and employees understand that we are a different Company with a new way of doing
business.

Change is not easy, but it is necessary, in life and in business. The
graveyard of American business is littered with the remains of
companies that, when faced with a challenge, refused to change.
PECO Energy will *not* be one of those companies.

The future of the electric and gas utility industry is challenging,
but it is also exciting. The employees of America's utilities have an
opportunity not seen before in this century. They can remake an
industry into one that is competitive and customer-focused—an
industry where employees find challenging and satisfying work—
an industry that keeps America competitive in the world marketplace of the 21st Century.

Chapter Three

The GPU Experience

James R. Leva

Leading an electric utility in this country today is a delicate balancing act. On the one hand, competition is forcing us to take urgent, drastic measures to survive. On the other hand, doing what's right for the people who will enable us to become competitive—our employees—is a compelling force as well. Tipping the scales to one side are the interests of our shareholders, to the other, the interests of our customers. When I'm asked which audience is most important, I answer, "All of them."

We are undergoing sweeping changes in our industry and at General Public Utilities Corporation (GPU). We face aggressive competition on many fronts, and to meet the competition and come out ahead, we must change, change drastically, and change now.

As my fellow contributors to this volume well know, changing a large, complex organization is not easy, particularly one with a deeply ingrained culture of regulation. While the business world around us has been competitive for decades, we have had the protection offered by monopolies, franchises, and regulator-allowed rates of return. With the passage of the Energy Policy Act of 1992, competition—real competition—entered our world, wailing like a newborn, demanding to be fed, clothed, and pampered.

How do we become competitive? By realigning our structure? By undertaking broad performance improvement measures? By effective strategic planning? By managing costs? By refocusing our customer service efforts? All are important in the drive to becoming competitive. At GPU, we've undertaken initiatives in all of these areas, but we're still not competitive.

To become competitive, the culture must change. The way employees think and behave must change. We must bring ourselves out of the cave of monopolies and franchises and into the bright light of the marketplace. We must talk—and listen—to each other. Our people will move the company into what is certain to become a ruthlessly competitive world. To paraphrase a thought often associated with President Clinton, "It's the *people*, stupid."

For the past two years, we at GPU have been balancing our actions between drastic necessities and the people who must take, or be the subjects of, such action. Yes, we must relentlessly drive down our costs, realign our structure, implement effective, aggressive strategic planning, and look again at our customers and their needs. Who will accomplish these difficult, essential goals? Our people.

As important as the strategies and the organization charts and the spread sheets and the budget and cost analyses are, it is the people who will make it work. They will force GPU to become competitive because, I'm convinced, in the long run, they want to be.

The balancing act has been difficult. But if we have tipped the scales, we have done so in favor of our people. We can create the finest strategic plan in the world, design the tightest budget, and construct the ideal organization. But if the people haven't signed on and believe in what we're doing, even the best programs will fail.

The process began two years ago with our employees answering a questionnaire about our future and participating in a series of focus groups. Then, about 60 officers and bargaining unit leaders met for a retreat to craft a "vision" for GPU using the information from the employee questionnaire and focus groups. Our process has been one of inclusion. And I believe it is working.

Are we competitive? Not yet. We've had some small victories, and we've made some good decisions. But we have a long way to go. In addition to wanting to save at least $80 million a year by the end of 1996, we must become quicker and more flexible in our decisionmaking, redefine our customer orientation and increase our willingness to take measured risks. And when we get to the end of 1996, we'll probably say "that isn't enough." So we'll save—and do—more. We *will* become competitive. Our people will make it happen, enabling us to fulfill our mission, "to be a premier supplier of energy and energy-related services through the skills of our employees and the excellence of our customer service."

The GPU Vision

To get an idea about how our thoughts on crafting a vision would play with employees, we decided to begin the process by sampling a portion of our employee population. We held focus groups for about 120 employees and sent questionnaires to about 10 percent of the workforce. We asked more questions and we listened. And we learned more about the company and how we were going to become competitive.

In the late summer of 1992, just before the Energy Policy Act was signed into law, our officers and union leaders began to chart a course to competition. Our goal was a vision, which included a mission, a purpose and values to help us work together.

Some resisted. Some were skeptical. Another flavor of the week, said others. Many adopted the familiar this-too-shall-pass attitude, asking "why all the fuss?"

The moment of truth came a short time after the act became law. One of our municipalities in our service territory in New Jersey approached a neighboring utility. Would this loyal and long-time customer really consider leaving us? Just to save money? You bet it would. And almost did, until we put together a competitive package it eventually accepted. Four other municipalities followed, and competition for GPU was born. Some of the doubting Thomases within the company said, "Well, that wasn't so bad. Now we can go back to business as usual." We had *responded* competitively, but we had not *become* competitive. The doubting Thomases, by the way, are still among us, but their numbers are dwindling.

The next step in the process was to invite another 350 senior managers and additional union leaders to the vision process, in a session very much like the one the officers and union leadership held.

More input, more suggestions, more insight, more exposure. People began talking about "the vision." What was it? A magic pill? Is this going to make us competitive? I was often asked, "Why should I believe this will work?"

This brings me to one of the many reasons for including employees in the process. Some companies have crafted a vision and handed it down like so many tablets of commandments. In fact, we tried that here at GPU some years back. That we had to start over again tells you how successful that earlier effort was.

Where are we now with our vision process? Despite our best efforts at inclusion, we still see a need to expose more of our employees to the process. So, we're preparing to offer a shorter, more intensive two-day vision meeting for the rest of our employees, some of whom are avoiding commitment by saying, "How can I 'walk the talk' when I haven't been to a vision meeting yet?" That's been another source of frustration for me, because I'm aware of just as many employees—who also haven't been to a vision session—who have enthusiastically embraced our process. Another challenge is keeping the original groups of employees engaged.

We have written about these successes in our internal publications, and asked these employees to meet with others to describe their experiences. Our Power Supply group holds periodic breakfast meetings for all employees to discuss current issues and foster the vision. Vision-related topics appear on staff meeting agendas.

That's the good news. The bad news is that some groups aren't doing these things. And that's the reason we're not competitive—yet.

It's no secret that the struggle for cultural change requires that we reach—and enlist—one employee at a time. When an employee attends his or her first Power Supply breakfast, that's a victory for change. When one supervisor places vision on the staff meeting agenda, that's a victory. And each win places us one step closer to understanding and preparing for a whole new set of truths about our business. And one step closer to being truly competitive.

Restructuring

This was the easy part.

Facing the realization that the generation of electricity would likely be the first part of our business that would become truly competitive, we formed a separate generation company, which will operate our fossil-fueled and hydroelectric plants. Recognizing that the successful companies of the future would "unbundle" their organizations and resemble less and less the traditional "vertical" utility, we needed to become more flexible.

Our generation unit has a clearcut goal: make electricity at the lowest possible cost. The transition team working with the president of our new company is shaping the organization to do just that. Costs that don't contribute to the least-cost generation of energy will not be allowed. Budgets will be among the tightest ever seen at GPU. And plants will be required to hit price targets that enable us to bring energy to the market at the lowest price possible.

A second key component of our realignment, announced last February, is the combination, without a corporate merger, of the managements of our two Pennsylvania companies, Metropolitan Edison and Pennsylvania Electric. Our goal here is to achieve dramatic economies of scale, starting at the top and working our way through the entire organization. The need for cost effectiveness and enhanced productivity does not end at the management of the company. We are asking our bargaining units to work with us for the larger good. I believe that our inclusion of the bargaining units in the early vision meetings will help ensure success. They are a part of the strategy.

A third element of our realignment that will have far-reaching impact is a comprehensive look at how we can improve our performance. Our financial target is to reduce costs by at least $80 million a year by the end of 1996. Our performance improvement effort goes much farther. First, we'll look at all of the tasks we do, and ask if we need to do them at all. Then, we'll look at how we do things, ask if we can do them better and listen to what our people tell us. We will improve both efficiency and effectiveness.

I'd like to share a story with you. At our western Pennsylvania subsidiary, Pennsylvania Electric, a group of our bargaining unit mechanics from several regional garages meets periodically to discuss common problems—and solutions. The idea for these sessions originated with the mechanics. They empowered themselves to work smarter. One of the supervisors said that this was one of the best things he's seen in his career. He said, "There's a lot to be derived from asking the people who are actually 'turning the wrench' to be part of the decisionmaking process. . . . It's the way of the future."

Related to our performance improvement initiative is an examination of the way we provide services, both through our subsidiary, GPU Service Corporation, and how we provide services in general. Many of our services are provided on a consolidated basis either through GPU Service or other companies in our system. These services include technology, accounting, purchasing, information, treasury and power supply.

We need to ask tough questions here as well. Are there other services that could be consolidated? Are there services that are now being provided on a consolidated basis that should go back to each subsidiary? As with our larger performance initiative, we will probe deeply, and not approach the effort with any preconceived notions.

The Human Element

The fifth element of our realignment deals with our workforce, what I call "people needs."

Throughout my career at GPU, I have always placed people first. Throughout our strategic planning process and realignment, I have continued to emphasize the importance of our people.

These times are especially tough for someone like me. Every day we read in the newspapers and business magazines of major layoffs and job reductions at companies around the country. Targets are set and met. In some cases, this has been an effective strategy. In others, people have to be rehired because the work wasn't getting done, or customers weren't being satisfied. The balance tipped too far the wrong way, and some have had to scramble to recover.

I decided that, at GPU, we weren't going to set a target for job reductions and announce it to the world. I've been telling our people, our shareholders and the investment community that GPU will be smaller in the future, but that we will let the needs of our new generation and combined Pennsylvania companies dictate the size of the organization, including GPU Nuclear and Jersey Central Power and Light.

I also determined that we would offer a voluntary enhanced retirement program to the 800 of our 5,700 non-bargaining employees who were at least 55 and had five years of service. As we looked at the bargaining unit population of some 6,100, we estimated that, if we offered them a similar program, an additional 600 to 700 could be eligible. This program will go a long way toward helping us achieve our target of $80 million in annual savings by the end of 1996. The balance of that goal will be met by reducing costs in other areas of the business.

I have also said that further reductions could be necessary, and that no one is guaranteed his current title, position or even job. We have realigned our performance management system to be more consistent with a competitive market. The old "contract" no longer applies. The quality of the work will dictate the compensation. Yearly raises are no longer automatic. And "average" is no longer good enough.

The employee who is not making a valuable contribution to fulfilling our mission is probably in the wrong job, and may be at the wrong company. It is not fair to such an employee to keep him or her on. And it is certainly not fair to the many others who are making valuable contributions. I'm sure our customers and shareholders would agree.

Balancing the needs of the corporation with the interests of our employees has been one of the biggest challenges I've faced in this process. And it won't go away. Fairness is paramount. And if the balance tips, I would hope to see it tip in favor of the employee. Our voluntary enhanced retirement program, as well as our programs for the employees who will constitute the new GPU after the early retirees leave, is designed to do just that.

We've put in place a number of special initiatives to help us create a rewarding environment at GPU today, while helping the employee face a future that is both exciting and uncertain. We have tried to instill in our programs the notion that if we can't keep our employees at GPU, we can do our best to keep them employable somewhere.

I referred earlier to an orientation session for the remainder of our employees who've not yet been to our vision sessions. This will be a more concentrated format than our original four-day workshops that will enable us to deliver our message while keeping costs low. As with our earlier sessions, the focus will be on inclusion, accepting accountability and personal involvement. Our vision is not something that others do for the employee, it is something each of us carries from the sessions.

An initiative that has been successful for us has been our Team-Power program. Clearly, teamwork will be one of the keys to our success in the future. Our TeamPower program uses cross-functional and cross-company teams to tackle problems, whether they are department or division-specific or affect the whole company.

I view the elimination of barriers that exist between functions and companies within the GPU system as another of my most important "people" challenges, and TeamPower has shown results. It's amazing what can be accomplished when people work with a trained facilitator who keeps the group focused on the problem that brought them together in the first place.

Another successful program worth mentioning is our Executive Institute at Penn State. Tailored specifically to our needs, this program was developed for some 200 officers, directors and managers, the "high potentials" who will be leading the company in the years to come. It provides our senior managers with the same foundation of customized business learning so they can think and act as a single System team. This approach will accelerate our efforts to respond to the challenges of competition, and complements, rather than replaces, some of the fine external programs we use for our officers.

A unique component of the program is the "action learning" team project required of the class members. This technique allows the teams to address actual problems facing GPU, using the knowledge they've learned in the course and their past GPU system experience.

We recognize that the competitive arena requires more of our employees than the traditional training and orientation programs we veterans attended. Conceptual thinking, along with the ability to see the big picture, and anticipate change will be among the special talents needed by our industry leaders in the years to come. Knowing all aspects of the wires business was important before competition. Foreseeing how that business will evolve will be essential to our survival in the future.

Strategic Planning

When we asked one of our officers if he would lead the strategic planning effort, he responded, "Only if you're serious about it." We were, and he took the assignment.

That was about a year ago.

Today, after much study, I believe we are on the right track. We know what the standout companies are doing, and we understand what we need to do to join their ranks.

But we are not there yet.

We recognize that strategic planning is a dynamic process, and we know that some fine-tuning will be necessary, perhaps even after the final decisions have been made. A good example: as this book was going to press, the California Public Utilities Commission had proposed a plan to implement retail wheeling for all customers by 2002. While some saw it coming, the news sent many others scurrying back to the drawing board.

To address the questions raised in our planning process, we established task forces to look at generation, bulk transmission, distribution and customers, products and services for the commercial market, cost identification, transition problems, human resources, and business scope and organization.

Last summer, I reminded our working groups that we couldn't afford to do lengthy studies of issues that were already affecting our business, and I think they responded well.

If one message emerged from our strategic planning process, it was that we need to look at the work we do as if we were running our own business. Ask any successful small business operator about costs, overhead, efficiencies and the competition and you will get a lesson on how to compete effectively. It is that kind of focused thinking we are trying to develop at GPU.

Maintaining Customer Focus

At last year's GPU management meeting, I told my colleagues that being profitable was our main concern, if we were to serve our customers, employees and the communities we're a part of. You could have heard a pin drop. "I guess the customer is no longer No. 1," some employees said. I responded, "If we are not profitable, if we do not drive down costs, if we do not work smarter, we won't have customers to serve."

This issue vividly brings the question of balance into the forefront, particularly in the new, competitive environment. We must keep the shareholders satisfied so they continue to hold—and perhaps buy more of—our stock. We must keep the customers satisfied so they continue to buy our energy. Sometimes that decision will be based on price, sometimes on customer service.

We've learned, for example, that providing services that we think the customers want may be the surest way to disaster. We have to find out from the customers what they want, how and when they want it, then deliver it to them at a price that's lower than the competition. In years past, we often didn't have to think about that last element.

A recent *Electrical World* poll showed that 56 percent of residential electric utility customers surveyed said that if given a choice, they would select their current supplier. That's the good news.

But, 43 percent said they would move to another utility if they could save just 5 percent on their electric bills. The firm that conducted the poll said "Customer loyalty is soft, and can be had for a relatively low price." Amen. Companies who ignore this kind of information won't be around for very long. Companies who listen at least have a fighting chance. I'd like to think that we are listening.

At the same management meeting mentioned earlier, we heard from three of our larger customers. One in particular didn't pull any punches. His message? "You have to listen to me." The economy was still struggling and his costs were skyrocketing . . . and our name was on his list of rising costs. The days of automatically setting rates for an entire class of customer and delivering uniform service to all have come to an end.

While I'm pleased to report that we still come out well in our customer approval ratings, the *Electrical World* Survey and recent news from California tell me we must roll up our sleeves and figure out how we're going to keep all those "loyal" customers. When switching electric utilities becomes as easy as switching long-distance phone companies, we'd better be able to beat the competition's offer with better prices or improved services—or both.

Competition—The Need to Change

The recent developments in California, traditionally a bellwether state in our industry, place even more urgency on GPU's plans than we originally envisioned. While I'm cheered that the key elements of the California Public Utility Commission's proposed rulemaking are consistent with *what* we want to do here at GPU, I'm concerned about the *when*. We may have to pick up the pace. Many of us had thought that retail wheeling, while a certainty, would be some years off. The California PUC proposal has changed all that.

Our position on the CPUC's proposed rulemaking, based on our very preliminary look, is that its stated objective of protecting a utility's potential stranded investments would provide a fair basis for the creation of a viable, competitive generation industry.

We would also support its intention to establish earnings ceilings and floors to balance risks and rewards to utility investors, as well as the provision allowing each utility to develop its own performance-based incentive programs to fit its particular operating needs.

And we might welcome the proposed change from traditional cost-of-service regulation to performance-based regulation that will enable utilities to compete in a changing environment and enhance earnings via superb performance. In New Jersey, GPU is supporting a measure in the state legislature to create "flexible rates" that would spur economic development.

There are questions that go unanswered by the CPUC, however. How will state and federal jurisdictional issues be resolved? How will the large-scale social programs that utilities currently fund be revamped and costs reallocated? Will the plan truly be able to deliver on its promises of lower electric rates, less regulation and the fair and equitable treatment of all concerned: utilities, customers and shareholders?

Utilities are becoming more aggressive in their dealings with regulators and legislators to shape the rules we will all have to live with in the years to come. We have to. We used to speak of a level playing field in our business. If anything, the advent of competition makes it imperative that we be well prepared internally to deal with the unexpected and bold externalities like the CPUC proposal. The flexible, agile and fit utilities will be able to respond to these kinds of developments in ways that benefit all the stakeholders I've identified. I suspect that in some cases, being fit and agile won't be enough. The truly outstanding companies will also be able to anticipate the next sea change and take advantage of emerging opportunities.

I'll close with another example of what we're doing at GPU to respond competitively to externalities as well as anticipate the next major developments.

Our nonregulated subsidiary, Energy Initiatives, recently acquired North Canadian Power, giving EI almost 1,000 megawatts of capacity at 11 plants. EI, as part of a consortium of companies, has been selected the successful bidder for a proposed 750 megawatt, $425 million repowering project in Colombia.

We are committed to making EI a more significant part of GPU's business, and we are seeking other opportunities in markets both domestic and worldwide.

I've told our employees that this is the most exciting time I've seen in the electric power industry. If someone had told me 40 years ago that we'd be competing with our neighboring utilities and investing in power plants overseas, I'd have questioned his sanity.

Handwringing has never been my style, so we're viewing the changes in our business as unparalleled opportunities. My job is to set the pace for change and ask my colleagues to join me. We could be dragged, kicking and screaming into the competitive arena. Or we can continue doing what we've been doing: setting our own pace, eyes and ears open, determined to make GPU one of the best.

Cultural Change at GPU—Some Final Thoughts

Another one of my roles at GPU is referee. With so many efforts going on at once, it is easy to lose sight of the final goal. My senior officers and I try to make sure that our efforts are aligned with our vision, even in the midst of realignment.

Although we have made some progress with our transition to competition, we recognize that we have a long way to go. There have been times when we took two steps backward after a giant step forward. There are still pockets of resistance to change. Having an inclusive process is one thing. Getting everyone to participate is quite another.

Among the changes in our culture still to be realized is breaking down the old parochial ways of thinking. We are often tempted to look at a problem or its solution with blinders on. And, we still look too often at our company through the eyes of the subsidiary we work for instead of the entire GPU System.

We must improve our ability to work in teams that cross departmental, divisional, company and state boundaries. Again, we must take off the blinders.

We must be committed to continuous improvement. These improvements need not be sweeping. I'd rather see frequent incremental changes than one a year. Then I'd know that we were really on our way.

We must frequently look at the best companies and understand why they are doing well, and challenge ourselves to do well, also.

We must rid ourselves of the entitlement mentality. We're not supposed to get raises, we're supposed to earn them. When we fail at a task, we must be told. We can't improve if we haven't been told we have to. We can no longer promote someone because he or she has been in the same job for 15 years. (If that's the case, maybe it's time to find something else for that employee to do.)

We must stop the "command and control" mentality of management. I want our employees to be empowered. Unfortunately, some of our managers don't.

Finally, we must learn to set objectives that make us reach. Generate electricity at 3 1/2 cents a kilowatthour? Why not 3 1/4 cents.

When Roger Bannister broke the 4-minute mile, did all the other milers stop running faster?

Our process here at GPU is really just beginning. We are still beginning to understand what we don't know. But we have learned some valuable lessons in the relatively short time we've been at this:

➠ This is a very difficult process.

➠ Our people need to understand what's in it for them, or they will not engage themselves.

➠ We must set objectives which are concrete and understandable.

➠ The leadership of the company must live the values.

➠ We have to emphasize personal responsibility.

And, I think we must remind ourselves that we have begun a journey. Our transition to being fully competitive will be a long one. We must get used to someone raising the bar after every jump.

Which brings me to one of my other roles at GPU. Some may call it "coach." Some may even call it "cheerleader." Whatever you call it, I must constantly remind myself and my colleagues that we will not give up. I'm committed to this process. I'm committed to setting an aggressive, competitive pace for our company. And I'm committed to making GPU a leader in the electric utility industry.

Chapter Four

Shaping a Competitive Nuclear Operation

William E. Davis

I spoke recently at a Nuclear Strategic Planning Conference devoted to "reinventing the nuclear organization." That's a clear acknowledgement of the need to change in an area of the electric utility industry where change does not come easily.

Change is especially difficult for those who are experts in an entrenched technology within a mature industry, as are utility industry nuclear executives.

It's tempting to deny the need to change, particularly when one has a big investment—professional as well as monetary—in the status quo.

For example, New York's canal system was once the jewel of a transportation system that moved the nation's goods to and from the burgeoning frontier by water. It was a good system. It worked. And it was a key to New York's economic dominance in the first years of the 19th century.

Some time ago, I ran across a letter from that period that makes a point about change.

It reads:

> Dear President Andrew Jackson:
>
> The canal system of this country is being threatened by the spread of a new form of transportation known as railroads. The federal government must preserve the canals for the following reasons:
>
> *One:* if canal boats are supplanted by railroads, serious unemployment will result. Captains, cooks, drivers, repairmen and lock tenders will be left without a means of

livelihood, not to mention the numerous farmers now employed in growing hay for horses.

Two: boat builders would suffer, and tow-line, whip and harness makers would be left destitute.

Three: canal boats are absolutely essential to the defense of the United States. In the event of the expected trouble with England, the Erie Canal would be the only means by which we would move the supplies so vital to waging modern war.

As you may well know, Mr. President, railroad carriages are pulled at the enormous speed of 15 miles per-hour by engines which, in addition to endangering life and limb of passengers, roar and snort their way through the countryside, setting fire to crops, scaring livestock and frightening women and children.

The almighty never intended people should move at such breakneck speed.

Signed, Martin Van Buren, Governor of New York.

The electricity business is going through a transition from monopoly to competition that to my knowledge has not resulted in letters from governors to Presidents, but which is nonetheless national in scope. And many observers would equate traditional utilities with the canal companies—on our way out.

I don't buy that. I think the electric utility industry is capable of reinventing itself to move at the breakneck speeds required to succeed in the competitive marketplace.

Some would also say that within a utility organization, the nuclear operation is the excess cargo that we ought to jettison to get up to speed.

Some of that kind of thinking undoubtedly comes from people for whom nuclear power remains a political and emotional, rather than a technological and economic, issue.

But there are others, and I include in that number some who will have a real say in the matter, who honestly believe that a successful transition to the competitive marketplace simply requires writing down high-cost nuclear or other generating assets.

I have trouble with that, for two main reasons. First, just writing down generating assets is a simplistic approach to addressing the costs of the transition to competition. Adopting market-based valuation just for generating, or even worse, just for *selected* generating assets, without recognizing the increased value of transmission and distribution assets in an increasingly competitive business, would not only be shortsighted but eminently unfair to shareholders.

Second, there's surely no prudence basis for writing down nuclear or other generating assets that have been examined by regulators and allowed in rate base.

One thing is absolutely clear, however, as we face the transition to competition. And that is that the issues are more manageable to the extent that we ensure our generating operations are as efficient, productive and cost-effective as they can be while, at the same time, maintaining high standards of safety.

Niagara Mohawk was required by the state Public Service Commission to do a comprehensive economic analysis of our Nine Mile One nuclear plant, completing the analysis early in 1993.

We concluded that the plant was economic to run, at least up to the next refueling in early 1995. But we made it clear that significant improvement in performance would be needed to justify continued operation beyond that point. The same kind of scrutiny is being given to our Nine Mile Two facility.

Certainly, close scrutiny is warranted, given the history of the plants. Prior to 1991, Nine Mile One had a lifetime capacity factor of 55 percent, well under the industry average. It spent two years on the NRC's troubled plant list, and suffered outages of 15 and 31 months.

Nine Mile Two had come on line in 1988, following a difficult and protracted construction period that resulted in a $2 billion cost disallowance. The plant struggled to a 43 percent capacity factor over its first three years.

Enter Ralph Sylvia, Niagara Mohawk's Executive Vice President - Nuclear. Continuing the work of his predecessor, Larry Burkhardt, Ralph has succeeded in reinventing Niagara Mohawk's nuclear organization over just a few years.

The fruits of his labors, and the labors of our dedicated nuclear workforce, are apparent in our 1993 operating results. By any measure, both units had the finest year in their history.

Nine Mile One compiled an 87 percent capacity factor, operating 309 of 310 scheduled days. Nine Mile Two ran for 327 consecutive days into its scheduled autumn refueling, and ended the year with an 81 percent capacity factor.

The refueling of both plants was an acid test of the organization. The slogan on the hats of the Nine Mile One crew tells the story: "55 to Stay Alive," a goal of 55 days for completion of the outage. They met that goal.

Nine Mile Two completed its refueling in 58 days, ahead of schedule and in less than half the time of previous plant refueling periods.

Both units finished the year under budget and received high marks for commercial, safety and regulatory performance. And they did it while in the home stretch of a staff reduction from more than 2,500 employees to about 1,450, which they're scheduled to reach next month.

Clearly, our nuclear operations are showing their mettle to the critics. And just as clearly, it will take continued improvement to hold that place, just as it will for all other segments of the organization. Because the transition will be—already is—a difficult time for all utilities.

Competition has made Niagara Mohawk into a different company than it was six years ago, and you probably won't recognize us six years from now, at the turn of the millennium.

One transforming factor is the intensifying competition from un-regulated generators, and Niagara Mohawk's efforts to meet it. The combination of federal and state law has required Niagara Mohawk to buy all the output from any unregulated generator at a minimum price of six cents per kilowatt-hour.

We managed to get the state's Six-Cent Law repealed, and to cut off the influx of new projects. Our actions have also reduced our future costs by some $1.7 billion dollars in cumulative net present value. But we're still left with about 2,400 megawatts of unregulated generator power, at a cost this year of about one billion dollars. We calculate that about $350 million of our 1994 cost is overpayment.

Unregulated generator costs are one of the two major cost categories that threaten our ability to offer competitive prices. The other is New York State's excessive utility tax burden. State and local taxes are twice the national average, and our total taxes have risen 42 percent in the past five years.

Added to those two are a whole range of costs placed on utilities over the years by law, regulation or just long-standing custom. These include the universal obligation to serve, cross-subsidized financing of all services, including demand-side management, and social programs such as assistance for the disadvantaged.

By and large, unregulated generators don't bear these same costs. Nor, as it now stands, would future competitors who will certainly enter the marketplace aided by the provisions of the Energy Policy Act of 1992.

An added challenge, particularly for a future that includes inter-utility competition, is that these costs vary widely from state to state. Regulators in the Northeast and on the West Coast have shown a greater tendency to impose societal costs on utilities than, for instance, in the South. That confers an automatic competitive advantage on utilities with lighter cost burdens.

So we're planning for a transition that includes competition from all directions, and for all customer segments—industrial, commercial, *and* residential.

Our strategic planning emphasizes three main elements: making internal cost cuts and efficiency gains to move our prices toward competitive levels; achieving external changes that will level the competitive playing field; and working to change utility regulations so we have the flexibility to compete.

We've had considerable success in cutting internal costs, to which our nuclear team has been a significant contributor. In fact, we'd be highly competitive right now, if our external costs were as low as those of utilities in many parts of the country. And that calculation includes continued operation of our nuclear facilities.

Our total nuclear revenue requirements are about $500 million a year, while our overpayments alone to unregulated generators are about $350 million. So even a major writedown of our nuclear assets would not take us close to the current wholesale price level. As to the third element of our planning, in February we sent forward to the PSC a five-year competitive rate proposal, which would give us the flexibility to offer competitive prices to industrial and commercial customers who have alternative supply options.

In the first year, the proposal would set our rates in the traditional way, to provide a base. For 1996 through 1999, the proposed methodology would set a cap on prices, tied to general inflation and productivity.

Beneath that cap, we would be free to set industrial and commercial prices competitively. The plan would also eliminate or modify some of the protection mechanisms of traditional regulation. Our financial success would be tied directly to our ability to manage costs and develop growth opportunities.

In our judgment, a rapid, unguided transition will visit most of the harm on utility shareholders and small, mainly residential, customers. Only a comprehensive, carefully planned transition can avoid damaging impacts.

We advocate a balanced approach involving reduction of some utility costs, and redistribution of others.

Reducing costs would allow utilities to use the savings gained to accelerate the depreciation of uneconomic assets, while at the same time minimizing rate increases.

Redistribution of utility costs should seek to share the pain, and the benefits, of the transition more equally. Redistributing too large a share of the costs to captive customers is not only unfair but in many jurisdictions a political impossibility. And there are competitive limits to rates even for customers now considered captive, given the ability of cities, towns and other political jurisdictions to form municipal utilities and gain access to generation at depressed market prices through open transmission access at the wholesale level.

And utilities should bear their share of the cost. A balanced transition plan might include some writedown of uneconomic assets, if it's fair and based on market valuation, and if it's accompanied by a *write-up* of transmission and distribution assets that would have increased value in a competitive market.

Our proposed approach to the transition would spread the costs and benefits among all competitors and customers. It would reduce burdens that have little to do with our business—like taxes.

However, we would advocate continuation of some environmental, energy efficiency and social programs that serve legitimate societal purposes and which are tied to the provision of electric services. Their costs must, however, either be reduced by moving to more market-based approaches, or spread more equitably among all competitors.

It is also important that those who benefit most directly from competition pay their fair share of the transition costs, through mechanisms such as exit and access fees imposed on customers who leave or return to the system.

We also believe the transition should proceed at a measured pace, so that Niagara Mohawk and other utilities can respond to emerging competition without having to abruptly reallocate existing costs.

Given the time, and the means, the utility industry and the other competitors can enter the competitive era on a more equal footing.

Niagara Mohawk's oldest direct ancestor was the Oswego Canal Company—one of those companies Governor Van Buren was trying to save.

That company survived by adjusting to competition, and so did the rest of the more than 500 companies that eventually combined into the Niagara Mohawk system. They survived by changing.

A surprising number of today's utilities also started out in other lines of business. So the electric utility industry has a history of adaptability that I think our competitors underestimate—just as I think they're underestimating the resiliency of nuclear power.

An industry that has survived the unfortunate expectation that it would provide power "too cheap to meter," can make a real contribution to the utility industry of the future by reinventing itself as "too cost-effective to write off."

Part Two:
The Union Perspective

Chapter Five

Labor and Competition in the Electrical Utility Industry

John J. Barry

The electrical utility industry as we have known it—especially in the past 15 years—has been like ancient Rome. It was a bastion of civilization compared to the brawling, deregulated world around it. It was an industry that was stable, profitable, and predictable. It delivered electricity efficiently and economically to any and all customers.

As in ancient Rome, the barbarians are at the gate. And our glorious civilization will never be the same. It need not be worse either.

Perhaps the reader might expect a union leader to take a strong stand against competition. Some may see the words "labor" and "competition" as a contradiction.

The fact is that organized labor's—and in the utility industry, that essentially means the International Brotherhood of Electrical Workers' (IBEW)—response to competition depends very much on how management acts in this new era. I can tell you that our union's experience in the telecommunications industry in companies like AT&T, NYNEX, Ameritech, and others showed us first hand the effects of deregulation on jobs and stability, well before the coming of the Energy Policy Act of 1992. In the electrical utility industry will we usher in the next dark ages or will we fast forward to the Renaissance?

The key word in that question is "we." You see, at this point in our history, labor and management at utility companies are kind of like a couple in a long-lived, but somewhat shaky, marriage. In this brave new world of deregulation, large customers may break away; investors may shy away; government might fulminate; residential consumers may rebel. But in the end, management and the workers have—or are stuck with—each other. So we might as well make the best of it.

47

How many utility executives share that attitude? The answer will go a long way in determining how well competition works as we lurch toward the millennium.

Our members are not the happiest campers in the world right now. How could they be? The rules under which most of them began their utility careers have changed rather suddenly. In those cases where arbitrary reductions-in-force and confused reorganization have become the rule, workers see that their individual and collective value is greatly diminished. Most of all, they are well aware of the history of deregulation in other industries. And they can read the signs in their own workplaces.

To what do the signs point? Well, if the history of the airlines, telecommunications, or trucking industries are any guide, the road may look something like the following. For purposes of this discussion, I am assuming that the trend toward deregulation is irreversible, and that government and judicial bodies will push in the direction of further competition, not more restrictions.

As deregulation takes hold, several things will probably occur. First, there will be a host of new entrants into the power production field, emboldened by the new rules. These new entities will be constantly pushing for greater access, at the lowest possible cost, to the grid which was largely developed and is owned and controlled by investor-owned utilities. They will attempt to cherry-pick the best industrial customers to the extent that they can undercut the prices of the utilities.

The previously franchised utilities, in turn, will be forced to lower rates, especially for their larger consumers, in order to retain any semblance of rate stability for their residential clientele and keep the political pressure at bay. This may buy some time, but it will make investors very nervous, as the realization sets in of the risk that accompanies active competition. Whether residential customers in some or all markets may ultimately choose electricity supply sources is a matter of regulatory debate and intensified interest.

This cycle will create a tremendous downward pressure on labor costs, as workers become viewed as another commodity in the profit wars. The contracting out of functions such as billing, customer service, and meter reading (which has already begun at some utilities) could well expand. Other job classifications—even those considered now as essential—will be carried out by untrained, inexperienced contract personnel who have little loyalty to the utility's goals or service standards. Utilities who take the hit of losing one or more major industrial customers may be forced to consider substantial layoffs that are beyond the current trend of downsizing.

Faced with cost pressures, the incentive for management at some utilities will not be cooperation with labor, but control. And that means confrontation with, and perhaps eventually attempts to break the union. Byproducts of this process will be the de-emphasis of quality in favor of expedition and economy and a weakened ability to respond to power outages or natural disasters.

After a few years of cutthroat competition, some of the IPPs and even large companies will give up the ghost. The field will be partly littered with the corpses of those companies and their workers who have engaged in bitter labor battles. The winners and losers will become more clear, and the human casualties will confront the reality of imposed unemployment, isolated from the corporate board rooms. The utilities with the deepest pockets and the shrewdest planners will begin the process of buying out as many of the smaller entities as they can. Some producers which started out small will thrive and become major players in their own right.

Eventually, the larger survivors will look for ways to combine forces through mergers and takeovers, be they friendly or hostile. Customers, whether industrial or residential, will find their choices of suppliers to grow increasingly limited, if not back full circle to regional monopolies.

This is what the utility industry will look like if it reflects what deregulation has wrought in the airline industry. I believe that such a scenario is likely to come to pass if government, labor, and industry cannot find sufficient resolve to avoid the predictable, negative outcomes of deregulation and unbridled competition. The effects will be felt by employees, some investors, and the customers who currently consider affordable, uninterrupted service as a given.

If the decision-makers in government and industry go a little slower, then utilities will bear a greater resemblance to present day telecommunications. It is not hard to imagine a system of regional power companies controlling the local markets for residential and small business, while larger companies are the object of intense competition involving power suppliers located anywhere on the continent.

A third possibility is that utilities become more like the trucking industry where cost becomes the single most important driving factor, no pun intended. Survival is assumed to be the reward of those who attempt to win the race to cut costs to the bone.

Maybe all of this will come to pass. Maybe only part of it. Either way, the view of those within the industry approximates what the Romans felt when they spied the Visigoths approaching their city.

There is little doubt that utilities and their workers are going to take lumps over the next few years. Pain is the inevitable byproduct of change. Speaking as a union official, however, I strongly feel that now is the time to take control over our own destiny to the fullest extent possible.

The past is gone for good. It would be a tremendous waste of time and energy to try to hold back the hands of time. Valiant wars in hopeless causes may yield great folk songs for posterity, but they do precious little to promote success.

Conversely, I would also maintain that utility executives would be wise to avoid the mentality conveyed by an energy consultant in a recent *Wall Street Journal* article about the age of deregulation in the utility industry. The article dealt with the effort by the city of Las Cruces, New Mexico, to obtain power from a utility other than the

El Paso Electric Company. It could have applied equally to other situations that are cropping up across the United States.

Noting that the loss of big customers would cause revenues to fall while costs remain virtually fixed, the consultant noted that either ratepayers, stockholders or both would suffer. He forgot a third, and equally critical group . . . the utility's employees. And that's the point—don't forget the tremendous resource that your workers represent. They could be the key to surviving in the age of competition.

Having been a business manager of an IBEW local, I know first hand that labor and management can work together to promote productivity, safety, and service. The IBEW has often supported its employers in seeking rate increases before state regulatory bodies to foster mutually beneficial growth. The IBEW has worked with progressive employers to bring improved technology and methods into the workplace and ensure that our workers are the best trained in the world. This training has allowed us to respond to crises rapidly and effectively to restore power and service that our society needs and demands.

Granted, it was easier to amass such a record of cooperation in a regulated environment. I maintain, however, that this history gives us a positive foundation upon which to build. We need to be honest with ourselves. It would be easy for the IBEW to fall into a totally defensive posture and fight to maintain the status quo to the fullest extent possible. It would be easy for utility companies to treat their workers like a drag on the bottom line and seek cut after cut in staffing, wages, and benefits. It would be predictable if utilities act like so many other industries and devote an inordinate amount of staff time and energy into the wheelings and dealings of the financial markets and less and less to their core business. I suggest, however, that it would be far better for us to confront our changing industry as partners, rather than as antagonists.

The first step we could take together would be to foster a vigorous debate, both within the industry and in the public forum, about the shape that society wants the electric industry to take. We need to point out that our utility companies have provided an uninterrupted and affordable source of energy to America for a century. We must remind government decision-makers that, through various entities, our industry has achieved universal coverage for virtually all who want our product. And it is a product that has become increasingly important in today's technology driven economy.

We must also challenge policy makers in Washington and state and local governments across the country to enunciate the standards they will demand of those who produce and deliver electricity. Uninterrupted service has become increasingly fundamental to our quality of life, and in some instances to life itself. To what degree do they want to ensure that the demands of the public are met? To what degree do they want to keep electricity affordable for private households? What about coverage of rural areas, or service reliability?

We can also work together to ensure a level playing field in the competitive age. We should push for industry standards in safety, quality, and service that will apply to all who participate in the industry. Of course we will welcome new competitors in to the game, provided that they abide by the same rules and standards that were put in place for the benefit of all concerned: consumers, industry, and workers.

We should demand that debate over the future of our industry proceed on intellectually honest ground. By that I mean that we should decouple the concepts of competition and deregulation. They are used synonymously, but in fact, their end results are not necessarily the same.

Competition has become an apple-pie virtue in America. It is linked with the solid values of free will, hard work, individual enterprise, in short, the American Way. Deregulation is something quite different.

Deregulation, in its extreme form, involves removing not only barriers to competition, but also undercutting the rules that ensure a degree of stability and reliability. Competition provides a spur to companies to be more efficient and better meet the needs of customers. Deregulation puts the emphasis on financial schemes such as mergers and takeovers at the expense of customers and the employees who serve them. As I noted earlier, deregulation in other industries has left only a few giants standing who control the market and strangle—you've got it—competition.

We need to spell out for policy makers exactly what it is they are unleashing in the name of competition. Do they want real competition, or are they serving the interest of the larger consumers seeking cheap power and the financial manipulators who are interested in new markets with which to play? The time to demand an answer is now, when the new age is taking shape. If we let them wait until a decade from now when the electrical system is in tatters, then it will be too late for our companies, our workers, and our customers.

In short, a key role that labor and management can play in this modern era is to fight for fair competition. If the new rules of the industry become everybody against the utilities and one against the other, then all we have worked so hard to build for decades will come tumbling down. If we work together for sensible public policy, we can truly compete and win in the industry of tomorrow.

In addition to the face we present to the outside, we must seek new ways of working together within our companies. The collective bargaining process should be looked upon by company executives and workers alike as an opportunity to promote innovation and efficiency. In the 21st century, these qualities will be the ultimate job savers. If each round of negotiations takes on the elements of a street fight, the competition will eat our lunch while we argue over the crumbs.

No one can say for sure what the future of work in a utility company will be, but we can examine some possibilities. To begin with, decisions on employment levels and compensation should be arrived at in concert with workers and their union. Management must realize that workers have a stake in the competitive position and long-term survival of their companies. However, decisions made unilaterally in the board room or the 9th hole at the country club and then imposed through intransigence will meet with the predictable opposition. This will benefit no one in the long term.

Likewise, labor and management should explore the implementation of new technology that will make the production and distribution of power and the servicing of customers more efficient. Along with that goes an ongoing commitment to training so that the workers remain prime assets to their employers, not excess baggage.

As utilities acquire new entities, more job opportunities may open up, as employment levels must adjust at the former core business activities. To the fullest extent possible, the existing work force should be retrained and redeployed at these new facilities. The more job opportunities remain in utilities, the better able the industry will be to continue to attract the high quality work force it has today. If utilities become a low-wage, low-security occupational category, it is hard to see how anyone but the bottom-line crowd will benefit.

Utility management must also realize that customer service and satisfaction, always important in our industry, will take on a new primacy. Who better knows the needs of customers than those who serve them directly? If workers are given more of a voice in how to provide the best service in the most efficient manner possible, companies can reap the benefit of the combined knowledge and experience of this work force. The real key to competitiveness lies not in trimming numbers, but in the fullest utilization of talent and resources.

I have discussed how management and labor can work together. Of course, we as a union have a task on our own as well. Our challenge will be to organize emerging power producers and suppliers and to introduce industry standards of wages, benefits, safety, and participation to these newcomers. The collective bargaining process is perhaps the surest and fairest way of creating a level playing field that will ensure that real competition, not the cutthroat kind that some may wish to become predominate in the utility industry of the future. That is our business, and you can be sure that we will tend to it.

And so we have a great task ahead of us. The IBEW must convince its members to seize the challenges that competition offers and turn them into opportunity. We will not and cannot do that, however, unless management reciprocates in kind. The more we can foster a spirit of cooperation within our industry, the better prepared we will be to compete and thrive. Otherwise, deregulation will become a mean-spirited free-for-all where the ultimate prize may not even be worth having.

Chapter Six

Cultural Change and its Impact on Labor/ Management Relations

James R. Pearl

"We don't see things as they are, we see them as we are."

Anaïs Nin

Re-engineer, reorganize, restructure. Rightsize, downsize, and lay-off. All these terms have become commonplace in today's business world. Companies across America are taking these steps to effectively change their operations and increase productivity. More importantly, though, these steps are fundamentally changing the corporate culture. The concept of, "changing the corporate culture," requires that employees understand and accept the need for change in *themselves* to align with business needs.

While some industries have always operated in a competitive environment, competition is relatively new to the utility industry. To survive in this new atmosphere, utility employees need to adapt quickly and be receptive to change. This requires them to take personal "ownership" of, and responsibility for, the overall change in their corporate culture.

Unions and Corporate Culture Change

The utility industry is more than 40 percent unionized. Labor unions, therefore, have a significant influence on culture change in a utility. As utilities try to accomplish change among their employees, this third party representing those employees must also be able and willing to accept and accomplish change.

Changing the corporate culture cannot be accomplished simply by an executive mandate. The only way to change the environment for all employees, and for union leadership, is through senior management's willingness to communicate honestly and openly with employees. A corporate culture, like individual paradigms, has a historical basis, something that has led us to believe that we know how our work environment should remain. Only through good communications, rationalization of the changes that are coming, and explaining legitimate needs to all employees, can a shift in corporate culture be accomplished.

Union leadership faces several challenges as they deal with a changing culture. They must accept change, internalize it, and then develop a philosophy on how to respond to it. This philosophy is necessary as they balance their members' fears with the pressures from the company for change. For successful cultural change, union leadership must internalize the necessary changes, both personally and professionally.

Communication is the Key

A key to positive corporate cultural change is how well the company ties together its goals and the reasons why change is necessary. Many employees believe their company has effective internal communications. Newspapers, bulletin boards, and personal contacts link companies with their employees in the workplace. However, these types of communications seldom connect the employees' culture with company or industry changes. Making new developments real for employees is an even greater challenge for union leadership. Rarely do union leaders have access to senior management for candid discussions on the company's goals, vision, or competition. As with all employees, union leaders need to be informed as changes develop. They need to know about changes in the industry and realize the challenges they must face together with the company.

At LG&E, we strive for good communications with our employees. Employees give our communication system high marks for advising them of changes in our company, its goals, its visions, and its future direction in a timely, easily understandable manner. However, a recent event showed us how far we still need to go in our efforts to change the culture for all of our employees.

Tough Decision for Tough Times

A management study indicated a surplus of employees in one of our divisions and a layoff appeared to be necessary. Before taking action, we discussed the matter with the union. We established a joint labor/management task force to study the potential layoff situation and to recommend alternatives to downsizing. This group was given extensive training in teamwork and team problem solving. Their challenge was defined for them and the parameters to solve the problem were established. An outside facilitator led the group and kept them focused on their objective.

The task force had access to all relevant information they requested, plus access to support personnel who could detail and explain the data. Management teams provided briefings to explain the internal and external pressures that would affect, or be affected by, a downsizing. For example, the task force was given an extensive briefing by the Regulatory Affairs division on how changes in the industry were developing. The task force learned about the probability of wholesale and retail wheeling, the company's plan to meet these challenges, and the effects on our rate structure. The finance group also explained revenues versus increasing costs, such as costs associated with health care.

Additionally, the task force reported weekly on their progress to an executive steering committee that included the union president and the company's executive vice president of human resources. The group also conducted focus groups in the workplace with their peers to develop solutions. After a six-week period, the group presented their findings and made recommendations to the steering committee. Although many of their recommendations had merit, the group was unable to develop a feasible solution to the overstaffing situation and the layoff was, unfortunately, necessary.

Although a downsizing was unavoidable, one of the task force's recommendations was implemented. The recommendation was for the company to provide a severance and outplacement package to employees affected by a layoff. The collective-bargaining agreement did not contain any provision for severance.

This recommendation became a reality when union and management negotiated a severance package at the time of the layoff, which lessened the damage to what had been a good labor/management relationship.

Lessons for the Future

Two important lessons for the company and union leadership about cultural change and union relations resulted from this process. First, with respect to cultural change, a union member of the joint task force explained to the steering committee how the company needed to improve its communications efforts for the sake of the employees. He said he had read in company newsletters about many of the factors presented to the task force and that he had heard some of the same information in small meetings with his supervisors and managers. But he noted that the lack of proper priority and emphasis on those factors in company communications, resulted in employees failing to appreciate the impact of retail wheeling on the utility business, the differences between wholesale power sales and retail wheeling, the problems associated with rising health care costs, and how these factors affect the utility's rates and its position in the wholesale market.

He reminded the committee that he and other employees were finding it difficult to understand how their individual efforts affected the company as a whole. He pointed out that they did not feel as if they were players in the "big picture" and that the company needed to "beat" this information into employees' heads, not just distribute information and assume that employees will assimilate it correctly. He asked the steering committee to help all employees understand where the company is going and how these challenges facing the utility industry relate to each other and to their company, so that layoffs in the future could be avoided.

The second lesson dealt with union leadership. Because the union president was on the steering committee, and one of his key business representatives coordinated the task force's development, they were able to understand and respond to the business challenges associated with the company's decisions as well as the company's actions regarding the layoff. The layoff, nevertheless, put some strain on labor/management relations. It was our genuine efforts to explain the business reasons for our actions and solicitation of help from the task force that were instrumental in salvaging the good labor/management relationship that we had enjoyed prior to the layoff.

The political impact of the layoff, however, seriously affected the union leaders' ability to deal with their members' attitudes about job security. Union leaders' active involvement in the task-force process enabled them to respond to their members' concerns by developing a professional union philosophy for addressing the threat of competition and communicating this philosophy to the membership.

The hurt of a layoff does not heal quickly, and it was difficult saying goodbye to long-time employees, but our communications efforts helped make an important and productive turn in our corporate culture. Our employees and the union leadership are learning that to survive in the changing utility industry, we must be able to accept change and to make changes in ourselves. We are also learning that the responsibility for changing our corporate culture belongs to each of us. By working together, we will be better prepared to meet the challenges that lie ahead.

Part Three:
The Right Compensation System

Chapter Seven

The Compensation System Meets the New Realities

Carolyn Kenady

The new realities of competition in the utility industry have led managers and employees in utility companies to question the value of their traditional entitlement-oriented compensation programs. As the controller at one company observed, "The base salary program rewards for hierarchy and the number of direct reports . . . we need to reward for good ideas, innovation, and customer service." A vice president noted that "People are still caught in career chimneys." And, according to a strategic planner, "We do not have the competencies we need to compete effectively: marketing, selling, managing risk, negotiating." "Our pay program does not connect pay with performance," says a manager, and employees often tell us, "I don't know what's expected of me."

Throughout the country, utility company CEOs, officers, managers, and employees all voice dissatisfaction with their pay programs. Why? What are utilities doing in response to the pay/performance disconnect? How can organizations use new pay programs to reinforce culture change? And what are the key success factors and pitfalls?

We offer two hypotheses. The first is that a new employment deal is a critical element in the process of changing an organization's culture. The second is that the process used in defining the new deal must model the behaviors needed for success in the new competitive environment. In this chapter we will explore these hypotheses using case studies of two companies—one a utility the other a non-utility—that designed new pay programs to support organizational change.

What happened to the old deal?

Managing and rewarding employees in a regulated environment was simple. Organizations were stable, jobs could be narrowly defined (and remained largely unchanged), employees expected to stay with one utility for their entire career, and the regulators did not expect or encourage experimentation in pay programs. In short, the employer/employee relationship mirrored the structure of the industry: stable and traditional. As illustrated in Figure 1, this arrangement was a good deal for both parties.

Figure 1
Elements of the old deal: Employee gets/company gets

Past Relationship	
Employee Gets	*Company Gets*
Job Security	Loyalty
Investment Training	Investment payoff due to low turnover
"Family" feeling	"Happy" employees
Pay security	Same fixed costs as competitors
Predictable career paths	Organization stability

The old deal was not unique to the utility industry; companies in other industries offered their employees a similar deal. However, as competition increased in other industries, they changed their employment deal to better reflect the needs of a competitive organization: streamlined, flatter, with less upward mobility and more performance-oriented rewards. Until recently, federal, state, and local regulation protected the hierarchical, highly structured organization that valued the elements of the old employment deal. Employees came to work for utilities because "I want a job with stability and security." For the most part, managers believed that "We need to take care of our employees." These values ended up becoming deeply embedded in the organization's culture.

However, competition has forced many utilities to abandon the "old deal." Management cannot provide the "old rewards"—merit increases, regular promotional opportunities, lifetime employment guarantees. All these promises worked in the past but don't work when the company has to compete with independent power producers or with other utilities that produce power at a lower cost.

The change occurred first at utilities that experienced financial problems because of high costs or a hostile regulatory environment. However, as more organizations felt the impact of competition, they were compelled to reevaluate and redefine the employer/employee relationship. Often the company introduces change in a piecemeal fashion—first instituting hiring or promotion freezes, then clamping down on perquisites and costs such as overtime, and later reducing merit budgets. Sometimes the changes are wholesale and dramatic, taking the form of layoffs, voluntary severance or open window programs, organizational restructurings, or pay freezes. Regardless, employees end up wondering why the change occurred and feel abandoned or cheated because the deal they "signed up for" no longer seems to hold—the implicit promises that the company appeared to have made to them seemingly betrayed by the company's own actions.

At the watercooler, in break rooms, and at the power plant employees speak in hushed voices—or complain loudly—about the new reality. "This used to be a friendly place to work . . . we were all one big family," is a common refrain. Or, "I'm working harder than ever without a raise in pay." Meanwhile, at management meetings and in planning sessions officers and managers search for ways to make sense of the new order. The business plan requires that employees think and act differently, yet the company's culture does not value or reward the desired behaviors.

Creating a new deal is critical to changing the culture because without it there is nothing to replace the "broken" promises of the past, and—without an employer/employee relationship that benefits both parties—employees have no incentive to modify their behavior (except in a way that works to the detriment of the organization).

65

Pay and performance systems send powerful messages to employees about what is valued and rewarded in the organization. A new deal based on a pay/performance contract offers the company the opportunity to communicate to employees:

➠ The new definition of "fairness,"

➠ What the company expects from employees in return for pay, and

➠ What employees can expect from the company in return for their time and effort.

Companies that are moving forward are doing so in part because they redefined the employment relationship to meet their business needs, reflect their cultural values, and create the perception of fairness among employees.

The second hypothesis—that the process used must model the behaviors and values required to compete successfully—helps support culture change. Competing successfully in the newly competitive environment requires that companies change—their cost structure, their customer orientation, and their ability to market, negotiate deals, and satisfy their customers. However, employees often do not understand the new realities and their implications for employee pay and career opportunities. All they see is that management is not playing by the old rules. Their sentiments sound like "The plum jobs go to the new hires," or "Management took care of themselves [during the reorganization] and the rest of us got the shaft." At many companies senior management has recognized the need to involve employees to increase understanding of and build support for the new pay/performance contract.

Defining a New Deal through Compensation Strategy

Employees may believe that they are getting the short end of the stick because their organization has not redefined its pay and performance programs consistent with the needs of the new competitive organization.

A compensation strategy can communicate to employees:

➥ What the company wishes to reward, and

➥ How it will reward.

The new compensation strategy will differ from company to company, but the basic elements are the same:

➥ It specifies the behaviors and results that support the company's business plan and cultural values.

➥ It lets employees know what they will be rewarded for (e.g., results, competencies) and how (in what form).

For example, as shown in Figure 2, the company may discard old forms of pay and introduce new, performance-based rewards into the compensation program.

Figure 2
Transition from Old Compensation Program to New Compensation Program

Past Relationship	To	Desired Relationship
■ If you come to work here, the company will take care of you ■ All employees are entitled to some market adjustment to stay "whole"	To	■ If we outperform the market, you will share in the benefits ■ We have to earn our right to competitive pay and a secure job

Based on longevity	**Trophies**	Self-funded at unit level	**Variable Pay**
Christmas "gift"	**Bonus**		Merit (increase or lump sum)
Average market increase	**Merit**	Funded by company performance	**Market Adjustment**
	Base Pay		**Base Pay**

The old compensation program is largely longevity-based; the new one is tied to market pay levels and company success. Many utilities and other organizations are adopting compensation programs that reflect a greater performance orientation. But the question remains: Can this change support the transition to a new (competitive) culture? Let's examine two case studies to see how different organizations designed the new compensation programs to support culture change.

The Case of the Forgotten Exempt Employees

Utility A was in deep financial trouble. Its rates were high; revenues were not meeting cash flow needs. At one point, its survival was in doubt. However, it got its financial house in order, initiated change efforts among employee groups, and revised some bargaining unit benefit programs to make them consistent with those of other employees. In the midst of redefining what it expected of employees, upper management realized that it needed the support of its exempt employees. This group had remained loyal to the company throughout its financial troubles and had worked hard to help it reach fiscal solvency, but these employees saw that their rewards were not consistent with the new needs being voiced by management. "We've never had goals . . . We need it tied together at the top to bring everyone together." Moreover, in improving the bargaining unit employees' overall package, upper management had eliminated the distinction and status traditionally accorded to the exempt workforce. This group felt abandoned by the new management.

Senior managers realized that their plans for change had not taken management employees into account. They had to pause and consider: What do we expect of our exempt employees and how are we willing to reward them in return? They set up a team of officers and managers to develop a new compensation program. Working with Towers Perrin this group developed a process for understanding:

➡ The new *behaviors and results*: What do we need to do to be successful?

➡ The new management's *values*: How do we want our managers to manage?

They began by looking at the company's business strategy to understand what was required of employees. The business needed employees who were more flexible and responsive. It needed fewer levels and more broadly focused positions. Although the company needed to manage costs more effectively, labor costs were not excessive.

Looking to the future, however, the company needed a sharper market focus on its programs, including employee pay programs. The management team then discussed how it wanted to manage. The new CEO spoke frequently of empowerment and of pushing down decision-making. In fact, he made a point of meeting with the rank and file and encouraging them to bring their issues directly to him.

However, as the team examined the officers' actions, it became clear that empowerment was in its infancy. The company was just beginning to introduce the concept of teamwork to bargaining unit employees, and exempt employees would continue to work in traditional jobs for the near term. Nevertheless, senior management wanted to introduce greater accountability for results and continuous improvement.

When the team had completed its analysis of management's business strategy and values, it set about understanding employees' definition of fairness. Focus group discussions revealed how well employees understood the new business strategy, their definition of "fairness," and problems with or inequities in the pay program. Employees understood that the company had to change to remain in business, yet they clung to the company's old promises: a promotion if you were "next in line," pay and service awards as a reward for loyalty and longevity, and overtime pay to reward for inputs. They also felt that pay opportunities did not reflect actual responsibilities.

On the basis of the fact-finding and analysis, it was clear that Utility A's compensation strategy should be to:

➠ Pay rates similar to those offered by utilities of comparable size and geographic market (for non-industry-specific jobs),

➠ Reward for innovation, flexibility, and contribution, and

⟶ Reward for company success and above-average results through variable pay.

To gain acceptance of the compensation strategy, the design process needed to address two issues:

⟶ Changing the exempt pay program focus from longevity to market,

⟶ Ensuring that job descriptions and job grades reflected what employees really did.

Utility A convened roundtable sessions with managers. Using a salary structure based on competitive pay levels, Towers Perrin educated the managers about market-based job grading. They graded jobs and took considerable time to ensure that they all could stand behind their decisions. They engaged in a number of debates about the relative worth of some jobs. They tested the validity and fairness of a market-based approach. At the end they agreed that the interests of the company and the employees alike were best served by using the market to determine pay opportunities. For the company, it meant that pay levels would not exceed those of its business competitors (other utilities) or power producers; for employees it meant that pay opportunities were comparable to those at other major employers. They all agreed to support the salary structure and proudly presented it to the management team. Utility A had achieved a milestone: it had gotten managers to understand, agree on, and support the job-grading process.

With the support and involvement of company managers, the rollout of the new program was easily accomplished. Utility A's CEO announced the new program to managers and supervisors in person and to all other employees by video. The management team and Human Resources briefed managers on how the program works and trained them to present it to their employees. Managers convened meetings of employees to explain the new program and held a one-on-one discussion with each employee reporting to them to explain the employee's new grade assignment and any impact on his/her pay. A subgroup of the manager roundtable meets regularly to grade jobs. And the managers revised the company's performance management program the following year.

Getting Pay to Fit the New Organization: A Matter of Survival

Company B had no choice. It had undergone a radical reorganization and downsizing. It staked its future success (and continued existence) on being a low-cost producer that could consistently meet customers' requirements. Company B is an aerospace manufacturer—another industry that is undergoing the pain of greater competitive pressure. The new organization was delayered, "leaders" replaced managers, employees were placed in self-managed teams; in short, the organization no longer resembled the old vertical hierarchy of an engineering-driven organization. And the old pay program no longer fit the new organization.

The old pay program rewarded employees for length of service, technical knowledge, rank in the hierarchy, and number of direct reports and/or budget authority. The new organization called for people who were willing to go above and beyond, to stretch, to contribute whatever is needed, and to work closely with both their teammates and the customer.

Towers Perrin and an internal design team worked quickly to assess the situation and to develop requirements for change. They conducted focus group discussions and an all-employee survey. Employees said that they felt cheated. They wanted jobs defined and wanted pay levels that recognized their new roles and contributions to the organization.

The design team interviewed members of the new general management team to understand their strategic objectives (what the organization believes it needs to do to be successful):

➡ Be a low-cost provider,

➡ Apply existing technology effectively, and

➡ Maintain customer satisfaction.

The design team also asked the general management team to define its values (how it wanted to manage). They found that the management team needed both to retain top performers and to recognize and reward group performance. It wanted to pay competitively but not exceed cost parameters. Finally, it wanted to ensure that employees understood the new career opportunities available to them since the dismantling of the functional hierarchies.

The design team then translated these strategic objectives and management values into a series of statements outlining the new compensation strategy, and tested them with the general management team. Because the leaders were new in their roles and had just developed a strategic framework for managing the new organization, gaining agreement on the new compensation strategy statement required several meetings. The management team and the design team then began to communicate the elements of the new employer/employee relationship via company newsletters, leadership briefings, and brown bag lunches. The compensation strategy contained three key elements:

➠ Defining new job families and career paths for a team-based organization,

➠ Providing employees with performance feedback and developmental support, and

➠ Tying pay levels (relative to its competitors) and employee rewards to company performance.

Then the design team set about involving employees and leaders in designing the new programs so that they supported all three elements of the strategy. First, they discussed with leaders what kind of job definition would fit with the new organization—traditional, functional, or generic. The leadership endorsed a job-family approach that was as generic as possible without sacrificing key distinctions between roles. The design team discussed this concept with a broader group of leaders, then convened a group of job experts from all areas of the organization and from all classifications to assist in defining new jobs by:

➠ Eliminating old job titles that no longer were useful,

➠ Grouping existing job titles into job families with more generic titles, and

➠ Identifying the number of levels for each job family grouping.

After the preliminary work was done, the design team used the initial framework to develop a questionnaire; the design team asked employees in every work group to complete it to obtain accurate information on jobs and roles. Using this information the design team drafted matrices describing the key dimensions of each job family—such as knowledge and skill, responsibility, teamwork, and leadership. It trained the leaders and job experts in the process, and convened a group of nearly 60 leaders and job experts, organized by area, to develop job family matrices. The completed matrices included a definition of job families and a leveling guide outlining the requirements for each level. The design team then used competitive pay data to design the new pay structure and assign jobs to grades.

The new program replaced the old hierarchical structure with one that collapsed narrow functional distinctions into broader jobs, thereby enabling employees to take on different roles without being concerned that their pay opportunity would be reduced. The new approach emphasized employees' knowledge, abilities, and responsibilities, and outlined the requirements for moving to a new job family level. The job experts and leaders felt that the job family matrices achieved some milestones—they defined new career paths for employees and reflected the flexibility required in the new teaming environment.

The design team concurrently tackled two other aspects of the new employment relationship—providing career development support to employees and rewarding group performance—by designing a new performance management program and a success sharing program. To understand the design requirements for performance management, the design team relied on the data gathered in the focus group discussions and the all-employee survey.

Its analysis of the information found that the organization did not give timely and relevant feedback to employees and that employees wanted development plans that helped them to understand how they can add value to the organization and what they needed to do to take on different assignments within the organization. To develop a new program the design team consulted with team leaders and resource leaders. The new performance management process consisted of three elements: a developmental discussion between the leader and employee to agree on needed competencies and areas for development during that year, a multirater form by which teammates could give feedback at the end of the performance cycle to the employee (and to his/her leader) on the employee's competencies and behaviors, and, following the feedback, a summary evaluation session and discussion between the leader and his/her employee. This enabled the employee and leader to focus on two aspects of the new employment relationship: individual competencies and employee performance and the behaviors that supported overall group results.

The final program, success sharing, was critical to the business strategy. Rewards depended on overall company performance and employees had to help the company achieve performance targets to receive future rewards. This aspect of the new employment relationship had to be explicit to gain employee commitment to the new business strategy and to ensure that employees did not feel cheated by the new performance-based relationship. It is a gamble. The organization must achieve certain sales and margin goals, but it enables employees to see how they contribute to the organization's success.

Keeping Pace with Change

Utilities face a challenging and uncertain future. Many already have made changes in their pay and performance programs. But the competitive world is not static. To ensure that reward programs continue to send the *right* messages, we recommend a continuous improvement orientation. Towers Perrin incorporates an evaluation and renewal process in the implementation of pay and performance programs. Key steps include:

1. Understanding the perceptions and needs of customers (both management and employee groups).

2. Building in quantitative performance measures that can be used to evaluate program performance.

3. Modifying the program on the basis of customers' needs and evaluation of program performance.

Lessons Learned

What are the key success factors in developing new pay programs to help support organization change?

➡ Involve employees in a process that models the desired outcomes,

➡ Test to ensure that programs:

    – Support business strategy

    – Are consistent with the organization's desired values,

➡ Outline a "deal" that meets the needs of the company and employees,

➡ Ensure buy-in and support at all levels, and

➡ Plan implementation carefully so that managers and employees fully understand the pay program and the role it plays in the transition to a competitive environment.

Chapter Eight

New Pay Programs: Reinforcing Cultural Change in a Transforming Industry

Jack McGourty, Richard R. Reilly, and Kenneth P. De Meuse

During the last two decades, American industry has undergone a dramatic transformation. Beginning in the late 1970s and throughout the 1980s, few industries escaped the influence of the merger and acquisition binge. An overwhelming number of companies became involved in what the press coined "merger mania." The dust hardly had settled when organizations, now loaded with debt, looked for ways to improve their financial conditions. "Merger mania" stepped aside for a new wave of organizational transformation—downsizing or (for the politically correct) right-sizing. At the same time, other changes were taking place. Technological innovations, globalization, and changes in government regulations coincided with a less stable marketplace and increased competition. Regulated industries, in particular, were forced to respond by changing both organizational structures and business processes. Total Quality Management and its successor Business Process Reengineering are two examples of initiatives that many organizations embraced as they moved to transform themselves into more efficient, flexible, and competitive companies.

These management initiatives focused attention on work processes and how they can be reconfigured to increase efficiency. But they also changed the way jobs are designed. Team-based work structures, probably the most notable example of this change, have brought with them a new set of human resource considerations. As employees become empowered to make decisions and manage their own work, new skills are demanded. Organizations need to modify their cultures, and in some cases completely alter them, so that these new behaviors can become accepted by and expected of all. Organizations urgently need to develop innovative management practices that will foster and reinforce fundamental behavioral change. This need is most evident in the area of compensation systems.

The Changing Nature of the Utilities Industry

Utility executives have predicted the coming age of deregulation for several years. During the past decade, lawmakers in states from California to New Jersey have been reviewing the laws that grant protective monopolies to utilities. However, the drive towards deregulation largely was inaugurated by the Federal Energy Policy Act of 1992. This Act forces electric utilities to open their transmission lines so that competing utilities can retail power over them. The impending age of deregulation and increased competition is causing utility organizations to take a hard look at existing structures, processes, and management practices. Utility organizations will certainly need to develop and foster a new employee culture—one that emphasizes different skills and competencies needed to compete effectively in today's marketplace.

New Contract for Employees

In 1956, William H. Whyte wrote a fascinating book, *The Organization Man*, describing a corporate America where an employee invested "himself" completely in "his" company—working 60 to 70 hour weeks, going on the road wherever and whenever needed, relocating on a dime's notice. In return, the employer provided a "good job" with "good pay," granted annual merit increases, and provided plenty of opportunity for advancement. The company offered financial security. It was a womb-to-tomb mentality!

This employer-employee relationship gave order, predictability, and stability. But such relationships do not (and cannot) exist any longer. Today, corporate restructuring and massive layoffs are everyday news. We live in an era of short career ladders and decreased job security. Moreover, we live in a time of increased individual leisure time, increased family demands, and rampant job/career mobility. In total, the work environment is weaving a new, dynamic employer-employee relationship—one built on self-reliance, independence, and mutuality. It is an employer-employee relationship that accommodates both sexes and integrates a mosaic of races, heritages, needs, values, and personalities.

The employer-employee contract of today's utilities requires the employee to take ownership for his or her work environment and career. Employees must continue to develop new skills and competencies, shaping and molding their jobs to new heights of efficiency. Employees need to take the responsibility for their work world. Rather than viewing their jobs in terms of "financial security bestowed by management," today's employees need to envision their role as an active partner with management to serve the customer. If they perform their jobs effectively, they and the company will prosper.

Consequently, utility companies today must select, develop, lead, motivate, communicate, delegate, reward—in other words, manage—differently than in the past. Today's organization must create a corporate culture that reinforces diversity, risk taking, teamwork, innovation, customer power, and flexibility. To remain successful in an era of deregulation, an organization needs a kaleidoscopic culture that institutionalizes change rather than a bureaucratic one that propagates the status quo. In utilities today, managers and non-managers alike need to behave differently and have new attitudes.

New Behaviors Required by All Employees

In the past, *managers* were expected to direct, organize, plan, budget, judge, and control. Non-managers were expected to follow orders, not make waves, show blind loyalty, respect the status quo, and listen without asking questions. American companies can no longer operate under such a system. Labor in the United States is too costly. We can no longer pay premium rates simply for "muscle activity." Employees need to also provide "brain activity" in their work.

As a Controller in a large midwestern utility asserted:

> It used to be once you were hired, that was it! Companies would never ask you to leave. Moreover, your job was so

79

comfortable you did not want to leave. Management had very limited expectations for employees in the past. That has changed.

Today, we are demanding much more from our employees. They must continue their skill growth, be receptive to cross-training, be responsive to customer service, and be an active member of a team. If employees are unwilling to learn new skills, they have diminished value!

In our interviews with several utility executives, we found they regarded three categories of new behaviors to be important to the success of utility organizations: Collaboration, Proactivity, and Customer-Focus.

In every case, executives discussed the importance of employees "working together" to meet marketplace demands. One example after another provided anecdotal evidence that multifunctional and self-directed teams are becoming commonplace in the re-engineered utility organization. Due to this new way of working, utility employees need to manifest critical team behaviors such as collaboration (McGourty and De Meuse, 1994). *Collaboration* is defined as demonstrating a commitment to the team's overall purpose, helping members to identify mutual objectives and be mutually accountable for results, working cooperatively with others and actively participating in team activities, and valuing the contributions of all members.

We classify the second critical set of behaviors as *Proactivity*. Proactivity involves both individuals and teams taking responsibility for their own and others' performance. Again, several utility executives discussed the need for employees to be self-driven, guided by established goals, and accountable for their performance. One executive described it this way: "We need to have the ability to confront each other regarding performance, not just as managers, but as peers...as well." Another interview revealed that utility employees must be able to view policies as guidelines rather than "gospel written in stone"—they must be able to deal with ambiguity and uncertainty. Proactivity involves team members working independently and interdependently toward established performance goals and evaluating new ideas in terms of these goals. Individuals and teams actively monitor their progress and use action plans and timetables to make sure they are meeting goals and objectives. In the new employer-employee contract, the employee's proactivity is an expected part of the bargain.

The final set of behaviors, categorized as *Customer-Focus*, involve employees' constant attention to customer needs. As one executive said, "We must not only ask the customer what they want, but when they want it as well." Customer-Focus behaviors include addressing the needs of the customer quickly, meeting the expectations and requirements of internal and external customers, frequently soliciting input from the customer regarding future products and services, and establishing and maintaining effective relationships with customers.

Problems with Traditional Pay Systems

Organizational theorists have long noted that rewards shape and motivate employee behavior. But understanding *what* rewards to give and *how* to give them is not clear. Whatever the reward structure, traditional pay systems are not the answer for today's dynamic, global marketplace.

Experts and practitioners alike recognize that traditional compensation systems are inadequate as organizations become more performance-oriented. Systems quickly become outdated as organizations redesign the way people work. Five problems often identified with traditional reward systems are:

➠ an emphasis on individual accomplishment,

➠ evaluations based only on the supervisor's viewpoint,

➠ the promotion of specialized skill development,

➠ the promotion of upward mobility, and

➠ a de-emphasis on performance.

Emphasis on Individual Accomplishment

First, traditional reward systems tend to emphasize individual accomplishment rather than collaborative efforts. If an organization's plan rewards *individual* effort, employees will focus their energies on *individual* accomplishment. This practice is troublesome now that working in teams has become pervasive in most organizations. Recent studies show that eight out of every ten U.S. companies have assigned people into designated work teams (Gorden, 1992). This new emphasis on teamwork is affecting productivity and profitability in large and small companies across every industrial category. Managing teams effectively is more than simply organizing individuals into groups and expecting team performance. Expecting people to perform as a team while rewarding individuals not only sends the wrong message, but can lead to breakdowns and ultimately failure.

Although it seems obvious that team-based organizations require different reward systems, many efforts to design and implement systems that promote teamwork have been unsuccessful. There even are critics who argue that incentives may be counterproductive to promoting any type of group or individual behavior (Kohn, 1993). This position is correct if the incentive system is poorly designed and implemented. However, incentive systems can and do work if they are communicated clearly and the right behaviors are measured accurately and rewarded fairly.

Evaluations Based on Supervisor's Viewpoint Only

Typically, an employee's raise is based solely on the supervisor's evaluation of the person's performance during the previous year. Critics have repeatedly attacked these "annual performance appraisals" for lacking validity and reliability. Even with specific training in how to effectively conduct performance appraisals, rating errors frequently influence the evaluation. For example, recent events may influence the supervisor more than events that happened earlier in the year. Furthermore, as utility companies become more collaborative and customer-focused, obtaining performance ratings solely from a supervisor becomes myopic. A more meaningful approach is to collect performance evaluations from fellow team members and customers. Pay increases would be based on information integrated from various parties who interact with the employee.

Promotion of Specialized Skill Development

Another problem with traditional reward systems is that they promote learning of specialized skills and disciplines within functional boundaries. Today, most people receive annual pay increases based on activities within their functional work area. An engineer's performance is evaluated by an engineering manager, who in turn is assessed by a technical manager, and so on. This approach, which was once perfectly reasonable, encourages the acquisition of narrow expertise in one area—exactly the opposite of what we need in today's world of multi-functional teams. Most traditional reward systems do not recognize and reward the acquisition of new skills outside the boundaries of a narrow discipline or function.

Promotion of Upward Mobility

Traditionally, reward systems have been inextricably linked to upward mobility, so that striving to move up the proverbial corporate ladder is both expected and encouraged. However, linking pay increases to promotions does not make sense in light of today's flatter organizational structures. Organizations need to encourage lateral movement instead.

De-emphasis on Performance

A final problem with traditional reward systems is that they usually do not emphasize actual performance. In many systems, pay increases are viewed as entitlements rather than rewards for effective performance. In fact, in most organizations, the phrase "merit increase" to describe a raise is probably a misnomer.

Increased competition in the utilities industry will require organizations to reward and recognize employees for their contributions to actual performance. Companies will no longer have the luxury (or the margins) to continually increase compensation based on entitlement and tenure. There are many challenges to face as you design and implement new pay systems. Foremost among these challenges is to design compensation systems that link rewards to organizational-level goals and objectives. When this is accomplished, rewards must be based on reliable, accurate measures of performance so that all organizational members will be encouraged to behave in the ways necessary to achieve the goals.

Implementing New Pay Systems in the Organization

The utilities executive needs a "road map" to follow when designing and implementing new pay systems. Based on our experience working with utility organizations and additional research on the best practices of benchmark utilities, we can suggest several steps to the successful implementation of performance-based reward systems. These steps can be divided into three major phases: assessment, design, and implementation (see Figure 1).

Phase One: Assessment

The *assessment* phase consists of these steps: evaluate the organization's readiness for a change in its compensation system, determine strategic pay objectives, and examine how employee behavior can contribute to these objectives.

Assess Organizational Readiness. When you plan to introduce a new pay program, an important first step is to determine how ready the organization is to accept it. As noted earlier, most utility employees have already experienced numerous changes in their work environment. Is the time right to ask them to accept more change? When assessing an organization's readiness for change, think about: the level of trust among organizational members, the history of employee involvement, and overall employee support for a pay system change. Consider how employee attitudes and past experiences will influence their acceptance of, satisfaction with, and commitment to the new pay system.

➡ The Trust Factor. Employee trust is perhaps the critical component when implementing new compensation programs. The degree of trust determines whether the new pay system

84

Figure 1
Road Map to a New Pay System

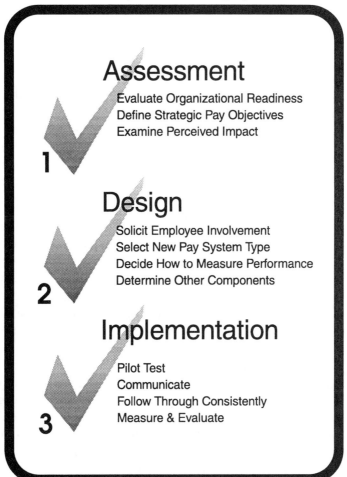

ultimately will be accepted by employees. Employee trust affects communication among all levels of employees. When trust is low, communication is less open and may be distorted, so that all issues regarding existing and new pay systems are difficult to discuss.

➠ History of Employee Involvement. As with other organizational initiatives, employee involvement ensures that those who will be most affected contribute significantly to the new pay program's design. When assessing whether the company is ready for a change in pay policy and structure, review the history of employee involvement. Question whether employee participation is part of the firm's culture and whether employees perceive past instances of involvement as meaningful. Do employees feel that their contributions are valued and incorporated in the decision process? Of course, employee involvement and trust are not mutually exclusive. A history of low employee involvement and failed promises may suggest that the timing for changes in compensation is wrong. Your efforts will be better spent to improve the level of trust as a short-term objective before changing the compensation plan.

➠ Employee Support. Another consideration is overall employee support for changing the existing systems. Today's work environment is subject to frequent, if not continual, change. However, people still perceive any tinkering with their compensation as a cause for alarm. Before initiating a pay change, managers must examine the degree of support from all employee levels, including management, non-management, and union representatives. You can encourage support for change by identifying "champions" in the organization. Champions from various departments, functions, and levels can help communicate and "market" the new pay program. In addition to these support issues, evaluate employee attitudes regarding existing pay systems. Questions include: "Do existing pay plans adequately address internal equity and external competition?" and "Are there clear, accurate, and reliable measures of performance already in place?" Ask yourself whether existing systems can serve as the proper foundation for supplemental pay programs.

Define Strategic Pay Objectives. The next step in the assessment phase is to define strategic pay objectives and how they are linked to overall business goals. The first and most important question is,

"What does the company hope to gain by changing its existing pay program?" As with any organizational intervention, objectives must be clearly stated and firmly aligned with existing business strategies. Clear pay objectives ensure two things: you get what you want, and you avoid getting what you don't want. The Sears Auto Service Centers organization provides an example of the latter. Intending to motivate service managers to increases sales, they placed incentives on the number of auto parts they sold. The plan backfired when some employees allegedly started to sell parts that the customer did not actually need. The result: Sears paid an estimated 15 million dollars in damages.

There are also many examples of reward systems designed to promote one behavior that undermines other desired behaviors. One organization we recently spoke to touted its success in improving the way employees from different business units cooperated. Through training and other management practices, the company had changed its competitive culture to a more cooperative one. With this successful change behind them, they offered a new pay program linked to overall business results—awarding stock options to individual employees for performance within their own strategic business units. This reward system precipitated enormous inter-team competition and a total breakdown of the cooperation the company had worked so hard to develop.

Strategic pay objectives can be defined in many different ways. Common objectives in business include financial results, quality improvements, employee safety, and customer satisfaction. These objectives are relevant for the utility industry, but you can also use pay systems to promote new employee skills and behaviors. As the examples above show, in addition to defining pay objectives in terms of financial performance, you need to identify the behaviors precipitated by the proposed pay system. However, there is one caveat: pay systems must reinforce behavioral and cultural changes, not initiate them. Behavioral and cultural change will not occur solely based on pay. Pay systems are only one way to inform employees which behaviors are expected and required for future organizational success. Behavioral changes occur when management provides long-term support and implements several practices designed to perpetuate change.

Examine Perceived Impact on Pay Objectives. A final area to evaluate during the assessment phase is the impact that employee behavior can have on the stated objectives. Compensation specialists have noted the importance of what is commonly labeled "line of sight" between the employee's job tasks and the actual performance objectives desired. The argument goes like this: when employees see that their actions on the job affect the actual objectives, rewards linked to the objectives will be the most effective. Assess the degree to which individual and team performance contribute to the objectives. Also evaluate how well employees understand their goals and whether they believe they can influence their attainment.

Phase Two: Design

During this phase, a design team composed of representative employee groups makes decisions on the type of pay system and other major design components. It is important to assemble a cross-section of employees from different levels, functions, and job classifications so all employees feel that their views are represented. The steps in this phase are: solicit employee involvement, select new pay system type, decide how to measure employee performance, and determine other design components.

Solicit Employee Involvement. The first step, getting employee involvement, is the most important aspect of the design phase. Experts agree that employee involvement is the key ingredient to any successful change initiative, especially when changes impact pay. There are many advantages to working with employees in the design of a new pay system.

Employee involvement helps to ensure that pay objectives are clearly defined in a way that employees will understand. Once the objectives are defined, an employee design team can help determine whether the future recipients will view them as achievable. If a pay system is founded on objectives that are perceived as too much of a "stretch," it is destined to fail. Also, employees can be the best source of information regarding how to assess whether objectives are attained. Most times, the people actually doing the work can describe measurable outcomes that are not apparent to individuals who are less directly involved.

Employee involvement also helps identify inequities the proposed pay program might create. Inequities occur quite frequently in organizations as cross-functional teams become more prevalent. By bringing employees from various departments and disciplines together to work on a project, a firm risks making salient any pay inequities that may exist. An example is product development teams where employees from marketing, finance, and research and development work together. Typically, marketing employees have been compensated based partly on product revenues, resulting in higher variable pay than non-marketing counterparts. Now that they are working together, this pay difference is brought into plain sight.

Employee involvement also ensures that recipients value the proposed rewards. A reward that is not valued by the employee will not motivate a change in behavior. This is a common problem with pay systems that are based on a percentage of revenues or profits. If potential earnings based on these calculations are perceived as negligible, employees will not be seriously motivated by them.

Select New Pay System Type. Once the pay objectives are clearly defined, the next step in the design phase is to select the type of pay plan that will best support these objectives. A problem in many utility firms is a long history of high employee compensation levels. The industry's regulatory nature made high wage rates possible because the utility simply would seek a higher tariff in its rate filings with the state commission or Federal Energy Regulatory Commission (FERC). Now, the question becomes how to align compensation levels to the marketplace so a firm can be more competitive.

There are several types of pay systems designed for new organizational realities. Recently, the Towers Perrin management consulting firm surveyed nearly 1600 businesses with annual sales ranging from under $100 million to more than $100 billion. They found that fewer companies are using traditional merit pay to reward employees for their performance. More than one-third of the companies they sampled offered variable pay options like lump-sum bonuses. These variable pay approaches are extremely helpful because they provide a one-time payment rather than a base salary increase. Utilities can use variable pay schemes to control their fixed costs and bring pay in line with pay in other industries.

Some pay systems are individual-based while many emphasize the performance of employees working collaboratively in teams. We will look at two types of new pay systems that are becoming common among utility practitioners: skill-based pay and team-based incentive pay.

Several utility organizations are "piloting" skill-based pay programs to broaden their employees' skills. Skill-based pay systems reward employees for learning and performing a variety of tasks and jobs as opposed to specializing in one area. This approach is more congruent with the needs of today's organizations. Employees often are made responsible for producing a whole product, completing an entire process, or delivering a complete service. Skill-based pay helps customer-focused organizations, like utilities, service their customers more effectively. These programs prepare employees to handle a wide range of customer issues without switching the customer from department to department. Also, when employees are multi-skilled and able to work interdependently, they can rotate among various jobs and assume responsibilities as needed.

Skill-based pay has many benefits for organizations within the utilities industry: it motivates employees to enhance and broaden skill levels, it measures employee value based on contribution rather than job value, and it creates career paths in a flatter, team-based organizational structure. Skill acquisition will become increasingly important as the industry undergoes significant force reductions (Fanning, 1994).

Team-based incentives are based on accomplishment of financial and/or operational goals defined at a *team* level. There are many team pay programs, including such group incentives as "winsharing" and "profit-sharing." Winsharing is derived from its predecessor, "gainsharing," which typically is based on a group's achievement above a historic operational benchmark. Gainsharing programs have been popular in the manufacturing arena for a long time. These programs usually provide group incentives associated with cost savings and increases in productivity. For many teams, historic benchmarks have become irrelevant because of such organizational events as reorganizations, process reengineering, and downsizing. Winsharing incentives are based on *future* financial or operational "gains." A common approach is to identify future objectives, put measurements in place, and base payouts on goal attainment. Winsharing plans are typically customized to "fit" the group's work activities and to ensure that the proper relationship exists between work activity and outcome.

Profit sharing is a common pay plan whose objectives encourage a broader level of involvement and concern for what makes the organization profitable. While this type of plan can provide employees with a common set of objectives, it does not necessarily drive the many specific behaviors that may be critical to the organization's success. The major disadvantage of a profit-sharing plan is that it is not flexible enough to motivate all employees who participate. Many employees cannot easily relate important job activities to profit outcomes. Thus, profit sharing can focus groups of employees on profits at the expense of other critical job outcomes like customer service.

Decide How to Measure Employee Performance. After selecting the type of pay system, the third step in the design phase is to decide how to measure employee performance. In most traditional pay systems, a manager's judgment of an individual's performance or skill attainment determines rewards. The measurement component is not well conceptualized, developed, or executed in most organizations. Innovative pay systems, if they are to be effective in changing behaviors, must be accompanied by innovative measurement systems. An effective measurement system has four key requirements: well-defined performance competencies, specific desired behaviors, processes that measure the behaviors fairly and accurately, and feedback to employees.

⇒ Well-defined performance competencies.[1] Definition does two important things: it helps to set the stage for measurement, and it provides a common framework for all employees to begin thinking about what they expect and what the organization expects of them. One note of caution. Companies frequently develop a complex, multidimensional system of competencies. We have seen models that include as many as 50 separate competencies. Such systems are difficult to construct, communicate, and use. The best advice is to "keep it simple."

⇒ Specific desired behaviors. It seems obvious that to measure something we have to be able to observe it. However, a common problem is the definition of competencies that are never clearly translated into "observable," or behavioral, terms. For example, many organizations today include competencies for "empowerment" and "managing diversity" but do not clearly specify how employees are to be measured. This situation can create confusion and lead to perceptions of unfairness. For any competency, a good test is to try to specify *observable behaviors* that can be used to determine effective performance or skill attainment. If it cannot be observed, it should not be included in the reward system.

An example of how to define a competency and then specify it in behavioral terms is shown in Figure 2. The competency is "collaboration," and several observable behaviors that can be used to measure an individual's or a team's effectiveness are described.

⇒ *Processes that accurately and fairly measure the behaviors.* Depending upon your organization's strategic pay objectives, you might use one or more skill-based, team based, and individually-

---

[1] The term competency is used here to refer to a well-defined category of behavior that can be measured. Other terms that are sometimes used are performance dimension or performance factor.

Figure 2
Behavioral Examples of Collaboration

Managing Conflict

➡ Accepts criticism openly and non-defensively

➡ Acknowledges conflict and works to resolve issues among team members

➡ Negotiates solutions and compromises that are acceptable to all team members

Creating a Team Environment

➡ Shares credit for success with other team members

➡ Is cooperative rather than competitive

➡ Encourages cooperation and participation among team members

Commitment to Team Goals

➡ Puts team goals over individual goals

➡ Understands the team's mission, strategies and goals

➡ Is committed to the team's goals

Valuing Diversity

➡ Respects and capitalizes on team members' diverse knowledge, skills, and abilities

➡ Values the contributions of all team members

➡ Encourages and accepts points of view different from his or her own

---

based reward systems. For skill-based programs, the measurement objective is to determine whether the competency has been sufficiently acquired. Certification programs are one way to accomplish this objective. For example "collaboration" will be an important and valued competency in a team-based organization. Managers might undergo training in collaborative leadership and then be reviewed by a certification board composed of experts who can evaluate their knowledge, skill, and behavior in the competency. Certification is a way to begin changing employees' behavioral expectations regarding the competency.

For team-based systems, 360-degree measurement is a flexible way to assess the extent to which both teams and individuals within the teams are moving toward the desired levels. Each team member should provide an assessment of every other team member. Further, other teams, internal clients, or external clients can assess the entire team.

At an individual level, input from subordinates, peers, clients and, in some cases, the attainment of specific goals can be measures of performance.

Research has consistently shown that the outcome—that is, compensation—does not necessarily determine whether employees will accept a system. Employees perceive a policy as fair if the *procedures* and *methods* used to arrive at the outcome are viewed as fair (Folger & Konovsky, 1990). As with other aspects of the compensation system, employee participation can help to foster trust and engender the perception that the measurement system is fair. In some cases, employees can be involved in developing the measurement methods. In other cases, they can actually be a part of the measurement process. For example, 360-degree performance appraisal systems may involve employees as subordinates, peers, or internal clients. Consider multiple measurements, wherever possible. This approach will allow more employee involvement and raise the level of accuracy, perceived fairness, and acceptance.

➡ *Feedback to employees.* All appraisal systems should be diagnostic. For an employee to improve his or her performance, feedback is essential. Certification programs, 360-degree feedback programs, and specific goal attainment have as a characteristic feature clear diagnostic information that can be used to plan developmental steps for performance improvement. Plan to provide feedback that constructively informs the employee of how he or she is doing and provides guidance on action planning to improve developmental needs.

When deciding how to measure employee performance, be sure to consider these four requirements of effective measurement systems.

In addition, for the measurement system to be effective, it is crucial that you communicate the plan effectively and follow through consistently in the implementation phase.

Determine Other Design Components. The final step in design is to make decisions on: the funding of new pay programs, allocation of pay, and the complexity of the new pay plan.

➠ **Funding new pay systems.** The funding of any new pay program is a critical decision. It not only has obvious financial ramifications, but sends a message to the employees about expected behaviors and performance. There are several ways to fund new pay systems, including from improved financial results, from added pay expense, and by placing base or future pay "at risk." Probably the most controversial method among employees is a system that places some component of their pay at risk. A more common approach is to design the program so that a variable portion of an employee's pay is linked to a specified objective. If the objective is met, the employee receives the pay. If the objective is not met, he or she does not. However, many new programs place either some portion of an employee's existing base pay or future pay increases at risk. When base pay is at risk, the employee must attain the specified goal to receive the full amount. If goals are not met, the employee does not get some percentage of base pay. This approach sends a clear message that base pay is not an entitlement and is linked to performance objectives. From a financial perspective, this type of pay program is useful when the organization needs to keep fixed pay costs to a minimum. This approach, of course, is highly controversial and only will be successful under certain circumstances. For example, a prerequisite is that existing base pay and other compensation are equal to or higher than the competition's. The latter plan, where future pay increases are placed at risk, complements a pay strategy focused on performance. Typically, this plan is designed so that an employee's base pay remains the same each year, and any increase earned is for a specified period of time. In this case, the message to the employee is: "an increase in base pay is determined by your contribution to the business's

95

financial results, not tenure." Financially, the plan ensures that any increased pay costs are in line with business performance.

➠ *Allocating new pay.* The second question is how to best allocate the new pay to the employees. The decisions usually involve how to allocate pay to individuals who are part of a larger work group or team. There are two basic methods for allocating pay: distributions based on some individual level of contribution or equal shares among all members of the given work group. This decision must be based on the degree to which the individual versus the whole group contributes to attaining the objectives in question. If a real team effort is needed to attain the stated business goals, then an equal share allocation method is appropriate. If individual effort contributes to the results more than team effort, then allocation on some individual measurement is appropriate. Of course, the breakdown is rarely that clean, and the best approach may be some mix of individual and team allocation.

One innovative approach recently piloted by a large chemical company was what they called a "pooled-bonus approach." Each member of a cross-functional team earned a certain number of "bonus points" for the team. These bonus points were based on the member's anticipated degree of contribution due to functional experience and the amount of time allocated to work on this team. The team, based on performance, could earn some portion or all of the pooled bonus monies. How the pay is actually distributed to team members is decided by the team itself.

➠ *Complexity of new pay program.* One common problem encountered when designing a new pay program is the potential to make it too complex and therefore difficult to understand. This practice is especially true with respect to pay funding, allocation, and measurement. When the components of a new pay system are difficult for employees to understand, the program's intent may be misunderstood and unexpected and undesired outcomes can result. For example, one organization, in an attempt to motivate employees to improve sales productivity, instituted a new pay program in which employees could earn extra income. As part of the design, the employees could earn this extra pay only if their department met certain financial criteria such as meeting defined "gross margin" levels. The organization's intent was to fund the rewards from increased sales, as well as ensure that employees did not overly discount merchandise in order to increase sales. In other words, sales needed to be profitable ones. The problem was most employees did not understand how gross margins were calculated. This lack of understanding, in conjunction with the added complexity of having to meet other criteria before any payout, resulted in the mass confusion over how the program actually worked. Employees did not understand when they were entitled to extra income and when they were not. Consequently, employees were very frustrated, especially when individual productivity increased and no pay-out followed. The pay program failed to produce any significant sales increases and caused many employees to resign.

Phase Three: Implementation

The final phase of establishing a new pay program consists of four important steps: pilot test, communicate plans, follow through consistently, and monitor and evaluate the system. No pay plan, no matter how well designed, can succeed without careful implementation.

Pilot Test the New Pay Program. We strongly recommend that any new pay plan be pilot tested in some sub-group within the organization. This step of the implementation phase allows you to examine all aspects of the plan to ensure that it accomplishes what it is supposed to do. In addition, it provides an opportunity to evaluate how well the system is implemented, understood, and accepted by employees—and whether administrative costs are as expected. One hint—choose a work unit that is somewhat autonomous but whose activities are relevant to the success of the entire company. Good examples are customer service and financial services departments within a larger organization.

A pilot test should run long enough to determine whether the program's specified performance objectives are obtained. For example, if performance objectives are measured annually, the pilot test should run for the year. For larger organizations, a phase-in approach may be appropriate. For example, many regionally structured organizations can implement the new pay program in geographic phases. This has an additional advantage of allowing the organization to compare performance between parts of the organization that are on the plan with those who have not yet begun. This is one of the best ways to evaluate the plan's actual impact on performance.

Communicate the New Pay Program. Communication of a new pay plan is critical to its success. Poorly communicated plans can cause disaster. Good communication involves describing to all employees the new pay plan's rationale, its critical design elements, and how it fits with existing compensation systems. It is critical that employees understand all aspects of how the plan works: how it is funded, how pay-outs are calculated, and what an employee must do to earn additional income. This last aspect is the most important. The organization must clearly communicate what the performance objectives are and what new behaviors are required to achieve them. Unless employees understand what is expected of them and how they will be assessed, it is not likely that change will take place or that the pay system will be successful. Remember, new pay sends a powerful message to all employees regarding organizational objectives and behavioral expectations.

It is important that communication be multidirectional. You should solicit support from employee "champions," people who are enthusiastic about the forthcoming change. Members of the original task force and employees who participated in the assessment and design phases are good candidates for this advocate role. The champions can help generate support at the non-management level. In addition, supervisors should be thoroughly trained in all aspects of the new pay program. All employees should be able to obtain information from their immediate supervisors regarding the plan and its ultimate impact on them. Focus training on the pay program's objectives and mechanics, and address how the supervisor should respond to questions that are likely to come up. Only through training efforts will you ensure that supervisors communicate the program consistently, thus reducing potential misunderstandings and confusion.

We recommend that you communicate in three stages. The first stage, *introduction*, allows the employees to become acquainted with the plan's objectives and learn how it works. In the second stage, *examination*, employees review the plan and ask questions after they have had time to think about it. The third stage, *on-going dialogue*, consists of continuous updates on how the plan is being administered and its overall progress. All employees should be part of the on-going dialogue, even if they are not directly affected by the new plan. This practice is especially helpful during pilot testing. Employees will be watchful of any change to their compensation. Frequent updates help reduce anxiety about potential change and promote the plan's acceptance when implemented throughout the organization.

Follow Through Consistently. Consistent follow-through simply means doing what you said you were going to do. If you change your mind, go back to communication. While this seems obvious, organizations frequently change their plans mid-stream without informing employees. Their expectations are not met and they are dissatisfied. If we lead employees to expect to be measured against certain standards with a specific set of procedures, we must be consistent and thorough in meeting those expectations. Careful, consistent follow-through builds the trust needed for a plan's ultimate success.

Monitor and Evaluate the New Pay Program. The final step in the implementation phase is to monitor and evaluate the new pay plan. Monitor the plan frequently, beginning with monthly reviews after inauguration. These early reviews focus on whether the new program is being implemented and administered as designed, and if not, why not. They should also capture employees' initial perceptions of the plan, their level of understanding, and preliminary satisfaction. Also, schedule periodic evaluations of the new pay program to ensure that it is accomplishing its performance objectives. For example, it makes sense to review pay program results in conjunction with the annual budgetary process, so you can make modifications and improvements for the following year. This is also a good time to evaluate whether the performance measures are still relevant and are accurately measuring performance. In general, select evaluation periods based on the ability to measure performance. The shorter the time period, the better. However, longer-term evaluations are needed to capture sustained performance gains. If you schedule frequent pay plan reviews and make appropriate changes, the plan will evolve with the organization and remain current, relevant, and aligned with changing business strategies.

Who should be involved in the evaluation process? When possible, make the original task force accountable for the on-going evaluation efforts. This group, representing all levels of employees, should meet monthly after implementation and also participate in an annual review of the new program. It is wise to add at least one or two new members, who did not participate in the original design, to bring a fresh and objective perspective to the evaluation process.

Conclusion

The 21st century will be an exciting, dynamic time for the utility industry. Certainly, the next decade will be a challenging period filled with new demands and different problems. But along with these demands come opportunities. These opportunities will affect labor and management alike. Old ways of conducting business, performing one's job, and managing and rewarding employees will need to change. One of the most powerful ways to influence employee behavior is by designing and implementing new pay programs. Those utility organizations able to successfully compete in the new marketplace will lead, motivate, communicate with, and reward employees differently. Management will need to revolutionize its practices just as it has installed new technology all along.

References

Fanning, T. (1994). Changing how electric utilities do business. In G.B. Enholm & J.R. Malko (Eds.) *Electric Utilities Moving into the 21st Century.* Public Utilities Reports, Inc., Arlington, Virginia, 93-137.

Folger, R. & Konovsky, M. (1990). Effects of procedural and distributive justice on reactions to pay raise decisions. *Academy of Management Journal, 32,* 115-130.

Gorden, J. (1992). Work teams: How far have they come? *Training Magazine,* October, 59-65.

Kohn, Alfie (1993). Why incentive plans cannot work. *Harvard Business Review,* 71(5), 54-63.

McGourty, J. & De Meuse, K.P. (1994). *Self-managed work teams: A conceptual model for practice and research.* Paper presented at the Annual Meeting of the Academy of Management, Dallas, Texas.

Chapter Nine

The Dynamic Staffing Model: Positioning People for Profits and Performance

Robert B. Marshall

One of the costliest mistakes utilities are making today is cutting staff to reduce expenses. Reducing head count treats the symptom, not the disease. It does nothing to win the commitment of those who continue working for the company. Traditional downsizing and lay-off methods have often been used as the answer to critical questions about how the electric utility industry can become more competitive in the '90s and beyond. These methods, however, often do not produce the results expected. Although short term financial gains may at first be encouraging, long term results are often disappointing. Employee morale and productivity suffer and sometimes never return to the levels enjoyed prior to downsizing.

Early retirement and voluntary layoffs often result in a skills shortage or mismatch when employees with critical and valuable skills opt to leave the company, usually with a severance package to encourage their departure. These incentives strip the company of valuable talent and offer no opportunity for management to control the outcome of the process. Involuntary layoffs, or percentage cuts, are often based on seniority—or worse, no constructive, defensible process—and can be significant morale busters. The result of a totally voluntary or involuntary layoff, is usually a workforce that is unbalanced in terms of skills, experience, age, salary distribution and readiness to move the organization forward.

Making decisions solely on the "numbers" may result in a smaller work force, but does not address the need for work elimination, changes to processes and procedures, and overall cultural transformation, all of which are critical to success in a more competitive utility environment. When the same amount of work must be done by fewer people, employee job satisfaction is affected and the potential for burn-out increases. When they feel they have no control over their future, employees may be afraid to participate in re-engineering efforts, or to generally offer innovative, labor-saving ideas, and become more adverse to taking risks. As Bill Ryan, Vice President of Human Resources, Sea-Land Service, Inc., Elizabeth, New Jersey, stated for a *U.S. News & World Report* article, "You can't just downsize your way to profitability."

Perhaps utilities are getting the wrong answers because they are not asking the right questions. The key questions are not just about how to cut costs or even re-engineer processes. The organization must also ask how it can position its people for profits and performance going forward. This question focuses on the future—and how to get the "right" people in the "right" jobs—aligned with the organization's strategic direction. The Dynamic Staffing Model (Figure 1) represents an ongoing process for transformational change designed to streamline and improve organizational functioning that has been used successfully by many utilities and non-utilities affecting more than 150,000 employees. These companies are positioning themselves for success in the '90s and beyond.

While addressing the future skill needs of the organization, this model also addresses the requirement for employees to have some control over their own destiny. The focus is on selecting the best qualified employees to fill positions in a new organizational structure designed to meet the fundamental needs of the business. Decisions about staffing the new organization are based on competencies derived from a strategic analysis. The approach focuses on selecting employees into the new organization rather than identifying those who should leave.

Staffing, or redeployment, is not a process done in a vacuum. Decisions regarding people do not commence until a strategic analysis of the business is completed. The first two phases of the model do not directly impact employees or production. During the Strategic Analysis phase, groups of senior managers work with selected employees to evaluate the internal and external business factors that created the need for change. Competition, new technology, deregulation, new and pending legislation, and

Figure 1
The Dynamic Staffing Model

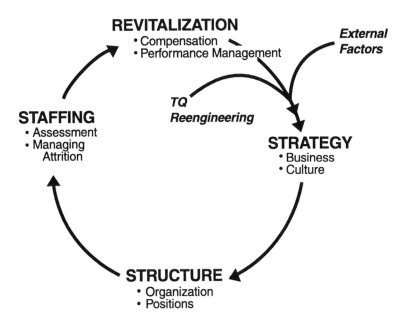

Copyright MGI, 1994

changes in ownership (e.g., mergers, acquisitions, etc.) are examples of such driving forces. The result of this participative analysis, usually conducted with the assistance of an outside consulting firm, is a new strategic direction for the organization. It includes a definition of the desired culture, (including competencies and behaviors) required to succeed in this new business environment. This analysis should be conducted openly, and employees should be regularly informed of progress and results.

Some organizations that have used this model have shifted from a paternalistic, risk-adverse, "command and control" culture to one where employees are more empowered and expected to take risks, make decisions, and achieve productive results. As Greg Nesbitt, CEO of Central Louisiana Electric Company (CLECO), Pineville, Louisiana, emphasized at employee meetings through-out the company: "Bosses are out and leaders are in." Mr. Nesbitt and his senior executive team went on to define and communicate a "New Vision of Leadership" at CLECO. This set of guiding principles requires managers and supervisors to set an example by their actions and add value to the people in their organization. Terms like "listen", "coach", "remove obstacles" and "getting results through teamwork" are taking on a new meaning at CLECO.

Once the new strategic direction is affirmed, the next phase involves organizational analysis and redesign. This redesign phase results in a new organizational structure, related operational recommendations and a transition plan. This requires an analysis of the organization's effectiveness to improve operational/management efficiency, eliminate low-value work and functional overlap. Cross-functional teams work with outside consultants and management to develop a design that ultimately includes defining each position's contribution to the new organization. In addition to defining position accountability in the new organization, this effort makes a statement about the competencies expected and what behaviors will be rewarded. The new position descriptions create a framework for behavioral and cultural change and are the basis for all staffing decisions. Again, employees should be involved in the process and apprised of progress through open, regular and timely communications.

Robert Kriegel (1991) says that "Sacred cows make the best burgers." He defines sacred cows as systems, strategies, policies, and routines that have become standard operating procedures. Employees take these practices for granted because "That's the way it has always been done." Kriegel recommends that corporations assess their present systems and culture, look for the sacred cows, and then round them up for a barbecue. In designing the new structure, there can be no sacred cows—areas of the organization, processes, procedures or positions that are "protected." All aspects of the work and the organization must be open to scrutiny and challenge.

Traditional downsizing methods often fail because they are not rigorous in their assessment and planning of the organization's structure. This may be the result not only of protecting sacred cows, but also of not separating organizational decisions (defining how the work gets done) from staffing decisions (the people who will accomplish that work). Bringing people issues into the equation too early in the process will cloud judgement and distort the results.

As the organization enters into the staffing or redeployment phase, decisions affecting people are now the focus of the process. This involves management at all levels and must be handled with great sensitivity, consistency and attention to detail and speed. An analogy to managing the staffing process might be the *Queen Elizabeth II*, a huge, oceangoing cruise ship, rapidly changing course by 180 degrees during a hurricane. It can be done, but it requires an effective captain and the careful attention and active participation of the entire crew.

Many organizations applying the Dynamic Staffing Model utilize the authors' concept of Zero-Based Staffing, which provides for all employees to be directly affected by the restructuring. Zero-Based Staffing means, in principle, that all employees are reassessed against the requirements of one or more positions in the new organization. It does not mean that employees are "fired" and "rehired." Indeed all employees are expected to remain on the payroll, stay productive and participate in the process. The principles of Zero-Based Staffing are not new to organization design, but have usually been limited to a new or newly-defined department or function. The difference here is that the entire organization is affected during a brief period of time (usually six to twelve weeks), thus requiring a disciplined, fair and fast-moving process.

In approaching restructuring, companies using Zero-Based Staffing avoid the question, "How many employees should we get rid of?" Instead, executives view the company almost as a start-up and ask, "What positions do we require and who can best fill them?" All employees are treated consistently. Only those employees with the necessary competencies and who are best qualified for specific positions become part of the new organization. Some employees may stay in their current or a comparable position, some may be promoted, some may accept a less-than-comparable position, and some may leave the company. The notion of a specifically defined "comparable job" is crucial. Employees offered comparable jobs are not eligible for severance. Employees offered non-comparable jobs have the option of rejecting the offer, considering other positions and being eligible for severance.

Employees who leave as a result of the staffing process receive a severance package with associated benefits and outplacement support.

The staffing process may sound overwhelming at the level of a large utility, but experience demonstrates that it can be managed in an orderly fashion. Staffing is implemented in a top-down fashion beginning with the highest management levels in the company. At Arizona Public Service, Phoenix, Arizona, staffing began with Mark DeMichele, the CEO, who was reaffirmed in his position by the Board of Directors. Because all employees are affected, lower level employees do not feel unnecessarily penalized, for they can see that management at all levels is in the same situation. A published schedule with milestones is imposed to avoid extended periods of uncertainty. The openness of the process helps to assuage feelings of guilt and remorse found among "survivors" of traditional downsizing practices.

Zero-Based Staffing is key because it helps maintain group attachment and cohesion while at the same time breaking up the old organization and providing an opportunity to create a new, fresh start. It sets the stage for a complete symbolic rebuilding of the organization from the ground up with a new strategic focus.

Although each company that has utilized the Dynamic Staffing Model is unique and has customized the process to its situation, some elements are usually common. In addition to Zero-Based Staffing, these include:

A philosophy that ensures people decisions will: (a) be based on the defined needs of the business; (b) be fair, objective and defensible; (c) be consistently applied across the organization; and (d) drive new accountabilities down and throughout the entire organization. This philosophy becomes the basis for a set of staffing principles and objectives, which are developed by an employee/manager team, approved by executive management and form the basis for the design and implementation of the staffing process.

A selection system based on the future needs of the business. This system begins with a one-page position description embodying the accountabilities and competencies that are required for success in that position. Each employee is assessed against these competencies on a position-by-position basis. Assessments are based on job-related examples of when/where the employee has demonstrated these specific competencies.

The selection system compares individual employee's competencies against the requirements of the position, not against other employees. A forced ranking system which compares employees to each other does not result in valid staffing decisions. The standard should not be other employees, but rather what is necessary for success. Although rare, it may be necessary to leave some positions open until the staffing process is complete and recruit from the outside to obtain the best possible candidate.

This model for matching the "right" people to the "right" jobs helps prevent the feelings of insecurity caused by a poorly communicated or seemingly random layoff and the loss of key talent through the open window of a traditional voluntary approach. It enhances the self-worth of individuals selected and reinforces their value to the new organization. It also focuses attention on behaviors that will be rewarded in the future.

A system for employees to express a preference for a particular function or location. This voluntary preference system allows employees to provide up-to-date and relevant (in their view) personal information to the organization, and direct that information to specific officers or directors, from which it is distributed down to the appropriate level of management. Human Resources also receives a copy, which facilitates placement of employees whose jobs were eliminated by the organizational design effort, as well as cross-fertilization of employees across business units and functions.

A targeted voluntary separation plan that determines severance eligibility on an individual basis. This seeks to assure that only those employees whose skills are not required in the future are eligible to leave the organization with severance benefits. All severance-eligible employees in this process are viewed as productive members of the organization, who through no fault of their own are at risk because of industry trends and specific organizational changes. This is not a process to deal with poor performers. Performance management is appropriately dealt with through an ongoing, fair and rigorous appraisal/development process, not an organizational restructuring. Employees who elect to leave the organization because they either were not offered a position or chose to reject an offer of a less-than-comparable position are eligible for a separation package which includes enhanced severance pay and continuation of benefits for a specified period of time. Full details concerning a severance-eligible employee's options and support services are provided during a decision-making window of approximately 45 days.

In most companies, a voluntary waiver agreement is used. Although the requirements imposed by the Older Workers' Benefit Protection Act (OWBPA) are stringent, with the assistance of Phoenix-based Snell and Wilmer and other law firms, these companies have crafted waivers that complied with the OWBPA and offered the company a higher level of legal protection than would otherwise be available. In fact, the OWBPA, which was intended by Congress to make waivers more onerous to management, if complied with fully (in terms of the *letter* and *spirit* of the law) actually has made the waiver more defensible. Of course, challenges to this legislation are only now beginning to emerge in the courts. The authors' experience is that "onerous" notwithstanding, applying the statute fully creates a fairer situation for employees and, we believe, more defensible position for the company. Companies that rely solely on a waiver are at risk if this key defense is subsequently compromised or limited by the courts. It is *due process* first and foremost, which creates the best legal defense and, as importantly, the perception of fairness in the workforce. Waivers, well-managed, are only the final measure of legal defensibility.

An involuntary separation plan for severance-eligible employees who elect to stay once the decision-making window has closed and who are subsequently unsuccessful in securing a position in the new organization. These employees are eligible for an involuntary separation plan which is less than the voluntary separation plan. The number of employees who are ultimately separated from the company, receiving the involuntary separation benefits, has consistently been negligible. In fact, the number has not exceeded two employees in any company.

A training plan which prepares managers at all levels to implement the staffing process. The training focuses not only on an assessment of competencies, but also on the human relations side of both decision-making and notifying employees of their status, in the new organization. All managers and supervisors in the current (old) organization are trained prior to implementation of the staffing process. Although all of these individuals may not remain in management, the training also acts as a communications vehicle and as such provides critical and timely information for all existing managers and supervisors.

Checks and balances to ensure fairness, consistency and legal defensibility. These checks and balances include multiple levels of management approval on all selection decisions as well as an independent review board, which audits the process. Each selection decision is audited by the review board. This board is not responsible for management's hiring decisions; they are responsible for ensuring that the process was followed consistently and fairly. Members of the review board represent a cross-section of the organization and, in the event one or more committee members has a close relationship with a candidate, other members step in to maintain objectivity. The review board monitors the impact of selection decisions on the demographics of the organization, the company's Affirmative Action Plans and its commitment to diversity. As a result of this staffing process, companies who use the Dynamic Staffing Model improve their diversity profile.

In addition, employees may appeal selection decisions to a separate appeals board, which will investigate their concerns. Because of the rigor of the review and approval process along with the manager training, the number of appeals are usually minimal. In general, no more than one percent of the entire population affected by the process files an appeal, and less than ten percent of these appeals are usually upheld by the board. In the event an appeal is upheld, executive management is expected to remedy the situation—to the mutual satisfaction of the employee and company.

An Internal Placement Program that assists severance-eligible employees in their search for positions within the company. An employee who is not placed in a position during the Zero-Based Staffing process will subsequently receive assistance in locating positions that are still vacant in other parts of the organization for which he/she was not previously considered and is qualified.

At Florida Power & Light (FPL), Miami, Florida, a utility of 15,000 employees that eliminated more than 1,500 positions in 1991, the internal placement program helped 300 displaced employees find new positions within the company, thereby retaining these valuable employees and avoiding the need/cost to recruit from the outside.

Detroit Edison, Detroit, Michigan, added an additional element to their internal placement efforts by establishing a team of in-house placement counselors, known as Human Resource Consultants (HRCs). Detroit Edison selected a team of approximately 20 HRCs who, in addition to their regular jobs, provide career assessment/counseling and internal job search assistance for displaced employees. Each HRC received more than 30 hours of special training by the Marshall Group (MGI) to prepare them for their new role. Of the first group of employees who entered the process, better than 50% were placed within the company. A similar process at Public Service Electric & Gas Company, Newark, New Jersey, where MGI trained over 40 HRCs, resulted in a placement rate of about 75%, and avoided the need for major lay-offs following a restructuring at PSE&G. Vacancies were created due to accelerated attrition resulting from changes to the retirement system. Northern States Power, Minneapolis, Minnesota, has also applied this process successfully.

Outplacement assistance. Outplacement services are available to all employees who leave the company as a result of the staffing process, either through the voluntary or involuntary separation plans. These services, normally provided by MGI, usually include use of a career center, job development, and referral to outside educational and other resources. A few companies have also added a tuition stipend of $1,500 to $2500 to offset education or retraining expense for departing employees.

A communication plan that ensures that employees, customers, and other stakeholders are kept informed throughout the transformation. Open and regular communication is crucial. These communication mechanisms provide an environment of openness and trust. Employees may not like what they hear, but they know they are receiving all the information that is available.

In addition to frequent group meetings, FPL distributed a series of print and videotape messages to clarify the process and to explain why a successful utility needs to restructure to stay ahead of the competition. These messages featured the CEO, the President, Vice President of Human Resources and other executives of the company, as well as managers and employees throughout the company.

At Arizona Public Service and Central Louisiana Electric Company, the CEO and executive team criss-crossed the organization to conduct employee meetings. Employee questions were dealt with directly and also were incorporated in regular Q & A news briefs.

Open, regular and candid communications are critical to the success of the restaffing process and the revitalization that must follow. As Alex Mandl, the then-CEO of Sea-Land Service stated during redeployment, "You can't overcommunicate during a difficult time like this." The Communications Director of CLECO put it another way: "Tell the truth and tell it three times. Employees need this information and don't always hear it the first time."

A business-based framework for revitalization for both individuals and the organization. Successful implementation of the Dynamic Staffing Model requires attention to the needs of individuals in transition and the organization as it moves toward a new culture. This framework or plan requires executive leadership, a focus on critical and measurable business goals, a series of organizational and individual interventions to assist with transition, and a complete review and assessment of Human Resource systems that will be needed to foster the desired cultural changes and support the new strategic direction.

As part of their study of transformational change, the authors conducted a survey in cooperation with *Electrical World* (1991), to discover how many utilities had carried through a major restructuring or downsizing in the past five years, what methods and approaches they used, the results they obtained, and what lessons were learned. Of the utilities contacted, 51 were willing to share their experience. These utilities did not use the Dynamic Staffing Model, but conducted their downsizings in a variety of other ways. When asked what they would do differently if given another chance to implement their restructuring, utility managers and executives made the following comments:

⇒ "We needed more and earlier planning of the reorganization process."

⇒ "We should have focussed more on work reduction, not just force reduction by the numbers."

⇒ "We needed more in-depth analysis of opportunities for consolidation of functions."

⇒ "Such an organization review should be a periodic process and not performed just at a time of crisis."

➟ "The grapevine had the news even before we released it in the house organ. The result was a longer slump in morale."

➟ "We relied too much on attractive (costly) benefits to generate needed exits."

➟ "We should have downsized selectively, instead of across the board."

The results of the survey confirm that utilities, like other companies, are responding to competitive pressure, industry changes and regulatory concerns. The clear theme is the need for strategies that foster continual organizational improvement and learning. These lessons indicate that the principles embodied in the Dynamic Staffing Model present an effective approach to align strategy, structure and employees' competencies on an ongoing basis.

The Dynamic Staffing Model is just that—responsive to a dynamic and ever-changing environment. The process of continually evaluating the strategy, structure and sizing, and the impact on staffing must be continually assessed. Both internal and external forces continue to impact the organization and create the need for ongoing change. This approach is fluid and flexible, while still maintaining its three critical components and the relationship between them.

The staffing phase may appear to be the most difficult because of the decisions that affect individuals in the organization; however, the real challenge is the revitalization of the organization once staffing is complete. Figure 2 graphs productivity and morale during the phases of a transformation of an organization as it implements the Dynamic Staffing Model.

Although there is a slight decline in both productivity and morale during the strategy and structure phases, the major impact is during the restaffing. This is the time of upset when employees begin to experience the effects of staffing decisions. The Critical Zone is the nadir of the curve which usually occurs once all staffing decisions have been made and those who are leaving the organization have left. Those who remain experience a variety of emotions that range from anger and guilt to excitement and anticipation.

Figure 2
Productivity and Morale During the Phases of a Transformation

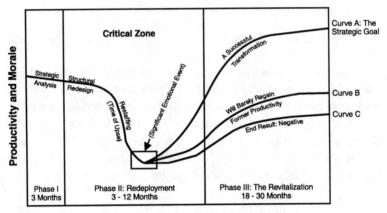

Approximate Time for Each Phase

The ultimate goal is for the company to be more successful after the process than it was before (Curve A). The model should position the company for the future and help make it more competitive in the marketplace. However, there is a risk that the company may never achieve this goal and may, in fact, return to its original status (Curve B) so the trauma was for nothing. Or, worse yet, the company may never recover (Curve C). A successful outcome depends on how well the Dynamic Staffing Model was implemented—the selection of most qualified employees, the respectful treatment of ALL employees, and on a framework for revitalization.

Successful revitalization also depends on asking the right questions at the start of the process. Asking questions that focus just on numbers, cost savings, headcount reductions, etc., causes those who remain in the organization to think about themselves as "survivors" of these (perceived) strictly cost-cutting measures. If, however, the focus is on positioning for the future, those who remain have been "selected" to be part of a new organization. The employees negatively affected are an outcome of a process rather than the objective. This distinction results in a subtle, but significant difference in how employees perceive themselves in the new organization and their willingness to commit to a new strategic direction.

Employees who remain as part of the new organization have experienced a "significant emotional event" that has shattered their feelings about the organization and its management and altered how they perceive themselves and their relationship with the company. Especially in companies with a paternalistic culture where layoffs are rare, a "Psychological Contract" existed—an unwritten agreement between the employee and the company that "entitled" the employee to a job for life. Any change process resulting in significant employee separations breaks this contract.

Some managers assume that remaining employees are automatically enthusiastic about being part of a new organization and are committed to a new vision of the company. It is often assumed that the Critical Zone is a temporary depression and the organization will move forward up the morale and productivity curve once employees are able to "get back to business as usual." This assumption can hinder the progress of the organization because it assumes that time is the only necessary ingredient. Other interventions and ongoing support systems are required for a successful transition.

The successful revitalization of the company depends on the extent to which the organization and its leaders are able to: 1) build a new relationship with employees that is based on performance and mutual trust; and 2) gain employee commitment to and involvement in the organization's success. Success means continuous improvement and learning rather than a guarantee of lifetime employment.

The Critical Zone is, in fact, *a window of opportunity* that management may use to help shape new behaviors. This window lasts for a while, but the opportunity is greatest during the first six to twelve months. It is a chance to re-energize, renew and redirect employees after a "significant emotional event." Failure to seize this opportunity slows and sometimes halts progress of the organization up the productivity/morale curve.

To maximize the window of opportunity, managers need to understand how a reorganization impacts employees, including themselves. Individuals experience various emotional stages during transition (Bridges, 1988) as they reattach to the new organization (see Figure 3). During the first phase, Holding On, people are reacting to the loss of what was familiar. Some people will attempt to hold on to what they know—their "comfort zone." Others may be angry at the company for fostering the change, at management for allowing it, and at co-workers who are accepting it. Others may be anxious about the future and have difficulty concentrating on work. Still others may withdraw or disengage. Whatever the reaction, the problem is the same: people are struggling to hold on to what was familiar. Their focus is on the past. Although these are very natural reactions to a reorganization, they may result in long-term difficulties when people get stuck in this phase. People who can't let go of their anger or move past denial do not adjust to the new organization and fail to commit to its new vision. Obviously, it is of great benefit to management and to the organization for individuals to move quickly through this stage into the next, what the author calls the Roller Coaster Ride.

In this second stage, the employee has made an intellectual decision to let go of the past but is not yet ready to commit to the future. This stage is important because people need the opportunity to work through the implications of the reorganization on both an emotional and intellectual level. This stage is somewhat chaotic because employees are in turmoil. They see value in both the new and the old. What they think and what they feel may be inconsistent. Employees need time to build bridges between the old and the new organization. Once employees have worked through the feelings of loss, let go of the old, and taken time out to reorient their thoughts and feelings about the change, they reach the third stage where they are committed and connected to the new organization. They are no longer confused; they have a sense of direction and know what is expected of them.

Figure 3
Phases of Personal Transition

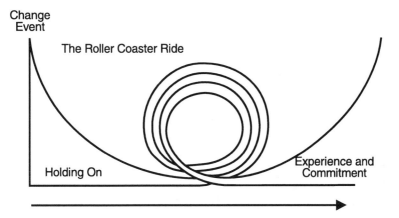

Copyright MGI, 1994

The experience of the reorganization is behind them and they have a sense of accomplishment for taking control and creating a positive outcome.

Since each employee is unique, there is no specific timeline for this personal transition. However, it is reasonable to expect most employees, with proper support and understanding, to complete this transition within three to six months. Employees who continue to exhibit these behaviors beyond this period of time may ultimately become performance problems. The transition of the majority of employees into the final stage is the driving force behind a successful, revitalized organization.

Organizations, like people, go through stages of transition after a "significant emotional event." The transition of the organization and its employees usually does not coincide (See Figure 4). There are three stages of organization transition: Disorganization—when roles, responsibilities, relationships and procedures

Figure 4
Organizational & Personal Transition

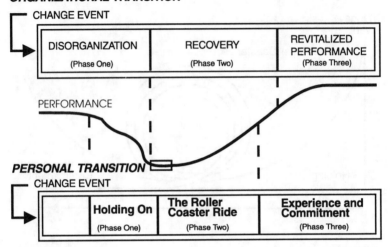

Copyright MGI, 1994

within the organization have changed; Recovery—when new roles, responsibilities, relationships and procedures have been established; and, Revitalized Performance—when productivity improves to a level exceeding that which existed before. In general, most people will not begin their own personal transition until they experience "Disorganization" within the company. Individuals then must deal with holding on (Stage One) to the old organization. When the majority of employees begin the roller coaster ride (Stage Two), the company begins recovery. Employees at this stage are seeing value in the new organization and are "back to work," with a new perspective on how that work should be done. The recovery of the organization is not complete until the majority of individuals have reached Stage Three and are committed to the new organization. Only when the majority of the employees know how to get things done in the new organization and have adopted the new culture will the organization enjoy revitalized performance. Thus, it is critical to the success of the organization that employees successfully manage through the transition.

This is a very critical point, namely—*executive management begins the major change event, but only employees have the ability to determine when it is over.* Very often, management loses sight of this fact and does not adequately address employee needs through the revitalization process. This is the reason why many companies never fully recover from a restructuring or ongoing re-engineering (major change) effort.

Some of the more critical needs of employees during transition are:

1. Clear understanding of a new vision. Without this understanding, employees are unsure and sometimes afraid of the future. Their attention is focused on the fear of another lay-off or reorganization rather than on ways to make the vision a reality.

This vision must be rooted in the business, communicated consistently and frequently. It becomes the basis for change. For example, at Arizona Public Service (APS), one manager felt the key to its success moving out of the Critical Zone stemmed from the ability of its CEO, Mark DeMichele, to effect the necessary changes:

> The biggest influence occurred when DeMichele communicated our goal as being "The Top 5 in 95." It was communicated to all employees. It became a motivating factor. Ultimately, we all understood how to contribute to that goal.

Almost four years after its major reorganization in 1990, APS is achieving the success envisioned and has already met its goal of being among the top five utilities in many of its targeted success areas. It was voted best investor-owned electric utility in the country by the Edison Electric Institute in 1993.

2. Role models of effective behavior. Leaders in the new organization must consistently and continually act and behave in ways that demonstrate their commitment to the new strategic direction. (This direction is usually embodied in a vision statement). The leaders' behaviors must exemplify what is expected of others and model what it takes to succeed. Beyond being role models, these leaders serve as a source of energy and attention to return employee focus to the critical needs of the business.

3. *Meaningful work that contributes to the success of the company and is tied to the new strategic direction (vision).* Employees need to believe that they can make a substantial contribution to the new organization and that they all are part of a team, each member playing a role in achieving a common goal. Measurable objectives that can be tied to the vision create the opportunity to celebrate success. These successes, however small, validate the effectiveness of the new organization and help to replace any fear of the future with feelings of pride and empowerment.

4. *Shared expectations throughout the organization regarding what actions and behaviors will be rewarded in the future.* Shared expectations provide guidelines and benchmarks for success. These expectations shape new behaviors and provide needed structure for employees in transition.

Some organizations selected three or four "Core Competencies" that were part of the selection process for each position in the new organization. One manager at Central and South West Utilities (CSW), Dallas, Texas, defined Core Competencies simply as: "When people think about our company, this is how they should view us. These are the strengths that we want to be self-evident." CSW selected customer focus, teamwork and adaptability/flexibility as its Core Competencies. These competencies are required (to some degree) in every position in the new organization and were included in every selection decision.

By communicating expectations of particular competencies required to some degree in ALL positions in the organization, the staffing process helps define and foster the emerging culture of the new organization.

5. *Strategies and techniques to deal successfully with change.* People react differently to change—some adapt quickly to the new organizational environment and others get stuck and may never recover. Managers and employees alike need to understand what happens to individuals during a transition. By understanding emotions and recognizing corresponding behavior, managers can take appropriate action to help employees and themselves should they become stuck or have difficulty coping.

These strategies and techniques encompass more than what is taught in a half-day "survivor's workshop" or a seminar on change. These strategies must address the unique dynamics when managers must play two roles simultaneously—both targets and agents of change. In addition to making changes in their own attitudes and behavior, managers are responsible for influencing the attitudes and behavior of those reporting to them at a time when they may still be dealing on a very personal level with their own reactions to the reorganization.

In fact, the notion of "survivors" is counter-productive and an anathema to the principles of a strategically-driven restructuring or a major re-engineering effort (transformation). Employees who act and feel like "survivors" will not tend to demonstrate the thinking and behaviors needed for organizational and personal success. The challenge is to relate organizational success and personal meaning into a single formula that is "win-win" for the company and employee. Individuals need to believe they are members of a new team, committed, accountable and rewarded/recognized for success.

6. Clarification of what is different and what remains the same. A clear understanding of what has changed provides guidelines for future behavior; a clear understanding of what remains the same provides a sense of comfort and confidence that all is not in chaos.

A challenge facing one company was to change employees' mind-set from an activities orientation to a focus on results. While this was very different, other of their best traditions stayed the same.

7. Reaffirmation of why the re-organization was necessary and closure on any questions regarding its purpose. Without closure, the reorganization continues to be the focus of attention. This closure must honor the past while communicating the need for change.

At Salt River Project (SRP), Phoenix, Arizona, Jack Pfister, the then-General Manager held an old-fashioned tent revival dinner meeting for his entire management team following SRP's 1990 restructuring. This meeting reaffirmed the accomplishments of the past, acknowledged the difficulty of recent events, and ushered in the new organization.

CLECO held a similar reaffirmation event during a two-day management meeting at the conclusion of their reorganization in early 1994. Along with a guest speaker, company executives shared their appreciation for the hard work of the management team and expressed their commitment and vision for the future. These same executives then participated as co-facilitators with MGI consultants and their business unit managers in a team building workshop focusing on revitalization.

8. Redefinition of a new "Corporate Compact" between employees and the company. A reorganization changes how employees feel about the company and how they believe the company values them. They may feel that an implied promise has been broken—the promise of continued employment in return for good job performance. Such feelings about a broken promise are based on reality. For many years in the electric utility industry, job security was a given.

Today, things are different. Few, if any, companies can guarantee lifetime employment. Thus a new relationship must be based on expectations other than "job security." Neither party can make promises it cannot keep. The challenge is to define a new relationship based on expectations that can be met in the current business environment. When neither the employee nor the company is "entitled," both must *earn* respect and loyalty based on performance and meeting mutual needs and expectations. An example of a typical relationship developed by our client organizations is included as Figure 5.

One important notion here is the difference between "employment security" and "employability security." The former no longer

Figure 5
Discovery of New Relationship

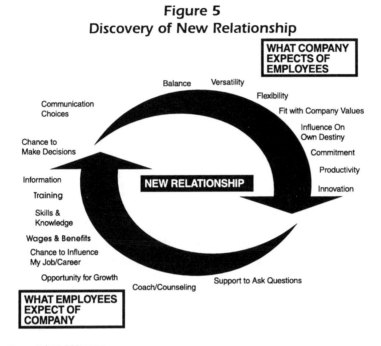

Copyright MGI, 1994

exists in our society, whether you work for General Motors, IBM, an electric utility or the federal government. The latter suggests that individual employability is the key to continued employment at your present company or elsewhere. This creates a shared responsibility—for the employer to create opportunity and challenge, and the employee to seize these to enhance competencies and demonstrate achievement.

9. Systems which support and foster the desired culture. Human Resources Systems such as Performance Management, Compensation, Career Development, Management Development and Training all need to be aligned with the new strategic direction and support/reward the desired behaviors. Some companies try to change culture and employee behavior without first assessing and altering their current systems. These systems shape behavior and must be aligned with the new strategic Human Resources (HR) direction. On the other hand, just changing HR systems will not drive a new culture or performance standards. A more integrated and holistic approach is required for a true transformation.

Results

Many organizations have achieved successful results from their application of the Dynamic Staffing Model. The concept pioneered at Polaroid in 1985, the first company to use the targeted voluntary severance plan and related management training. And it worked. The Salt River Project applied those principles successfully in 1989 and was the first to begin the application of Zero-Based Staffing. Sea-Land Service, an international transportation company, applied the model in 1990, eliminating five layers of management and reassigning half its workforce to new positions. Four hundred employees left the company. Sea-Land has continued to apply the model and has significantly increased shipping traffic and operating income with a workforce that has continued to decline over the years.

FPL attributes, in part, its ability to restore power to 1.4 million customers in the wake of Hurricane Andrew in an unprecedented 35 days to its new structure and an empowered workforce. In its restructuring, FPL set out to centralize its operations, then broaden and flatten the organization. FPL cut its layers of management in half and reorganized along functional lines. And in the process, FPL implemented new compensation and performance management systems to support its new culture.

Other electric utilities that have adopted and applied elements of this process include CLECO, APS, Central & South West Services, Northern States Power, Public Service Electric & Gas Company, Texas Utilities, Detroit Edison and Potomac Electric Power Company. The value of the process and its contribution to organizational success can only be evaluated by the management of each company. Certainly, the Dynamic Staffing Model was but one of many interventions that have been applied as these utilities effectively respond to an ever-changing, more competitive marketplace. It is true, however, that each and every organization that has applied the model across the organization, has experienced dramatic and positive results. Perhaps this is because, Zero-Based Staffing represents a turning point in an organization's history. It symbolically closes a door on the past and prepares the organization and its people for the future. With its emphasis on productivity, accountability and matching individual competencies to organizational needs, it offers a foundation to improve processes, reduce costs, develop new competencies, and redefine the employer/employee relationship.

Summary

The Dynamic Staffing Model provides an alternative to traditional downsizing or restructuring methods. Before implementing such a model, organizations should learn from others who have used it. With each organization, the authors gain new experience and insights, and they consistently are reminded that the process must be approached with rigor and serious attention to detail. Short-cuts and deviations do not produce the desired results. Also, the process must be tailored to the unique needs of the organization. To succeed, it cannot be a Marshall Group process, but rather the result of collective thinking and deliberations of key HR and line executives within each organization.

Positioning people for productivity and performance means committing to a new strategic direction, continually aligning the structure of the organization with that strategy, selecting the right people to staff it, and supporting their ability to be committed and productive in an ever-changing environment. Cost and head count reductions have been a result in many instances, but they have never been the specific objective. The ultimate goal is a more viable organization, poised to continually improve its processes, customer satisfaction and shareholder value. This requires that employees be fully committed and appropriately developed, recognized and rewarded. It also means treating people with respect and dignity; the future success of the organization and individual self-esteem depends on it.

References

Bridges, W. *Surviving Corporate Transition*. New York: Doubleday, 1988.

Kriegel, R. *If It Ain't Broke. . . Break It!* New York: Free Press, 1991.

Marshall Group. *Restaffing/Transition Manuals*. Scottsdale, AZ: Marshall Group, 1993.

Marshall, R. and Yorks, L., What Utilities are Learning About Lay-offs, *Electrical World*, McGraw-Hill, June, 1991.

Boroughs, Don L., Amputating Assets, *U.S. News & World Report*, May, 1992

Kilmann, R. and Kilmann, I. and Associates, *Managing Ego Energy: The Transformation of Personal Meaning into Organizational Success*, San Francisco, CA: Jossey-Bass, 1994.

Marshall, R., and Yorks, L., *Making A Reorganization Work For You*, Scottsdale, AZ: Marshall Group, Inc., 1994.

Marshall, R., and Yorks, L., What Utilities Are Learning About Lay-offs. *Electrical World*, 1991.

Marshall, R., and Kelleher, L., A Test of Restructuring Success. *HR Magazine*, August, 1993.

Greengard, S., Don't Rush Downsizing: Plan, Plan, Plan. *Personnel Journal*, November, 1993.

Part Four:
The People Impact

Chapter Ten

Challenge for the '90s: Creating Social Contracts that Reflect the Times

Shirley Richard

For more than a decade, the winds of change have been steadily changing the course of utility marketing, construction plans, rate-making, and regulatory, political and customer relations. In the 1990s—joined with the forces of changing social values, new technology, the entry of baby boomers into positions of power, and a more competitive, global economy that is forever altering the structure and culture of American business—these winds have reached hurricane proportions. They've grown faster, stronger and seemingly less predictable.

The impact of change on the structural and financial aspects of our industry (i.e., mergers and consolidations, more flexible construction and generation plans, and the restructuring of individual utilities) is being well documented in utility journals. But what about the impact on people that electric utilities employ and serve? This chapter examines the human impact of change—how changes have affected individual and corporate values as well as how changing values have affected the ways in which we work.

The Old Contract is Gone

One of the most difficult changes for utilities has been the need to renegotiate the social contract between employee and employer. Since the industrial revolution, this unwritten contract had guaranteed American workers a regular paycheck, steady advancement and lifelong employment in exchange for eight hours work each day and loyalty to the company. In virtually every major industry, utilities included, that contract no longer exists.

For example, continual job creation, which enabled steady advancement for workers, has slowed and/or been reversed. As a result, advancement into management—once an indicator of success to which many employees aspired—is less of an option than ever before. Wholesale layoffs, once unheard of in the utility industry, are now a fact of life.

Employees know that the old contract is obsolete, but they're uncertain what kind of contract—if any—will take its place. As a result, regular paychecks are no longer enough to buy employees' loyalty. Loyalty today is to the individual, not the company.

At the same time, a utility's contracts with other publics, such as regulators and customers, also are changing. Utilities are no longer guaranteed service territories, individual customers or rate increases. Expectations are changing in such a way that promising reliable service at reasonable rates is no longer enough to keep a utility in business. Competition has emerged, and it is quickly increasing. Utilities no longer have large blocks of customers —residential, irrigation, and commercial/industrial. Instead, they have many, diverse and demanding segments within each of these blocks. If utilities are to succeed in this new world, they must quickly learn to create and operate within a whole new set of contracts—with employees, customers, regulators and others.

Changing Values Dictate New Terms

People's values—simply defined as basic beliefs about something—affect every perception, decision, judgment and relationship in which they are involved, including social contracts. So to succeed under the terms of new social contracts, utilities must begin by understanding the human values that drive behavior.

New information on Americans' values (as well as the political, marketing and social trends driven by those values) is constantly being accumulated by firms like DYG, Inc., a New York-based national opinion polling firm. Since the mid 1980s, DYG has provided regular briefings to Arizona Public Service (APS) executives as well as marketing and customer service management.

APS began tracking values to better understand the thinking of decision-makers, and thus better predict changes in the industry and competitive environment. We recognized that a new breed of decision-makers was emerging. From offices of corporate executives, state regulatory agencies and legislatures all the way to Congress and the White House, positions of power were being filled by baby boomers. What's more, this generation of some 77 million individualistic and demanding men and women, born between 1946 and 1964, makes up 44 percent of American households.

We also recognized that boomers, because of their sheer numbers, have long been setting the political and marketplace agenda. But, in the 1990s, as they have begun to take over positions of power in business and politics, their voices have become even louder. They are influencing utility pricing, negotiations with key customers and economic development prospects, even environmental legislation and utility deregulation. Understanding how their decision-making process differs from past or future generations is a powerful marketing tool.

Changes in our workplace environment (the same changes affecting many other American industries) gave APS another reason to study the boomers: Their values are changing how, why and for whom they work. By understanding the values of today's primarily boomer workforce, we can create a more suitable social contract between employer and employee.

Values Vary by Age

To understand how boomers differ from other generations (and how those changes might affect social contracts), let's first examine the values of those generations:

Depression babies, born between 1929 and 1933, possess values that enabled our economy to prosper after World War II. Valuing conformity, savings, a strong work ethic, delayed gratification, clear sex roles and traditional family values, they know little about self-fulfillment and define success as doing better than their parents.

Baby busters, born between 1965 and 1975, see boomers as having partied through two decades, sticking them with the bill. Often the children of divorced or dual-income parents, they suffer from being the first generation of latch-key children, often raised on Sesame Street or at the malls. Because they don't believe the marketplace is paying attention to them (boomers have more clout), they have become savvy, cynical consumers.

The children of boomers, *baby boomlets,* born between 1976 and 1994, are expected to number 50 million by the time the boomlet is over. Because their parents have raised them to think for themselves, boomlets are smart, independent consumers with tremendous marketplace power. Born after everything (after Watergate, after the Beatles and after the boomers), they also have a fix-it mentality and are expected to create major social and political change.

Finally there's the *wedge group,* born between 1940 and 1945. Caught between two larger generations, this group often feels out of sync with societal values. Known as "the quiet ones," their most enduring value is a longing for how things were in the 1950s—when life was simple and everything came together in a wonderful way.

All these generations, whether depression baby, boomlet, buster or wedge group, have little choice for the next 15 years, but to follow trends set by boomers. *Because what boomers want is what the marketplace and social-political leaders deliver—particularly now that boomers are beginning to dominate business and political leadership positions.*

The Boomer Agenda

Whether you are dealing with an employee, residential customer, legislator, regulator or key commercial customer, odds are you are working with a boomer. Not only do boomers possess different values, they expect businesses, including utilities, to understand and cater to those values.

Their values, which are constantly changing, are an outgrowth of their life experiences. For example, boomers grew up taking the American dream and the economy for granted. In the 1960s and

1970s, when the economy was expanding rapidly, they not only believed they were entitled to getting what they wanted and *thought* they needed, they believed that *everyone* in society should also have their needs met. In the 1980s, realizing they couldn't have it all (there would be winners and losers), boomers worked around-the-clock to achieve and flaunt material rewards. By the 1990s—with wake-up calls sounded by global competition, belt-tightening by industry and the stress of dealing with a changing world—boomers began shifting from valuing work and material things to valuing balance and quality of life.

Among their defining characteristics:

➠ *Impatient.* Boomers, who live for today, aren't accustomed to compromise or waiting. They've been catered to by parents, marketers and politicians. Instant gratification and attention is a baseline expectation.

➠ *Highly Individualistic.* As youth, boomers were the "me" generation. They wanted to "do their own thing" and get their own way. Decades later, those attitudes prevail. These are demanding, often cynical consumers.

➠ *Activists.* Social activists in their youth, boomers are expected to renew their activism. Besides having the numbers that forced political, business and social leaders to listen to them as youth, boomers now have an added advantage with peers as leaders.

➠ *Environmentalists.* Having started the environmental movement, boomers haven't stopped caring. While they won't generally pay more for environmental products, boomers believe government and business should take more responsibility for the environment.

➠ *Technology Junkies.* They grew up with televisions and microwaves, and now consider fax machines, computers, modems and other technology as basic necessities. Because boomers use technology to increase their speed and efficiency, they expect businesses to do likewise.

➠ *Smart, Savvy Consumers.* With at least 20 years experience as adult consumers (in an age of consumption), boomers know what they want from companies as well as how to get what they want. As a result, the 1990s will be the decade of value, with value largely defined as more benefit for the consumer dollar.

➠ *Home Centered.* Boomers, who put off having families because of career commitment and over-indulgences in spending during the 1980s, are now having families, spending more time at home and striving for more balanced lives. As a result, issues like home security and protecting families from crime are increasingly important.

➠ *Pursuing Balance & Control.* After the fast-paced, do-it-all 1980s, boomers yearn for less stress and increased control over their time, finances and relationships.

➠ *Middle-Aged.* With a record number of boomers turning 40 each year, the gravity of America is shifting to the second half of life. *The most significant impact is that boomers are moving into positions of power in politics and business.*

➠ *Health Conscious.* As boomers age, new images of health, beauty and age will emerge. The new status symbol will be "looking good for your age." Combined with their environmental values, boomers will begin spending more on staying healthy.

New Opportunities for Utilities

By better understanding the boomer's demands, whether as employees, residential customers or business and political decision-makers, utilities can create tremendous competitive opportunities. For example, those utilities who recognize the value that boomers place on time, can redesign processes and use technology to provide convenient products.

The smart utility will realize that boomers (who have always had their way in the marketplace) are savvy, experienced consumers.

Because of that realization, they'll provide hassle-free service. They'll also recognize that the values of boomers aren't restricted to their personal lives; those same values are brought into workplaces, legislatures and hearing rooms—places that greatly influence the future of utilities.

The implications are enormous. Boomer employees will have different motivations, for which they will demand different incentives, rewards and ways of working. How they deal with customers and other publics also will change—not only because of their own changing outlook, values and experiences, but also the outlook, values and experiences of those with whom they work. This includes internal and external customers and decision-makers.

Customer Service Implications

Pollsters say the extreme cynicism, which started this decade, is easing. Boomers are regaining their common sense, saving more and applying a cost/benefit approach to everything. They're also spending more time at home with families, and using sophisticated electronics while there, to achieve more balance and control. For utilities, that means reliability (and power quality for electric utilities) is more noticeable and important.

One of the greatest benefits a company can offer boomers is time, which translates into convenience. Whereas past generations may have valued do-it-yourself activities like weather-stripping or been willing to wait hours for a utility representative, boomers want work done for them on the schedules they consider convenient.

Boomers also expect our employees to provide more information, whether on the technologies we use or how long outages will last. Since they are accustomed to receiving on-line information at the press of a button, utilities may want to rethink how they bill and communicate with boomers. On-line information systems, like the voice mail systems now being implemented, may be an idea whose time has come. Some boomers already use computers to pay utility bills.

Because boomers have the education and the technology to track utility usage and expenses, home electronics have become essential tools. The same considerations electric utilities once gave only to life support customers, such as advance notice of planned power outages, may be needed for persons who depend on computers.

Aging boomers also will be increasingly careful about how they spend their money. They'll use technology to save time and improve decision-making; they'll put more pressure on regulators to ensure utilities are meeting their needs; they'll want green products, and they'll expect businesses to pick up the tab for those products.

Meanwhile, where boomers live is changing. There's a "Country Living" renaissance, especially among well-educated boomers with household incomes of $75,000 to $100,000. Extending utility service to more remote locations, and ensuring these boomers get the same high reliability and quick service they've come to expect in more populated areas, will be a major issue.

Finally, as boomers age and pay-off their homes, they will spend more on health and place personal comfort as a high priority. This group—also a generation of environmentalists—will be increasingly interested in products like electronic air cleaners, which improve home health and comfort. They'll also pay more attention to the environmental impact of products they use or things they, or utilities, do in their neighborhoods. Issues like electromagnetic fields or siting of utility facilities will grow in importance.

Instead of seeing their homes as temporary abodes in which they are reluctant to invest, boomers may now consider long-term home improvements, including home security alarms and other products requiring utility service. They are more likely to notice and appreciate a knowledgeable, lasting contact at their utility who can provide needed guidance.

Work Force Implications

The boomer values that are changing the marketplace are changing the utility workplace as well. Boomers, who comprise more than half of today's workers, hold new beliefs and expectations about their jobs and their work.

The most significant trend is a waning of corporate loyalty. Employees realize their job is no longer theirs for life. One's job is no longer the primary source of satisfaction and reward. And just as consumers want more control over their lives, so do employees.

Taking control often means exploring choices. If working for a utility no longer promises economic opportunity or security, employees would prefer to do something rewarding, like working for small businesses, where individual contributions are noticed.

Along with a shift from materialism to quality of life, many employees are choosing lower incomes in exchange for greater personal satisfaction. Instead of climbing the corporate ladder, the new American Dream is to own one's own business.

Besides worrying about job security (and busily exploring options outside the corporation), employees worry about child care, financing children's college and caring for elderly parents. To meet these demands, more employees will choose to work out of their homes or join the contingent or part-time labor force. They'll also look for cafeteria benefits that meet new household needs.

Meanwhile, those employees who remain with a utility after massive layoffs or change will develop new, different attitudes. These survivors often feel guilt, burnout and lingering insecurity. They'll be looking at their jobs, their company and their co-workers through a new lens. Survivors are likely to be skeptical, especially if they feel layoffs were unfair or that their co-workers were mistreated. The more loyal that employees were to the old company and old contract, the more they will feel the abandonment.

These new values are creating a different set of workplace needs. Because they are feeling confused and upset, employee survivors expect their leaders to provide and promote a compelling vision and mutually acceptable values, and they will want more communication and interaction with leaders. They may require boosts to their self-esteem. Plus, they'll want assurances that the work they do matters.

Recognizing that they can't be guaranteed employment, survivors also will look for more balance—the same kind of balance sought by those who leave large corporations. Family, friends and a sense of belonging will be more important than ever. This sense of belonging will even reach to work relationships. Working in self-directed, empowered teams, employees will hold their peers directly responsible for performance. And because employees at all levels will be working on the same team, they'll value fairness and expect management to deal with non-performers.

Needed: A New Workplace Contract

Just as employees are looking to simplify their lives, our industry is becoming more complex. To inspire employees to take on new challenges, utilities must compete with the pull towards home, family, leisure and personal control. And because boomers have shifted toward prioritizing quality of life, companies also must find new ways to attract, motivate and retain the best and brightest employees.

How can utilities meet this challenge? First, recognize that a gap does exist; that the old contract of lifetime employment and regular paychecks in exchange for the 40 hour work week and loyalty of employees is outdated and ineffective. Employees have new values and new needs, and so do the companies for which they work.

There are two forces at work here. First, layoffs and restructuring have introduced insecurity into the workplace. At the same time, workers today are not willing to live to work. They now work so that they can live. Work is becoming a means to an end, not an end in itself.

Having accepted that the old contract is obsolete and that work no longer comes first for most employees, utilities must create a new contract that is based on the new values of both employer and employee. Instead of an organizational compact that asks employees to sacrifice their individual needs and rights in return for the employer contract, these two groups—employee and employer—must seek a middle ground. They must strike a balance in which the individual and the company can grow.

For example, since utilities can no longer offer job security, try appealing to what boomers (the majority of workers and the trendsetters) say is important to them: quality of work life. You can bridge the gap between employee and employer by offering flexible work hours, more meaningful work, opportunities and recognition of individual contributions, improved communications, and less command and control management.

What about utilities? What can they expect in return for offering employees an improved quality of life? The answer is simple. Employees who are offered the opportunity to learn and are treated as thinking, responsible adults will return to their employers more creativity, enthusiasm and productivity—all of which are vital to a competitive utility's success. By pursuing learning and increasing their individual potential, employees will increase the combined ability and potential of the employer's team.

The New Contract at Work

APS, by creating a new social contract with our employees, quickly discovered that the gap between employer and employee wasn't unbridgeable. We simply needed to build new bridges. Like our employees, the new APS was looking for ways to deal with change, increase our potential and find new opportunities in a very different world. Our new social contract needed to reflect these common needs.

For example, when we began creating our new contract, we identified flexibility as one aspect of our culture that would need to change if employees were to buy into any contract. Employees defined flexibility as more time for family activities, extracurricular activities, community service and personal professional development. The company, on the other hand, needed employees to be more flexible in their willingness to cross organizational boundaries, question assumptions and help customers or co-workers with problems. As a result of restructuring and reengineering, we also needed employees to be flexible in terms of how they did their work, the technologies they used and the people with whom they worked. In short, we needed people who could accept and thrive on change.

In examining the old APS culture, we found a lack of flexibility on everyone's part. APS had rigid work schedules, and this affected employee morale and willingness to try new things. Likewise, the company had rigid policies that discouraged risk-taking.

Once we identified these and other gaps between our desired future and what currently existed (for both individuals and the company), we worked with employees to brainstorm ways to close the gap. Employees wanted APS to better define what we meant by things like value added; they wanted cross-training in jobs; and they wanted to know that they could take risks and make mistakes. In return, APS wanted things like assurances employees would be personally accountable for results, that they would learn from mistakes and that they would adjust their actions accordingly.

The result of these efforts is a new social contract, which we have incorporated in our 1995 Strategic Plan. Titled "Our Company/Employee Understanding," it reads:

> We demonstrate commitment to our Company vision, mission and core values. We understand our jobs are not guaranteed—our employment is dependent on adding value to the organization and success of our company. We are personally accountable for continuously finding ways to add value.
>
> We are committed to a work environment and culture that encourages us to make choices to achieve harmony and fulfillment in our work and personal lives. We are rewarded fairly, work in a safe and healthy environment, and pursue personal and professional development opportunities.
>
> Together, we are the future of the Company.

At APS, we believe this understanding marks a new beginning. We have not completely bridged the values' gap, but we have made an important step in identifying terms for a new social contract. The more we work to understand and accommodate the needs of employees, the more employees are working to understand and meet the needs of APS and its publics. The key is that both sides—employees and employer—are willing to make tradeoffs to make this contract work.

Competitive and Policy Implications

In a more competitive environment, utility employees at all levels will be challenged and tested as never before. This is particularly true when dealing with commercial business leaders, regulators and political leaders. That's why an effective contract between employees and employer is critical. Without such a contract, utilities are unlikely to create the kind of strategically directed and empowered workforce needed to serve more demanding customers.

For example, boomer customers who move into senior management and other leadership positions are likely to be even more demanding of your company and its employees than are other boomers. Your employees will be asked to meet increased demands for personal attention, instant gratification, time and convenience—especially at the boomer's office, where profitability and accountability are at stake.

When a business loses utility service, they want to know from your employees—and know immediately—when power will be restored. If your employees can't provide the answers (much less ensure reliability), boomers will find someone who will. Remember, boomers grew up in age when new product choices were introduced by the hour. They know that when they have a need, someone will take the opportunity to fill that need.

Utilities who wait until there's a problem to develop relations with boomers also are likely to fail. Boomers—especially those in leadership positions—want your employees to pay attention to them right now and on their terms. If your employees fail to do so, they'll find someone who does.

Just as with residential customers, price will be a warpath issue with your business customers. Boomers have put their households and their companies on an economic diet, and they're expecting utilities to follow suit. As part of a decade-long quest for value, they demand efficiency of the businesses with whom they deal, then expect prices to reflect those efficiencies. Even your employees will not tolerate waste or unfairness in pricing.

Finally, boomer leaders expect utilities to understand their business. Because of their personal comfort with, and awareness of, information technology, they'll expect utilities (and those who work for utilities) to use information to better meet their specific business needs. As a result, utility employees must understand the work processes, competitive forces and financial situation of each major business in each segment we serve.

In short, boomers not only understand utilities (and competitive options to their local utility), they also expect us, and our employees, to understand their business needs. Individual attention is the kind of value-added service needed to build relations in a competitive environment.

Besides moving into power positions in business, boomers also are being elected and/or appointed to state legislatures, regulatory agencies and other public policy making positions in record numbers. Once again, they are bringing with them their boomer values. Activists in their youth, they are active again—this time, with power to enforce.

The decisions of these policy makers and regulators affect virtually all aspects of the utility business. Utilities need to look at the values and experiences of leaders, who are likely to be boomers. The activism of their youth hasn't died; it's been redirected. How we lobby and keep legislators informed will have to change. We will also need to revisit how we approach regulatory requests and work with regulators.

Utilities also must face some cold realities. Since rising prices are inconsistent with their values, boomer regulators will be more scrutinizing of how and where we spend money. Utilities must hold the line on costs, and possibly even lower prices.

The manner in which utilities deal with environmental issues also will be scrutinized. Just as they have begun balancing material and quality of life needs, boomer policy makers and regulators will demand a better balance of economic and environmental needs. Because they're used to getting what they want, they'll expect proactive environmental action by utilities.

All boomers, meanwhile, will pressure utilities to fulfill their commitments as never before. To ensure you "do the right thing" for them and society, boomers, even those who aren't yet leaders, are more likely to participate in political and regulatory decisions.

The Forces of Change

New technology, combined with the middle-aging of America and the ascension of impatient, demanding boomers into positions of power, is forever altering how utilities do business. So whether you're dealing with employees, customers or policy makers, understanding values can help you define new, more targeted competitive strategies. Conversely, if you fail to consider values, you're likely to widen the gap between your company, your employees and your customers.

Price and reliability (because of its impact on convenience) will continue to be warpath issues for boomers, many of whom are living with or running companies with less capital than they were raised to expect. Price, speed and reliability all impact perceptions of the value (cost-benefit) utilities provide.

Meanwhile, utilities must segment, and service, customers as never before. Boomers value taking control, being first in line, and quickly making changes when old ways don't meet their needs. Depression-era executives must acknowledge these different values, and begin dealing with boomers on boomer's new terms.

They must revise the social contracts that have long dictated how utilities deal with their own employees and world outside.

Changes to these social contracts must begin in the workplace. If your employees are to understand and live up to the terms of new social contracts with outsiders, they must first be provided with an internal contract that meets their personal needs. For employees to deal honestly and productively with customers and others, they must believe that their employer is showing the same considerations. Only then can new social contracts and changing utilities succeed.

Chapter Eleven

Aligning Human Resources to Meet Changing Business Needs

Judy Zanotti

> *It's not so much that we're afraid of change or so in love with the old ways, but it's that place in between that we fear . . . it's like being between trapezes. It's Linus when his blanket is in the dryer, there's nothing to hold onto.*

> Marilyn Ferguson, American futurist

Utilities around the nation are facing new and unfamiliar pressures as deregulation and reregulation occur. These organizations, once known for their staid, unchanging approach to systems improvement, are now turning to redesign and reengineering to create "leaner and meaner" organizations. With almost 17,000 utility workers laid off or undergoing early retirements in 1993, and many others affected in 1994, Human Resources departments are struggling to keep pace with increased demands and decreased staffs. Many departments have outsourced some services and this trend will doubtless increase as administrative staffs are cut.

Human Resources organizations are faced with other challenges, as well. As the work force grows more diverse, its needs are changing. As companies grow more competitive, a higher need is created for the retention of highly-skilled and well-trained employees. Human Resources plays a key role in providing services its work force needs and, in doing so, helps to actively retain its "best and brightest."

Getting Started

Getting started on a department redesign is often the biggest hurdle. Utilities, unused to the risk-taking and creative thinking required for the process, must be led rather than forced to make the leap.

In mid-1990, Public Service Company of New Mexico hired a new Chief Executive Officer. Prior to the change, Human Resources departments resided in three different areas of the company—electric operations, gas operations and the corporate office. Each had separate policies and procedures.

The new CEO decided to combine the three departments. But while some efficiencies were gained by the consolidation, the effort was not a true reorganization. The services and functions remained the same and only a few positions were eliminated. The newly-consolidated Human Resources organization operated in this manner for about two years, when I initiated a Human Resources (HR) Redesign Project.

When the project began, the company had 3,100 employees at 26 locations around the state. The company had a recent history of downsizing—one-quarter of the work force had been laid off in one day in 1988. In addition, the company offered a voluntary severance plan to all its employees in March of 1993, soon after the HR Redesign Project was initiated. Many employees took advantage of the offer, and 523 employees left the company by May 1993. The HR department lost 23 employees during 2 months in 1993.

More changes were in the offing. The CEO announced that he would be retiring from that position in January 1993, and a search for a new CEO was underway. By August of 1993, the new CEO was hired from outside the company (a first) and in place.

With the upheaval of downsizings and layoffs as a backdrop, the HR redesign effort was not an easy task. Department members questioned the need for such an effort. My view was that change itself was driving our need to redesign—as we moved into a market-driven, competitive environment, change was a must. We had to accept that further reductions in our HR work force might be necessary.

Human Resources as Overhead

Staff support functions, as with most companies, are often viewed as excessive overhead. It was apparent that Human Resources needed to make a comprehensive review and analysis of the Human Resources support systems which we provided to the company. Our primary goal was become more customer focused and service oriented. Like many regulated monopolies, our department had not recently surveyed our internal customers to determine if our services were of value to them. We also believed that HR had a role in moving into the competitive marketplace and being successful in it. Because our part of the business was responsible for placing the correct people in the correct jobs and assuring that these people have appropriate skills and training, we are a source for competitive advantage.

Three "C's" drive our business as we transition into a reregulated industry:

➠ Customer

➠ Competition

➠ Changes

Improving the quality of customer service is a clear focus for our company and for our Human Resources department. The company began to strategize around competition for its electric operations prior to the passage of the National Energy Policy Act of 1992. These strategies further impelled Human Resources to think "ahead of the curve" in designing a more efficient and effective department.

A New Model

Survival, for our department, was dependant on our ability to be flexible and proactive. The changing environment also presented us with the opportunity to model successful change for the company. Driving our change was the need to find ways to improve the service to our internal customers while reducing the cost of providing this service. Such change is a double-edged sword, for while we tried to manage the costs of people, we also struggled with how to invest in them.

After an HR staff strategy planning session, we settled on a model for our department that looks and feels like a consulting agency. This led to our redesign project clearly focusing on the needs of our HR customers. The services we wished to provide should be perceived by our customers as "value-added" services to ensure their worth to customers and the company.

In addition, we needed to develop and retain core competencies to ensure the quality of our services. We also wished to develop a more diverse work force within our department and company-wide while respecting different and often conflicting values.

Four Major Objectives

Our four major objectives were to:

1. Evaluate existing systems, activities, functions and services.

2. Determine short-term and long-term opportunities for reengineering.

3. Review existing resources and respective skills required to accomplish tasks.

4. Develop and implement the systems, processes and training necessary to create an effective, responsive service organization.

The original scope of the redesign analysis included the following functional areas: Benefits, Compensation, Human Resource Information Technology, Employee Relations, Placement, Employee Assistance Program and Occupational Health and Safety.

Initially included were two other areas which subsequently moved to another reporting structure in the organization during the early 1993 reorganization. These areas, organizational development and technical training, and general services, are not included in the overall Human Resources Redesign Project.

The Nuts and Bolts of Change

A Human Resources Redesign Team was created, consisting of nine staff members from HR and two members from Organizational

Development. In addition, the team has an executive sponsor, which is the role in which I served, as vice president of Human Resources. My two direct reports and two team leaders, each from the HR and Organizational Development areas, formed a sponsor board with me.

The nine-member Human Resources Redesign Project Team worked directly on the project two days a week. This team reported to the sponsor board and worked with the feedback groups. These team members required extra support from coworkers not involved in the project in order to accomplish the ongoing tasks of the department. With our staff already reduced by the voluntary severance, it wasn't possible to free them up completely for the team project.

Each of the nine team members reviewed and analyzed a specific area. Periodic feedback meetings were conducted with a larger group of department staff, and a user group was also formed to provide feedback from our internal customers. Retirees were included in this customer group; with more than 800 retirees, they are a considerable constituency group. A number of methodologies were used to review and analyze areas identified for redesign. Basic system flows were developed within areas and the major services provided were reviewed. Benchmarking information from outside companies was researched and provided. Outsourcing information on major services being redesigned was also researched. Surveys were distributed to HR staff (only 27 percent returned them, a sign of their apprehension) and retirees.

The Redesign Team developed a charter and assignments were made. A clear assessment process was developed to assist the team in redesigning the various processes. A timeline of four to six months was established, with implementation of a newly-developed restructuring being the final step.

Communication of the Process

From the beginning, a great deal of communication, via staff meetings with myself and managers, and with the entire HR staff, was necessary. We provided memos, small group meetings, and advisory meetings, as well. Senior management also received regular status reports on the project.

In retrospect, even more communication would have been helpful. Face-to-face meetings with small groups in a question-and-answer format, should be scheduled frequently and regularly. The communication process must be built into the planning process, and should occur throughout the entire process, not just when "there's something to announce." The goal is to solicit feedback and then act upon it. This can't occur without communication planning.

As a part of communication, the flow for the redesign effort was prominently posted in our HR area to help everyone understand the process. A key events schedule was also created and distributed, as well as the development of key milestones.

Training for the HR Redesign Team was created to provide the skills and tools necessary to work in each functional area and assess redesign possibilities. Each of the nine members reported regularly on their particular area so the full team, including the sponsor board, could take a cross-functional view. Data analysis focused on processes. Opportunities and barriers for each phase of the redesign effort were identified where possible, acknowledging that some might reveal themselves later in the process.

The Pressure of Change

> The world fears a new experience more than it fears anything because a new experience displaces so many old experiences. The world doesn't fear a new idea. It can pigeon-hole any idea. But it can't pigeon-hole a real, new experience.
>
> D.H. Lawrence, English novelist

Any serious attempt at cultural change causes a tremendous amount of pressure. The emotional climate was highly charged. Staff questioned the motives of the effort ("they're just doing this to justify another downsizing" was a common sentiment). The approach, and those leading the effort, were heavily criticized. The literature on reengineering often refers to the experience as "gut wrenching." It's an accurate description.

It is very hard for employees to see the big picture when their jobs are at stake. Many felt they could not adapt to a new working environment or even to a new job within the company. The biggest challenge for leadership in this situation is to be sure the reasons why the changes are being made is fully understood by those affected. Even those unaffected personally by these efforts can raise the level of skepticism and doubt. The general work force doubted the sincerity of our effort and whether real change would come about. In an organization unused to meaningful change, such skepticism abounds. Most saw the attempt as another "program of the month" that would not ensure cost savings or better service.

These external influences only exacerbated the HR staff's questioning. "Why us?" they wanted to know, "when others aren't doing it?" Many believed that our earliest consolidation in 1990, when three separate HR departments were combined, was sufficient. Most saw that consolidation as reengineering.

Changes are Substantial

By the spring of 1994, about one year into the process, the redesign review and analysis was completed. Our first area of emphasis was to reduce the layers of management from four to two. We also reduced the number of managers from 13 to just five. The work force was reduced from 82 1/2 people to 51, resulting in a $2.2 million savings.

Organizationally, the changes were just as great. Functional areas— Benefits, Compensation, Information Technology, Employee Relations, Employee Assistance and Occupational Health and Safety—were transformed into three customer service teams, one strategic services team, and one customer/technical services team.

The intent of the redesign was to align these newly-formed teams with the realigned organization of the company they serve, assuring that provided services are value added, and that the processes are efficient and effective.

We had an opportunity in this redesign effort to realign responsibilities and activities while broadening the span of control and eliminating layers of management. Our strategy was to eliminate the familiar bureaucracy our internal customers had to combat to obtain service, and to bring decision-making closer to the customer.

But, without the systems and processes in place, such change would be "in name only," with the same people, rearranged, covering the same duties. A period of transition is now underway. Initially, the effect of the redesign, with fewer managers, means that many more decisions seem to float upwards, into my own office. As we transition to our redesigned organization, more and more of this decision-making will occur at lower levels. Shifting responsibility—and accountability—is a current issue as we work our way out of our old bureaucratic ways.

Keeping the Vision Alive

Redesign projects are disorienting to the employees they affect. Employees often feel demoralized, rather than energized, by the process. Within our group, after downsizings and the voluntary severance, a "survivor mentality" had set in. In this atmosphere, how do leaders crusade the change effort, champion the cause?

The key is to communicate consistently throughout the entire process. The leader must be thoroughly committed to the plan and implementation. He or she must inspire his or her direct reports to convey the same vision. It can't be done alone. And setbacks and criticism must be recognized for what they are—part of the process. Leaders of such change are under a microscope, as are everyone on the team. "Walking the talk" is never more important than at times like this.

Because the process is likely to be long and the transition difficult, emphasizing that employees are valued and recognized for their efforts is also a key component. Celebrating milestones of the re-design project offers great possibilities of recognizing the team's efforts and underscoring the importance of their work to all staff.

Our transition also includes a basic HR 101 training course for all employees, including managers. Training increases core compe-tencies and offers employees the assurance that they are valued and valuable. Our personnel will be required to cross-train, in-creasing their versatility within the company, and their value outside it.

Redesigning Jobs

Part of the process includes the task of redesigning the jobs them-selves. In our redesign project, we developed new job descriptions for all of the new jobs in the department. We "dehired" our employees, posted the new jobs, and underwent a rigorous selection process.

As a result, Human Resources emerged as a new department, with a new structure and a clear mission and vision. Our mission states, "Human Resources is dedicated to lead and partner with our cus-tomers in aligning the Human Resources strategy with the com-pany's business strategy in a manner that values the dignity of each individual."

Human Resources' new vision is to operate as an expert consult-ing agency. We believe our experience in and understanding of the company's culture and environment provides our employees with a core competency which is increasingly valuable—as change agents and leaders for the company in the Human Re-sources field. As a model consulting agency, we are cost-competi-tive, responsive and flexible. We seek to minimize bureaucracy and market our services. Meeting our customers' needs is our top priority.

To achieve our new vision, Human Resources will:

➠ be a strategic partner in the company's planning process,

153

➡ be multi-skilled in providing quality human resources services to meet the needs of our customers,

➡ be perceived as leaders who are credible, accountable experts in our fields and change agents for the company,

➡ provide creative options and solutions that meet our customers' needs,

➡ be able to measure what we contribute to our customers and to the company, and

➡ shift resources where they are needed based upon business needs analysis, customer needs and feedback.

These core values serve as our guide to decision-making, how we work and deal with people, problems and opportunities. They serve as an anchor that represents the commitment we make to ourselves and others. Teamwork, individual initiative and risk-taking will be rewarded in our new environment.

This new culture rewards individual and group successes. It assures integrity, fairness and confidentiality to its customers, and mutual respect between co-workers.

Our ultimate goal is to transition our HR Specialists into HR Consultants who can provide "one-stop shopping" for their customers. The combination of increased training as well as the creation of customer-focused teams will facilitate this transition.

The difficulties inherent in all transitions still remain, and will linger for some years. Anxiety and its attendant resistance to change still exists. Some are excited by the changes, and their enthusiasm is contagious. Others feel pain over lost identities, from their old job title to their old work group. With more than 30 co-workers gone over a short period of time, some still grieve this loss. Yet others recognize an opportunity to grow personally and professionally. Their confidence grows with their skill level, and there is less apprehension about whether they will have to look for a job outside the company.

Critical Periods

The process of change passes through some critical periods. The first came after people left our department through the voluntary severance plan. Those left behind deal with additional work loads and the work of planning and implementation of the redesign. This period presents the opportunity to initiate and reward new behaviors and build new relationships with employees based on desired performance.

It is important in this first stage to clearly identify what is different about the organization and what will remain the same. In this phase, the department's (and company's) vision must be articulated. We should emphasize why change is needed, what each individual's part in that change is, and how this change is rooted in the business. The *whys* and *hows* must be clear to everyone involved. And they must be expressed consistently and frequently.

In our department, we have continually emphasized our opportunity to be a role model for the transformation and change for the entire company. Our systems—performance management, compensation, training and staffing—don't necessarily drive cultural change. But they are its underpinning, supporting and helping to define the desired culture. These systems must change if a cultural change is to occur.

Today: Sub-Process Redesign

Our redesign tasks are far from over. Today, teams are redesigning sub-processes, such as staffing, regulatory reporting, the resignation process and performance management. These teams have been trained in total quality transformation materials and tools. They're applying the knowledge they gained during our initial phase to system improvement processes. We continue to focus on customers' needs, redesigning, realigning and improving processes. We've learned the "lingo" and understand the differences between system improvement and system alignment. We have the skills to analyze a specific process and find solutions.

We continue to evaluate ourselves to assure that we are staying focused on business practices while still aiming high. Marginal improvements can sometimes create more problems than they solve, so we've learned to evaluate which processes have the potential for profound improvement.

We've learned that resistance is part of the process and should not dissuade us from our desired results. Most importantly, we know that reengineering or redesign is an on-going process. It requires a great deal of its participants, from continual evaluation to a complete change in mind-set. On the positive side, many find letting go of the past is rewarding, and new challenges are indeed exciting.

The goal of our redesign effort is to create an HR support system which improves customer satisfaction and the quality of our services. We need to be flexible to suit the individual needs of our customers and the company as a whole. We continue to evaluate the costs of providing services, and whether these services are delivered effectively.

As a result of our on-going redesign, we've been able to provide a full range of innovative HR consulting services, products and outsourcing support. We're continuing to develop programs that are high on quality and customer-driven. And, we want our staff to find professional growth and development in their roles. They are themselves changing from a "staff mentality" to a "business mentality."

Rather than seeking consistency, we strive for responsiveness. As our company refocuses its strategies, we must be flexible to respond. In short, our role has changed—we see ourselves as partners in our business, rather than servants to it.

Alvin Toffler wrote, "Our moral responsibility is not to stop the future, but to shape it . . . to channel our destiny in humane direction and to ease the trauma of transition." The partnership role is one for which the Human Resources function is well suited to provide leadership. We are a role model for the entire organization.

Chapter Twelve

The Reality of Teams

Jean M. Dickson

Four years ago I was hired to facilitate problem-solving teams at Boston Edison Co. The intent of this chapter is to relate my experiences in working with teams at Boston Edison, to discuss what works, and what doesn't. I have presented the results of teamwork in a narrative style rather than in quantitative terms.

I have identified factors or conditions that make teams successful, highlighting when to use teams, because they are not the solution to every problem. Each condition is illustrated by a brief example. Additionally, I have discussed the practical aspects of using teams, including considerations when forming joint teams of union-represented employees and management personnel. The names of the employees in the cases are fictitious.

Definition of Team

There are many ways to define a team. It can be set up functionally to meet a goal within a work unit or composed of members who report to different organizations. For the purpose of this chapter I define a team as a group of interdependent people focused on a common goal. This definition distinguishes a team from a collection of people by the interdependence of the members in reaching their common objective.

Background on Boston Edison Co.

Boston Edison Company is a publicly owned urban/suburban utility founded in 1886. Its service territory is 590 square miles serving 40 cities and towns with 651,000 customers. Two locals of the Utility Workers Union represent 66% of the 4,300 employees of the workforce. One local represents the production and maintenance employees and the other represents the office technical and professional workers. The company is one of the most extensively unionized utilities in the country. Kilowatt-hour sales have been flat for the past five years.

It took me some time and experience to understand how different the team approach was for the existing culture. When I first began, I was struck by the rigid functional lines that were drawn and observed how little crossing of the lines occurred. It was a traditional company with little diversity reflected in the management ranks. The organization structure was heavily layered, in some parts up to ten, with an authoritarian style of management. The relationship between the unions and management historically had been adversarial, sparked by perceived injustices and mistrust. Neither side believed what the other said.

As the lessons of competition are being learned, we at Boston Edison have begun to change and look at our business differently. The company has evolved over the past few years, shifting from an orientation of "cost plus" to focus on running an efficient business. There is new leadership both at the senior management level and in the unions.

A team approach to problem solving has support from the top. Senior management initiated teams to conduct reviews of organization effectiveness, examining each organization's strengths and areas for improvement. Teams have been formed to review and streamline work processes. Joint union/management teams have been established to examine changes in job functions prior to negotiations.

Not surprisingly, there are both detractors and supporters among union and management personnel. As with any new approach people are still evaluating the costs, the benefits, and how the team approach affects them.

When to Use Teams
Using a team is not always the best or most cost-effective way to solve a problem. However, there are situations where putting a team together is the best approach.

Complex Issues

If the problem is large and complex, one person will not have a complete understanding of all the details, impacts, or nuances. To fully define, diagnose and solve a complex issue takes the collective understanding of many individuals. A team approach may be a faster method to reach problem resolution. A team can shorten the time for researching and evaluating the components of the problem. Team members also bring their own perspectives and are able to anticipate potential problems with the proposed solutions.

A team was formed in the Transmission and Distribution Department (T&D) to address the inconsistent availability of stock items at various service centers. The first inclination was to blame and find fault. Through research, the team members found that some service centers were stockpiling and in some cases, hoarding stock, making some items unavailable for use system wide.

They further found that the problem was caused by inefficiencies within their own internal processes: they were not managing contractors well; the contractors were taking weeks of supplies out of the yard at one time. Their internal system of inventory control had broken down: the computer system was not always updated when items were removed. Therefore, the service centers responded by ordering ahead and overstocking necessary items.

The team addressing this problem consisted of employees from the five different service centers. By talking to their colleagues, they were able to quickly assess the situation and determine the issues.

Crossing Functional Lines

The use of teams is also effective when the problems cross functional lines. Each team member brings functional knowledge of his/her area and experience with how the problem affects them. They will either know how people have tried to solve it in the past or have access to that history. In these cases the team pools its expertise to identify the root cause of the problem rather than just addressing the part of the problem that lies in each team member's own jurisdiction. By using a cross functional team there is a better chance of developing broad workable solutions.

The Transmission and Distribution team working on the stock issue decided to expand its membership. They invited representatives from the Stores and Services Department to form a joint team to resolve the issue.

Through further research, cross-functional issues were identified along with the ones internal to T&D. There were inconsistencies in the way stock keepers at the different service centers used the computer system to handle items that were not in stock. Veteran stock keepers knew the quirks of the system and how to get around them, while the newer clerks didn't know how to effect short cuts. There were only two inspectors serving all the service centers; when they were backlogged, some items were reported as out of stock. The clerks didn't "speak the same language" as the T&D workers: T&D used slang words to describe items; the clerks spoke in code numbers.

With this joint team issues were identified and addressed that the Stores and Services Department "owned," as well as issues that were "owned" by the T&D Department. The team developed solutions that addressed the root causes.

When Buy-in is Required

When you need buy-in for successful implementation of a change, a team approach is advisable. Employees feel that it's not being "done to them." People are involved who really know the business, impact and processes.

Over the past two years teams have been formed to review the effectiveness of the organization (called Organizational Effectiveness Review Teams). Specifically, the task is to examine work processes for efficiency, costs, and customer satisfaction to make recommendations for redesigned processes with new organization structures to support them. When the team begins to examine department structure and work processes, employees' anxiety levels are guaranteed to rise. Appointing team members who are respected by employees in the work unit can help with this anxiety. Also, this team approach includes methods for obtaining input from colleagues and their reactions to the proposed solution before the team makes its final recommendations. While these steps are not panaceas for managing anxiety levels, they do help in providing forums for employees to voice their concerns and be heard.

When a New Solution is Required

Teamwork can be a good way to foster innovation. A mix of people with different backgrounds, orientations, values and styles creates the possibility for new ideas and innovation to emerge.

A multi-level and multi-department management team conceptualized a new work order process. Members of the team were of varying ages and had diverse interests, each bringing their unique perspectives to the project.

After mapping out the current processes for installing small, medium, and large KVA services, the team developed a simple new concept. Order-takers and order-fillers would simplify the front end of the work order process to serve the different customer needs.

The team began by developing an understanding of the current situation, and identifying barriers that existed in meeting customer needs. They explored concepts and broke out of functional roles and thinking. Each team member took risks, while team members confronted each other and piggybacked on one another's ideas. They felt they had the freedom to look at new ways of doing business.

What Makes Teams Successful?

Putting a group of people together in a room does not necessarily make a successful team. There are seven factors or conditions that influence a team's success.

1. Team Culture

A culture that supports teams is an important ingredient. In order for the concept of a team approach to work, there has to be clear support voiced and action to follow it up.

That combination worked for the Meter Department. Department members had been part of early teamwork efforts and had received additional training in a problem solving approach. They wanted to apply what they learned and looked for opportunities to do so. One supervisor approached his manager to set up problem solving teams within the division. He and his colleague acted as facilitators for eight union/management problem-solving teams. Their objectives were to identify and resolve barriers to workplace efficiency.

Teams met once a month for an hour and a half for approximately one year. One team made a day-long site visit to a manufacturing plant that was designing a new meter trough with their input. This allocation of time required the support of management. The teams made recommendations that again required management support. Support from union leadership was also received as members of the local union needed their blessing to participate.

Getting a culture that supports teams takes more than senior management saying it is so; employees must understand why there is a need to change and how it will happen. They need to get behind the process improvements, believing that the company and, ultimately, they will benefit.

During the beginning stage of a joint union/management team, competition and cost-effectiveness were discussed. One union-represented employee stated she didn't believe competition was real, "It's something that management made up." Several others agreed. This statement reflected the history of union/management relations. These team members were expressing their distrust of a team approach as well as their distrust of management.

One of the union-represented employees on the team later brought in a newspaper article on competition in the utility industry. Yet, it did not resolve the larger issue of distrust.

Middle management is key in the support of teamwork. This level of management has direct influence on the day-to-day operations.

When this group is behind the effort, the team has a better chance for success.

One department manager chose not to include his two subordinate middle managers in the team process. He had determined they were unwilling to try new things and felt their participation would be detrimental.

When the team made its final recommendations, the department manager assigned implementation responsibilities to the excluded middle managers. It came as no surprise that the recommendations were being stonewalled by the managers.

The team reconvened for a status meeting with all parties attending including the middle-level managers. During this meeting we developed clear action items, accountabilities and time frames. It was important for all to be part of this planning and to commit to the implementation. It also helped to have a clear, simple plan that was not time consuming. The implementation plan moved forward after some initial resistance.

Middle management often feels most threatened by the use of teamwork. This level is responsible for the day-to-day operations. When a team is formed to address an issue, they believe they may be blamed because they haven't solved it.

Bob is a new division manager in a largely clerical function. His manager had a positive experience using teams in another area and wanted him to implement a problem-solving team. Bob dutifully set up the team and, as he heard of the issues they raised, he went about solving them himself. He thought the issues raised were a reflection on his ability to manage. The process was a threatening one for him; he took the issues personally.

2. Clear Roles
One of the biggest factors in successful teamwork is clear roles and an understanding of what each member brings to the team.

Clarity around role definition includes the sponsor's role, team members' roles, and the facilitator's role. The sponsor sets the mission and goals, clarifies decision making, and establishes any parameters. The sponsor provides resources and recognition and "walks the talk."

One department in the nuclear organization provides support to operations. It uses one major process to deliver its service. The issue was how to provide timely, cost effective support to the customer. A team was given the directive to re-engineer that process and design a structure to support it.

The sponsors, the department manager and his boss, had previously discussed possible solutions. They, along with the V.P. of Operations had concluded two departments were the best solution. One would focus on short-term projects and the other on long-term ones. This solution also solved another dilemma, providing department-level opportunities for two managers in the organization.

The team was not informed of these possible solutions, but had heard rumors of a two-department structure. When the team questioned the sponsors, they gave no indication of a new organization with two main departments.

The team spoke at length with their customers, wrestled with their current process, and finally had a breakthrough developing an innovative re-engineered process. They designed one department to carry it out.

When the team presented the recommendations, the sponsors were remarkably quiet. The team had not come up with the "right" answer. The sponsors were looking for the two-department solution. While they understood the value of the new process, there was that "promise" of career opportunities for those managers. The sponsors did some soul searching. Then they asked the team leader to help them "sell" the team's concept to the client. This team and its sponsors visibly struggled with their roles, team objective, and "walking the talk."

Team members also need to understand and implement their roles. I worked with one team that had agreed to "speak with one voice." They would report to the sponsor at agreed-upon milestones and would communicate concepts, as opposed to "who said what ." One member of the team, Brad, broke the confidentiality by reporting to the sponsor "who said what" after one particularly heated meeting. When the project leader learned of this, he called Brad on his broken agreement and told him he was no longer on the team. Brad replied, "But everyone knows I'm Bob's (the sponsor's) eyes and ears!" He saw his role as an informant first, team member second. This role definition was in conflict with the norms the team members set for themselves.

3. Clear Achievable Purpose

A team needs to understand its objectives and to see the value in resolution of the problem. The team further needs to believe it can solve the problem.

A field service project set out to combine job functions. The objective was to provide efficient seamless customer service in the area of metering. This team was asked to make recommendations for combining jobs of the union-represented employees. The idea of combining jobs was driven by a new automated scheduling technology for field service work.

One of the legal requirements of joint union/management teams is that the selection of the team members be made by the unions. Unfortunately, no one explained to the union officers that team members needed to be well acquainted with the jobs under discussion and understand the need for flexibility in the job specifications.

Without that guidance, the union leadership set its own criteria. They wanted members of their executive board on the team to hear the discussions and the positions voiced. This would provide valuable background when the time came to sit down at the bargaining table. Some of the team members selected by the union had never worked in the area of metering and were, therefore, unfamiliar with the jobs being discussed.

165

Another nuance made this a challenging team. Some of the union board members were up for re-election during the time of these team meetings; there were some in the union membership who thought cooperating with management meant selling out union jobs. Therefore, it was important to the board members who were up for re-election to maintain distance from management. They did not want to appear to be siding with or cooperating with management. At times, it seemed as if they were using the team meetings as a campaign platform by showing how scornful they were of this "new approach."

For some, the goal of the team, creating flexible job specs, was not achievable. Being a member of the team was in conflict with how they viewed their roles as union members and negotiators and, therefore, they would not participate.

Although a great deal of work had gone into setting up the union/management team, this joint work was "a reach" for many. The conflict in roles and desired outcomes soon became clear. To deal with this we acknowledged the conflict during one of the early meetings and asked the team how they wanted to handle it. They redefined the outcomes. The union-represented team members agreed that they would contribute to understanding the current job functions, but they would not be part of any recommendations for job combinations. When this front end work was completed, a second team of only management personnel continued with the recommendations and the implementation plan.

4. Right Team Members

For a team to succeed the members need to be knowledgeable about the project. They also need to be able to "think outside of the box" and set aside their own agendas and to work for the team's goals.

The work order process, how a customer gets hooked up to the power delivery system, had been conceptually re-engineered by a cross functional management team. An implementation team was formed to refine and develop the concept and the steps necessary to implement it. The team members were union and management personnel most of whom performed their own job functions in the process.

As the team began, there was skepticism expressed by the union members. The group continued their work identifying the eleven different job classifications and the fifteen steps required for the simplest overhead tap service. Some of the union team members became angry and hostile. The conflicts heated up even more as the team discussed how to streamline the process.

Some members believed the team was meeting to eliminate union jobs. Again, this belief was rooted in history. This belief was so strong and anxiety so high that at least one member couldn't see any other purpose or possibility. Nor could he shift his thinking and see that even if the team outcome did mean loss of jobs, he could have input into how that might be minimized, or best be handled; e.g., through attrition, or early retirements. This belief prevented him from participating.

It became clear how novel and unusual it was for union-represented employees to work together with management.

In some cases, however, employees rose to the occasion. On one joint union/management team the union-represented employees were asked to measure their own productivity. This was not their usual role. But their tasks were complex and had many steps; it would be difficult for anyone who did not actually do the work to know all the details and special conditions.

This team was exceptional; members understood the value of what they were asked to do. The supervisors were very supportive of the complexity of the task; the union-represented employees put aside their traditional concerns and tapped into the value of wanting to do what was right. They completed the objective and delivered a superior product.

An early team consisted of members who were "veterans" of the company. Most of these men came to Boston Edison after high school and worked their way into management. The team was dealing with the issue of how to meet in-service dates for customers. They had a wealth of experience in their fields, but they had trouble breaking out of the familiar systems and processes to be truly customer focused.

They took the initiative to invite some customers to meet with them: two contractors, a town wiring inspector and an electrician. These customers provided very graphic feedback on the level of service they were experiencing. They also provided contrasting information on their experience with one of our competitor utilities. For this team it was a critical juncture. We were not doing a very good job. Hearing from the customer directly drove home the need to make dramatic changes. The team went on to develop an innovative concept for completing work orders.

5. *Clear Process*
To work effectively a team needs a good structure. It needs a road map or a template to help get started outlining the issues. It needs a structure to help determine what data to collect for its research. And finally, it needs a framework within which to develop solutions or recommendations.

One of the first Organizational Effectiveness Review teams I worked with had been formed six months before I began working with them. The sponsor did not see any significant progress. I was asked to consult with him and the team regarding the work to date.

The project had been divided into three segments: one team was to review complement with the task of identifying personnel and areas of the department to cut; another team was to review processes and make recommendations on how to increase efficiencies; the third team was to develop implementation plans. Overseeing the project was a steering committee comprised of the three section managers in the department.

The section management level had been specifically targeted as an unnecessary level as the company reduced layers of management.

The teams had been struggling with their tasks; the first didn't have a consistent process to identify where to reduce complement. The second team had no framework to help them identify what their customers wanted, to determine if what they were doing met those needs or added value. They further had no clear methods to identify process redundancies or inefficiencies. The third team did not know how to integrate what the other two teams had produced.

Finally, the steering committee had little incentive to oversee the project. As section managers they knew their jobs were targeted for elimination and they did not want to take the lead in moving the project along.

This project clearly exemplifies the need for a team to have a clear structure and process when undertaking a large, complex objective.

To resolve this stalemate, the sponsor and facilitator reworked the project plan to integrate the three objectives of the teams and to clarify their process. The sponsor named a new team, putting one of the section managers on the team. This man was well respected in the department and, ultimately, played a major role in leading the team to an innovative process re-engineering solution.

The facilitator worked with the project leader to set up phases of the project. The team first identified their major deliverables and met with key customers to obtain feedback on how they were doing to meet the customers' needs. The second phase was to map out the steps required to produce the deliverables, identifying issues, inefficiencies, or redundancies. The next phase was a look ahead to the future to determine how the business needed to change to meet that future. The fourth phase was to re-engineer the processes and design a structure to support those new processes. Finally, the team planned for implementation.

This structure enabled the team to meet its objectives in an integrated way and to develop a dynamic organization with re-engineered processes designed to meet customer needs.

6. *Facilitation*

A facilitator, while not essential, can help with teamwork. The facilitator is a content neutral person who works with the team to provide a structure and to help them stay on track. The facilitator is also a process observer; that is, as the team works, the facilitator helps members work more effectively together. This help may include assisting team members to resolve conflict, providing ways to help them if they get struck, or teaching them to use tools to analyze and address the issues.

To be effective the facilitator must remain detached, or be very clear when he/she is stepping out of role and offering an opinion. There are also skill requirements that enable a facilitator to be effective, such as, good communication skills, ability to synthesize and gain consensus, and being comfortable with conflict resolution.

7. *When is it Over?*

Teams need to have clear measures of when they have reached their goals. They need to know when they are finished. If the end goal is not clear, they will not know what they are working toward and will end up unsuccessful.

In my early work with teams at Boston Edison Co., supervisors in one department spent some time identifying issues the department faced. Several teams were formed to deal with the problems identified. One was the issue of field personnel working in the high crime areas of the inner city. They had identified a complex social issue that had political implications within and outside of the company. The team eventually put this issue on the back burner because they had not pared the issue down to make it relevant to the department. They had not determined what a successful outcome would look like.

Sometimes teams are unable to reach their goals. Sponsors need to be aware of this and know when to "call it a day."

Practical Aspects of Teams

As with any work, we have learned both from experiences that have been successful and those that were more challenging. Consider the mechanics of teamwork as you get started.

Preparation for Teamwork

➠ Meet with sponsor to clarify expectations

In Boston Edison, using teams is still a new venture. Some sponsors have easily taken to their roles and been comfortable with a team approach. Others are less familiar and unclear about their involvement.

Before I accept a team facilitation assignment, I meet with the sponsor to clarify expectations and to surface concerns. This is when I establish a contract to work. I define my role, verbalize wants and needs both for myself and the sponsor. This is also when I consult with the sponsor to make recommendations on how to proceed or the criteria to use to select team members.

➠ Address concerns head-on

I also meet with the members of the team. Again, the purpose is to define my role and to learn of any concerns members might have. It is useful to know of any potential problems up front and to then plan to deal with them.

➠ Establish check points with the sponsor

When developing a project plan, establishing check points with the sponsor has several benefits. This practice keeps the sponsor informed, helps keep the team focused on a milestone, and can promote dialogue between the team and the sponsor on the direction and outcomes to date.

When the sponsor sets a team in motion, there is a bit of faith and trust involved. The sponsor is turning the issue over to others. He has to trust that the team will do the right thing. If he truly has empowered them, he will have to live with their recommendations.

Check points are also vehicles for the team to bounce ideas off the sponsor and to get a reality check. At the end of each phase of an Organization Effectiveness Review Project, for example, the team meets with the sponsor to report its findings. At the same time members ask the sponsor to provide them with feedback and general direction.

⮕ Define the parameters

If there are limits or boundaries for the project, they must be stated up front. Without this information, the team could be headed in one direction, while the sponsor has another vision.

Sometimes sponsors are hesitant to state their constraints. They may be new at their role as sponsors and feel they shouldn't dictate to the team. It's much more productive to be clear about any limits or boundaries than to have a reluctant sponsor implement team recommendations that he/she is not comfortable with. It is more damaging to send a team back to the drawing board when the recommendation is not in line with the sponsor's unspoken expectations, which can give teamwork a bad name or increase cynicism among employees.

⮕ Confront and support

When a team begins to concretely examine their work processes or methodology, they don't always like what they see and they may resist. The facilitator needs to confront resistant behavior while offering support at the same time.

⮕ Involve key people

As issues are identified, it is important to involve key stakeholders as soon as possible. People who have a vested interest in how an issue is resolved need to take part in the up-front discussions and the planning of the solutions.

There have been teams for which the criteria for membership is one's role in the company or office in the union rather than one's position or knowledge of the process being addressed. In these teams there is less partnering and, therefore, less successful resolution.

Union/Management Teams

We are a company where two thirds of the work force are represented by two unions. Working with joint union/management teams requires other considerations.

➠ Involve labor relations

Before any joint work is agreed to, Labor Relations should pave the way to avoid overlapping and conflicting efforts to obtain union agreement. In the joint union/management teams it is beneficial to have a Labor Relations representative attend meetings. This provides first hand knowledge for the Labor rep to keep the union leadership informed and "in the loop" where the team's progress is concerned.

The joint teams cannot discuss wage, hour, or working conditions as these are only handled through negotiations. These parameters are set up front.

I learned early to involve Labor in any joint team efforts. One afternoon after beginning work with a joint team, I received a phone call. The union president identified himself and wanted to know what I was doing working with his employees. He was most upset at learning about the team from one of his stewards. He rightly felt he should be the first to know. This conversation quickly taught me to involve Labor Relations early in any joint team efforts.

➠ Assess readiness

When a team approach is new for employees, they are venturing into uncharted waters. One important factor, especially for union/management teams, is to assess the readiness for this work. The degree of openness to participation and the employees' comfort level will affect the teamwork.

I would also add that team competencies and orientations make a difference for successful teamwork. Therefore, selection of team members is an important ingredient. It is also very difficult to tell the unions who should be on the teams.

In two instances, when we received the names of the team members, we revised our expectations and outcomes. We didn't think we had the right members to complete the objectives. Our previous experience gave us information for assessing the readiness of some of the team members and their ability to participate fully.

Conclusion

There have been many positive changes at Boston Edison Co. We have made a great deal of progress in changing the way we work together. Teams have made a difference in improving our competitive position.

The tangible results of teamwork include inventory reduction and increased availability of stock at the service centers. We have streamlined work processes and eliminated delays for customers. Teams have developed flexible job specifications increasing efficiency and customer focus. We have increased billing dollars. We have reduced layers of management and increased spans of control.

There have been less tangible benefits: *i.e.*, there is increased communication and increased employee involvement. The teams in one functional area have such "esprit de corps" they now print an internal quarterly newsletter to keep each other informed of their team's progress. There is a marked increase in employee input to decision making.

Teamwork has helped us with our need to focus on customers. Through working on teams, we have become more aware of our customers and their needs. Every team has a customer. Even if team members do not have direct contact with the external customers, they soon become aware of their internal customers and their needs.

Teams continue to promote organizational learning. Members learn about other areas and disciplines, their concerns and problems. They also learn how to work with people with different orientations or perspectives and see how others around them move to improve work practices.

Teamwork has provided a structure for union-represented employees and management to work on common problems and forge solutions together. We are working collaboratively.

During the early team efforts, when we first brought people from the different functions together, we heard comments among participants like "I haven't seen you since we worked in the manholes in '72," or, "Do you still work for the company?" or, "What have you been doing with yourself?" Now that we've been using teams, the greetings no longer sound like a twenty-five year high school reunion.

The culture is changing.

Chapter Thirteen

Driving Transformational Change Through the Organization

Dr. Jo-Anne Pitera

In business, there is a well-known theory. The "kick-in-the-butt" theory. Although the name couldn't be less technical, the results are impressive.

Whenever an industry receives a kick in the butt, it wakes up, revitalizes itself, and often goes on to record earnings. A prime example is the auto industry. It sauntered through the fifties and sixties, producing standardized cars for an accepting and eager market.

Then the Japanese invaded, U.S. manufacturers' market share plummeted and it took numerous layoffs, numerous turn arounds, and massive losses until U.S. manufacturers became competitive.

What did it take to achieve an impressive turn around? One day, automakers woke up and realized that it took more than just machines and factories to build cars.

The company culture had to be changed; employees had to buy into a new vision, a new way of doing business. Employees, long protected by powerful unions, had to learn that they weren't entitled to a job, they had to earn it every day.

In fact, General Motors Saturn factory, where both the factory and company culture were built from scratch, shows how critical people are in helping a company to succeed.

And once the major car companies understood that cultural transformation and retooling went hand in hand, they were able to go from "bolt-them-together" Chevettes to state-of-the-art Saturns.

Answer the Wake-up Call

The electric utility industry has recently received its own "kick-in-the-butt." Competition, heightened by new wholesale wheeling laws and possible retail wheeling transactions, is as earthshaking to the electric utility industry as Japanese cars were to American automakers.

Fortunately, utilities have one strong advantage. Carmakers did not understand the threat of foreign cars until it was almost too late.

But utilities across the U.S. are listening carefully to their wake-up call. By making everyone in their companies understand the competitive threats and by helping all employees understand the attitudes and behaviors that are necessary to succeed, utilities can begin to transform themselves into successful, competitive companies.

Instead of going through the Chevette-building stage, they just might take a quantum leap to the Saturn-building stage.

Plant the Seeds of Transformational Change

Now, executives may see the importance of cultural transformation. They may understand that the right company culture, accepted by their employees can help them achieve their goals more quickly. Yet, seeing the need to transform and having the necessary skills to transform are two vastly different subjects. It is easy to say that change must start from the top, that change must be sponsored by the top. It is easy to say that with strong sponsorship, a clear vision, a clear strategy, and milestones to measure the progress along the way, the seeds of transformational change are planted. Yet, beyond merely planting the seeds of change, more must occur for a successful transformation.

To elaborate on the agricultural metaphor, it is easy to demonstrate and convince anyone that planting a seed is just the first step in a series of pain-staking and time-consuming cultivating processes needed if the seed is to grow and thrive.

Yet, all too often, organizations feel that once the vision is set, the strategy determined, and the mission announced, the seeds of change not only will grow, but also magically transform the work force into powerful, proactive employees.

Unfortunately, cultural transformation, as too many frustrated companies can attest, just doesn't happen that way.

Every company must determine the cultivating processes that increase the probability, while decreasing the time frame, for organizational change to take hold and to transform the culture.

Establish an Entrepreneurial Framework

In the days of the "rate-case mentality," employees didn't need to understand the entire business of running a utility. Their world was fragmented, some were content to keep the books, others were content to buy fuel, yet others were content to keep the steam generators in peak condition to turn out kilowatts.

As utilities shift to more entrepreneurial enterprises, they must understand that a good entrepreneur sees relationships. He understands how environmental laws, fuel costs, accounting procedures, responsibilities to customers and shareholders, among many other factors, all affect the bottom line.

Above all, an entrepreneur, especially one who has struggled to build up a business over many years, understands the need to· "earn."

Every business needs to earn customers', regulators', and stockholders' trust. Every employee, by making that company as efficient and as cost effective as possible, earns their paycheck.

In short, the feeling of entitlement to one's paycheck (long held by utility employees) must be replaced by a feeling of, "I must go in every day and earn my paycheck."

Employees have to see how their individual contributions fit into the entire company structure.

179

Organizations need to define and communicate about the company's cultural transformation. Information that once was reserved only for board rooms and held close to the corporate vest needs to be shared and understood throughout the organization.

Employees need to see the big picture, and know for what they are accountable and responsible. Also, they must understand *why* they are accountable and responsible.

In other words, the focus of the successful utility employee must shift from entitlement, to an attitude of performance.

Help to Shift Attitudes

How does this "attitude shifting" take place? First, every employee must be given a set of agreed upon indicators. Call them milestones, call them critical success indicators, call them targets . . . the theory is the same. These indicators are known by every employee and every employee understands that performance is geared towards success, which is defined by the indicators.

For example, indicators can range from striving to achieve 100 percent satisfaction to achieving an Equivalent Availability Factor of 85% at the power plants. Indicators can range from striving for a successful safety record to keeping costs at 4 cents per kilowatt hour produced.

The point is, employees who see the big picture, will find it easier to understand and strive toward achieving their indicators.

But above all, pressure should be steadily applied. There must be a carefully scheduled, monitored approach to achieving success that the employees understand and accept.

Without such an integrated approach, employees become confused or cynical about the cultural change efforts and think that these efforts are merely another "management fad of the month."

They adopt the "kidney stone mentality." If you ride the latest management wave, keep a low profile and talk the right talk, this too shall pass.

So yes, vision, mission, objectives, goals, and milestones, key responsibility areas, and key competencies are all crucial to an integrated transformational culture change.

But at the very foundation must be an entrepreneurial group of employees who understand that their efforts must be performance based and result oriented. They have to understand why they must earn their paychecks and why the era of entitlement has vanished.

Bring Out the Leader in Everyone

The pain, hardships, losses, and sacrifices involved in downsizing organizations have left a wounded work force. Many employees have lost the confidence and courage to fight the corporate war.

Thus, utilities are now fighting on two fronts. They are fighting the enemy of competition on the outside and worse, they are fighting an enemy within. Employees have a sense of helplessness and hopelessness that is paralyzing organizations.

A sense of hope and confidence needs to be rekindled back into the work environment and the work force. This is an important component of transformational change and can be a powerful curative factor in organizational recovery.

This sense of restoration can only be found through the leadership abilities of employees. Leaders must be relied upon to lead employees out of the desert of despair into the new promised land of competition and success.

But to achieve this transformation of spirit, it must be recognized that leaders should be cultivated throughout the organization. Leadership can no longer be confined to titled positions. Mobilization of the energy and leadership of all employees is required.

Organizations need titled leaders committed to, first, their own development, then to all the employees they are responsible to for coaching and support.

Yet, this "soft" side of the business environment, competence in people skills, is difficult for many managers who grew up in a traditional corporation saturated with command and control edicts.

Executive development in core leadership competencies has to become a top organizational priority. Weak links, those afraid or those not wanting to develop the necessary leadership and people skills, can no longer be tolerated.

Leaders must be trained to convince employees to commit to the new organization. That is difficult because commitment is something that employees have to give willingly.

The challenge, therefore, becomes encouraging the hearts of the work force, while focusing on business results.

Leaders charged with convincing employees to commit to the new organization, face obstacles. For example, commitment may now be perceived in organizations as a one-way street with little investment on the side of management in the individual employee.

The perception exists that everyone is expendable; there is no safe haven for retreat. How can leaders stop this downward spiral?

Understand the Importance of Values

The downward spiral can be stopped when values are taken into consideration. High-performing organizations are driven by a set of values that determine behavior. As employees are asked to change their behaviors, there is an implied request for them to change their values. They must be convinced that changing their values is worthwhile and an important thing to do.

The importance of changing values and behavior can be demonstrated only by the leaders in the company. Specific leadership behaviors have to be identified and reinforced at all levels of the organization, beginning at the top.

Leaders must understand that to get employees to buy into the new culture, it is no longer enough to insist that they, "do as I say."

Identified leaders, whether it be by position or title, have a tremendous obligation and responsibility not only to inspire others, but to model the way everyone is expected to behave to support the company's vision and new corporate culture (Kouzes and Posner, 1987, 1993).

By serving as an example, leaders can regain employees' faith and the credibility of the new company culture will be greatly enhanced.

But it cannot be stated enough that leaders are believed when they demonstrate a change in their behaviors while conducting their daily business and facing challenges that arise.

Articulate and Communicate a Compelling Reason for Change

To further ensure a successful cultural transformation, as part of their role modeling, leadership needs to continually articulate and communicate a compelling reason for change. This reason becomes the foundation upon which challenges to the processes and practices in the company are based.

In addition, leaders need to transmit a sense of urgency. A sense of urgency is critical in a competitive culture. Your company cannot afford to reserve leadership practices only for critical incidents that have far-reaching impact. Failure to achieve cultural change will have a far-reaching impact on utilities that minimize the need for clear, consistent leadership.

Leadership, quite simply, must be practiced each day in seemingly inconsequential interactions and exchanges. And soon, employees' confidence will begin to take root.

Expectations of leadership practices must be clearly defined, so that the organization will know which behaviors to support. Making those behaviors everyone's responsibility and accountability will increase the likelihood of successful cultural change. As employees take responsibility for the desired behaviors, they gain a sense of control over the outcome.

A sense of confidence, control, and commitment slowly begins to revive the individual and the organization. Hopelessness and helplessness are replaced with a new vision and empowerment.

Take a Systematic Approach to Changing Culture

People receive culture cues primarily from three sources in organizations. The first, already discussed, is leadership behavior. The second are programs and systems that are put in place to support the norms and expectations in the organization. The third source of cultural cues is the formal and informal communications systems that deliver the corporate message throughout the organization.

All these culture cues must be managed and all of them have to be in alignment if change is to propel an organization forward.

Never forget that people receive their communication cues from what is said and what is done. High-performing organizations realize this and work hard to communicate a focused message throughout the organization.

They realize that commitment to change requires providing the work force with information so that intelligent decisions are made. Confronted with decisions, employees then can choose to be a support or a barrier to the new organization.

The infrastructure and support systems serve to support the message and to channel the message into specific behaviors and actions in which employees can engage.

Organizations will find it productive to offer rewards and recognition that will support the identified behaviors and help those expected behaviors become the foundation for sustained cultural change.

Far-reaching Implications for Human Resources

Human resources plays a vital role in putting the proper systems in place to support the new culture.

A systematic approach has far-reaching implications for human resources. All human resource processes and programs need to point people in the same direction.

Recruiting and selection, compensation (rewards, recognition systems, performance management), benefits, training, and development must provide a competitive advantage for the organization and individuals.

Transformational change requires envisioning where you need the culture to be, assessing the gap between the current and future culture, designing a change strategy, and redesigning all processes and systems in support of the change strategy.

Enable before You Empower

Organizational culture change will be slow to take hold, unless each individual in the organization feels a responsibility for the change process at a personal level.

Momentum needs to build in the organization. That momentum builds with the singular actions of individuals and continues to build with the cumulative actions of the collective work force.

Bringing change down to a personal level will require a commitment from people in positioned leadership roles. Enabling requires fostering collaboration and joint problem solving with common goals and agreed upon objectives.

Without enabling, empowerment will remain an illusive, intangible buzzword, which will produce more cynicism than change.

And, of course, employees will have to assume their share of responsibility for change, too. When your employees share the responsibility—and your organization assures that the necessary resources, materials, training, performance expectations, rewards, incentives, teamwork, innovation, and creativity are in place—you are well on the way to a successful cultural transformation.

Part Five:
Communicate, Communicate, Communicate

Chapter Fourteen

Communicating Culture Change: A Practical Guide

J. Kimball Hansen

Communication is often called the lifeblood of organizations. If that's the case, and I believe it is, many of today's corporations are in desperate need of a transfusion. Their anemia is stress-induced. A major cause of that stress, ironically, is the whole gamut of today's consultant-prescribed corporate 'cures.' Downsizing, reengineering, restructuring, business process improvements and cultural renewal are just a few sources of serious organizational tension. Tension that, if not tempered in constructive and productive ways, can lead to critical breakdowns of trust, credibility and human relationships within organizations.

Good communication is the balm that can help soothe the strains organizations sustain as they experience rapid culture and business process change. On the other hand, communicating poorly during times of great organizational change and stress is like throwing handfuls of proverbial salt into the wounds that will inevitably open within the organization.

I do not mean to imply that the changes we are going through in contemporary organizations are not beneficial in the short or long run. I'm only saying these changes exert enormous pressures on organizations and their members. If left unchecked, these pressures can thwart the gains we hope to achieve through our organizational and culture change efforts. Perhaps at no time is good communication needed more in organizations than at times of significant change in culture, in structure, in technology, in market conditions, or in any other way.

As Robert Levering, co-author of *The 100 Best Companies to Work for in America*, said, "Employees don't expect the impossible, but they do demand the possible. And good, two-way communication is probably the most important thing companies can do."

Fortunately, there are lessons of good communication that we can apply in our organizations to more successfully introduce, manage and anchor change. This chapter briefly describes eight of these lessons gleaned from companies that have traveled or are now traveling the roads of change. It is not meant to be a primer on the process of organizational communication, but merely a few key concepts to think about as you manage your changing workplace.

Lesson 1: Remember Proverbs

"Where there is no vision, the people perish . . ." These are ancient words with current relevance from a wise King Solomon. To that, I would add my own corollary, "Where there is no communication, the vision perishes."

Today's successful organizations do at least one thing very well—they instill within the hearts and minds of their members what the organization stands for and its overall direction—its purpose. Values and vision drive the successful organization's decisions and actions. And communication plays a leading role in ensuring common understanding and commitment.

When she was interviewing for jobs a few years ago, Heidi Catano met several CEOs who asked for her analysis of their companies. Armed with an MBA and a computer programmed with performance ratios from annual reports at home, Heidi knew the numbers.

But when she interviewed with Tom Chappell, president and co-founder of Tom's of Maine, he asked her: "What do you do in your life that contributes to the common good?"

"I'd never been asked anything like that before," remembers Heidi. "Tom said, 'I know you're an expert in the job. But what's in your heart?'"

Now when Heidi interviews prospective employees, she too looks for people who share the company's values and are passionate about social responsibility. "I know they'll do a good job for us."

Using the founders' vision as the basis for making decisions is an everyday occurrence at Tom's of Maine, a producer of natural personal care products founded in 1970 by Tom and Kate Chappell on the twin values of respect for people and the environment. That makes the culture of Tom's remarkable, in an age when mission, vision and values statements are often little more than pretentious documents slapped on a wall only to be greeted with the cynicism of employees.

Not here. The managers and employees at Tom's use the mission statement to make decisions every day on everything from advertising budgets to product ingredients. What the Chappells learned from their experience at reinventing their company through a sense of shared purpose and values will be useful to anyone involved in managing change and renewing a stagnant workplace.

Among their discoveries and conclusions:

➠ "If the company has no principles other than maximizing profit, or if its values are not stated, workers will limit themselves to the least creative principle in business: please the boss."

➠ "Common values and a shared sense of vision and purpose can turn a company into a community where daily work takes on a deeper meaning and satisfaction."

➠ "The mission of the company shapes the hopes, expectations and aspirations of this business community in non-economic terms."

➠ "The best way to get beyond titles and the intimidating factor of corporate hierarchies is to trade stories with the people you work with."

➠ "Customers care that the product is good, but they seem to care even more that the company is good."

➠ "Diversity is a value that creates excellence."

➠ "Real business leaders seek their worthiness among their employees. We visit our employees; we talk to them; we find out what's going on in their lives; we're part of them. We stand with them."

Of course, these are all conclusions drawn from a long, ongoing and, at times, messy process. On their journey to corporate renewal, the Chappells learned hard lessons; that people will not immediately greet the vision and mission statements with the same enthusiasm as those who drafted them; that evolving standards of competence may mean leaving behind long-time associates; that veering too far from the middle course between profits and the common good can mean sluggish growth—or the loss of consumer confidence.

There are many lessons for communicators and organizational leaders that can be learned from the Chappells' experiences: the central role of listening and storytelling in building trust; the moral responsibility of supervisors to their employees; the company as a place of education; the importance of drawing everyone into the process of formulating cultural statements; and the value of incorporating cultural statements into orientation, performance reviews and hiring decisions.

Finally, this advice from Tom Chappell: "The company is not an organizational chart but an interdependent system. What you do in the company in one place will have an effect in another place. We have to care about each other as fellow humans, and—absolutely critical—we have to be interconnected through a good communication system."

Lesson 2: Leaders are communicators

James O'Toole in a recent issue of *Fortune* magazine wrote, "Ninety-five percent of American managers today say the right thing. Five percent actually do it." While this chapter is about saying the right thing—communicating, the words will be void of meaning and credibility unless they are brought to life by the leader's actions. In today's business jargon, it's called walking the talk. A leader at a southwestern electric utility has the following words of wisdom posted on her wall: "Communicate culture change; use words if necessary." Actions do, in fact, speak louder than words. But words are also needed in large organizations where not all members can personally witness the actions of their leaders.

Leaders are, by definition, communicators. They may not always live up to that high calling, but it is theirs nonetheless. Roger D'Aprix, former employee communication manager at Xerox Corporation and one of this country's most experienced authorities on organizational communication says "management *is* communication." Leading and managing people, individually and in groups, are principally acts of communication. Successful organizations are full of leaders, formal and informal, who take personal accountability for their responsibility to communicate to their people about their group work, about their organization, about their markets and industry. Effective leaders know the importance of leader communication, they accept their role and they know how to do it.

Members of organizations look to their leaders as the most preferred source of important organizational information. People want to hear from their leaders; they want to talk with them, ask them questions and come to a shared understanding of the organization's vision, mission and values. In other words, they want their leaders to care about them as people and make them feel like they are an important part of the organization.

A large amount of data exists that verify these assertions. Research conducted within single organizations and across multiple organizations and industries over the past decade consistently concludes that employees' most preferred source of organizational information is their immediate supervisor. They also viewed their supervisors as the most credible source.

Research conducted at Arizona Public Service (APS), an electric utility with about 7,000 employees that is currently undergoing significant culture and business process changes, goes one step further. That research showed a relationship between the content of the communication and employees' most preferred medium or source. These findings were not surprising. As the complexity of the information increased, employees increasingly preferred personal sources, i.e., their leaders. That's because complex information—and culture change is a complex process—needs translation, explanation. Employees need someone to put that information into a context and language that they can relate to and understand. Their own leaders are best positioned to fulfill this communication responsibility.

What happens when leaders don't fulfill their responsibilities to communicate the business and cultural issues to their employees? An information and communication vacuum is created that quickly fills with rumor, speculation and misinformation—the breeding ground for distrust and breakdowns in leader credibility.

APS, when faced with a reluctance on the part of many formal leaders to fully assume their role and responsibility as principal communicators in the organization, recruited an initial group of about 250 employees and initiated a concept called Breakthrough Leadership. These Breakthrough leaders—formal leaders and frontline employees—were chosen on the basis of their demonstrated commitment to the cultural changes taking place in the organization. They were given communication tools and training and empowered to cross organizational boundaries and serve as "communication catalysts" to precipitate more and better communication throughout the organization. Among other things, they set aside time to assist other formal leaders in the communication process. And they both solicited and responded to invitations to participate in staff meetings to present information and answer questions about the company's culture change strategy.

To prevent the perception that a class of cultural elitists was taking root, APS encouraged all employees to become Breakthrough leaders. Employees—including formal leaders—could appoint themselves as Breakthrough leaders by demonstrating an understanding of and commitment to the changes happening in the organization and positively affecting the change process in their work teams.

Breakthrough leadership is a "culture change intervention" that's working at APS. To be successful, organizations must capture the commitment of their formal leadership and hold them personally accountable to fulfill their communication responsibilities.

Lesson 3: Choose the right channel

When it comes to changing an organization's culture, there is no more effective communication channel than good, solid, down-home, face-to-face communication. Leaders at all levels of an organization, yes, even those at the very top, must talk to people regularly in large groups, small groups and one-to-one. As Debra Shutt writes in *The Williams Report*, a communication newsletter published by Joe Williams Communications, Inc., "Nowhere to hide. Every tell-tale facial expression on display. Every word taking on a life of its own—colored by presentation, augmented by intonation. No chance for rewrites, editing, cuts—just the naked, spoken word delivered first-hand." It's culture change communication at its best.

It is risky and leaders too often shun the opportunity to communicate in this way, but the benefits in building trust and credibility far outweigh the risks. Employees in today's corporations hunger and thirst for information that can help them make sense of their ever-changing environments inside and outside their companies. Joseph Conrad, author of *Heart of Darkness*, said back in 1898, "There is a weird power in a spoken word . . . And a word carries far—very far . . . ." Organizations that want to negotiate the waters of change must use the power of the spoken word to lead them safely along their course.

There are, of course, multiple communication channels to choose from in large organizations. And each one serves a useful purpose in reaching an audience with important messages. But in times of transformational change, face-to-face communication should be your flagship channel supported by newsletters, videos, e-mail, voice-mail and all the rest.

At Texas Instruments (TI), corporate internal communications manager Kerry Miller uses face-to-face because it gives the communication experience an added authenticity and sincerity that other channels cannot provide. TI's face-to-face program is based on a foundation of policy-mandated monthly and quarterly meetings.

Once each quarter, every department level manager conducts a one-hour meeting for all employees. The managers direct these meetings and cover updates on particular departmental issues, overall corporate activities and general news. They also talk about the "burning issue" for the quarter. On an every-other-month basis, the CEO meets with all levels of staff. He steps into departmental meetings (which can involve from 40 to 500 people). Miller coordinates the logistics of whom he will visit each month, and ensures he has the background on the department or organization he is visiting.

Another service provided by Miller and his communication staff is the preparation of presentation packages used by managers and supervisors as they conduct their department meetings. These packages of information usually focus on single topics important to the organization. Issues that TI has communicated in the past through this face-to-face approach include drug-free workplace policy, alternative work schedules, sexual harassment and flexible benefits.

Arizona Public Service president and CEO Mark DeMichele holds monthly breakfast meetings with employees selected at random. "These are open, frank discussions," he says. "I have no agenda other than to try to answer any question that has anything at all to do with our business and our company. If I don't know the answer, I'll find out and get back to the person who asked it that same day, if possible." Other APS leaders have begun to follow DeMichele's lead and create more opportunities to talk with employees about current issues and concerns.

To facilitate leader communication, many organizations publish newsletters or other publications specifically designed to support leaders in their communication efforts. Often these publications are formatted as discussion guides with bullet points, supporting information and anticipated questions and answers to help leaders prepare for and present the information in an effective manner. The document serves the added purpose of providing a control mechanism to make sure the messages being communicated are as consistent and timely as possible throughout the organization.

A critical element in successful leader communication programs is accountability. Leaders must be held accountable for communication within their groups. At APS, communication is a part of every leader's job description and quarterly performance review. Leaders must produce results in the technical aspects of their jobs as well as the cultural aspects, including communication. Those who do not or cannot perform in both areas up to expectations are moved out of their leadership positions if they do not improve within a specified time.

Face-to-face communication need not be the exclusive domain of leaders. Frontline employees at one western utility, with the support of their leaders, organize weekly brown-bag lunch gatherings to talk about current issues facing their company. They select their own topics, invite members of management to take part in the discussions and do their own publicity. The meetings are informal, but serious. And they represent a new level of trust between leaders and employees that didn't exist in the company just a few years ago.

One last word about face-to-face communication—and that word is dialogue. Face-to-face communication should never be one-sided. It is not speeches and lectures and slide presentations. Face-to-face implies two-way communication—dialogue, and lots of it. As one employee said, "We don't want to just listen to our leaders, we want to talk with them."

Lesson 4: Focus on the forest

Changing an organization's culture is usually a multi-faceted, wide-ranging effort. Everything from leadership styles to compensation systems to business processes are often affected. Simultaneous change on many fronts can be bewildering to members of the organization, especially if change is introduced into the organization at a rapid pace. As confusion increases, so do stress, skepticism and doubt. A core strategy in communicating culture change, therefore, should be to keep things as simple as possible and never allow people to lose sight of the big picture. In a rapidly changing environment, people do have a tendency to forget the forest (the reasons for making the changes and the ultimate objectives) when the organization is introducing so many new trees.

During the high tide of its cultural transformation, Arizona Public Service was busy implementing more than 20 culture change "interventions." These interventions included a new "pay for performance" system, a new performance review and measurement system, reengineering core business processes, changes in leader expectations, changes to vision, mission and values statements, emphasis on diversity and the list goes on. The organization was flooded with information on each of these efforts.

To manage the volume and pace of the communication flow, the APS culture change strategy was focused on four main themes. Each of the themes was linked to the overall corporate mission and values. Those themes, and their links to the corporate mission and values, provided the framework for a reasoned and measured approach to communicating culture change to APS employees. Information was consistent, messages were clearly tied to the big culture change picture and employees were able to put things in the right context relating to their jobs and area of the organization.

Remember, however, people learn at different rates and adjust to change in different ways. Walk into any bookstore, stroll through an airport terminal or open the comics section in your Sunday newspaper and you are likely to find a 3-D picture puzzle. You've seen them. They are computer-generated images which, on the surface, appear to be a random pattern of multi-colored shapes, lines or dots. But if you stare at them long enough while relaxing the focus of your eyes, something else begins to emerge from the random field—a seemingly three-dimensional object. Maybe it's a whale breaking the surface of the ocean or a vase of flowers or the profile of a person. No matter what it is, however, the moment of discovery brings feelings of wonder and excitement. It's as if scales fall from your eyes giving you the power to see things in ways you've never seen them before.

"Seeing" our organization's new vision and culture emerge from a background of traditional patterns can be a similarly exciting and energizing experience. But, like the 3-D picture puzzles, not everyone can see the depth and dimension of the "hidden" object quickly and easily. It takes work and practice to develop the ability to look at our environment differently—with new eyes attuned to the new wavelengths of work. And it takes patience, understanding and perseverance on the part of both the organization and its members.

A cohesive and coordinated culture change communication strategy stems from good planning and research. In efforts to change the corporate culture at US WEST's Marketing and Information Services business, the communication staff recognized that "good communication is the key to making [those] efforts work. If we don't communicate effectively," says Robin Baca, director of corporate communication, "all is for naught."

Given the go-ahead to develop a comprehensive communication program, Baca and his staff first turned to the internal research material to see what employees really wanted. From that data, they developed their proposals. They reviewed the strengths and weaknesses of the U S WEST Marketing Resources communications and came up with a proposal called Project Cascade, named for the notion that good communication should cascade down the corporate ladder. Backed by facts and figures, the proposal spelled out two ambitious goals:

➠ Within two years, establish a systematic, integrated, interactive communication process that provides honest, accurate, timely information that people want and need to effectively contribute to and share in the company's success.

➠ Within five years, offer comprehensive interactive menu-driven communication that allows employees to get the information they want, when they want it, in the format they choose.

Management accepted their proposal and authorized the formation of a comprehensive communication program. "Our first job was relinquishing our role as being the company's key communicators," said Baca. "Instead, we facilitate communications and position managers and leaders as communicators. At first we thought, 'Are we putting ourselves out of business?' But there will always be a need for people to facilitate communications."

Facilitating means monitoring and continuously improving the communication channels within an organization, including the all-important feedback channels. It also means helping to set the corporate agenda, to formulate messages and control the timing and pace of the overall communication effort in accordance with the culture change strategy. Facilitating also includes the responsibility for coordinating and integrating communication activities covering a wide range of interrelated organizational projects and functions. In short, while leaders should be at the forefront of communicating culture change within an organization, communication professionals play a vital behind-the-scenes role to develop overall communication strategy, then coordinate and integrate the work needed to implement that strategy in a comprehensive and consistent manner throughout the organization.

Lesson 5: Localize your messages

Large organizations are varied and diverse. They are communities composed of people with broad ranges of education, skills, experience and culture. Organizations can derive great strength and resources in these differences but such variety also poses great challenge, especially when it comes to communicating. That's why leader communication is so important. Leaders know their team members, or should know them. Leaders can receive information from the organization and translate or customize it to fit the needs and characteristics of their teams. They can put the information in the right context to help their teams better understand their contribution to the total organization's mission and purpose.

Most employees need answers to a few basic questions to feel like a valuable and contributing member of an organization. What is my job? How can I do it better? How does my work contribute to the overall purpose and success of the organization? Where are we going and how will we get there? What challenges and problems do we face and how can I work with others to help solve them?

Traditionally, managers and supervisors communicated only as much information as was needed for an individual to perform a given task. Today's employees demand much more from their leaders. Enlightened leaders now will make sure employees understand the mission and values of the organization and how their work contributes to the overall purpose. Such a perspective gives employees a greater feeling of self-worth and value to the organization. It also makes employees better able to make decisions on their own within the framework of the organization's broader goals and objectives. As one leader once said, "Teach people correct principles and let them govern themselves."

Are all leaders able to communicate to their employees in this manner? Not likely. All too often, leaders in organizations are still selected not for their ability to lead and inspire people, but for their technical accomplishments. Fortunately, leadership, and the ability to communicate effectively to groups and individuals, can be learned. But to learn, leaders must be given the tools, training and opportunity to customize corporate messages to fit the needs and characteristics of their people. Then they must be held accountable.

Culture change is really nothing more than a community of people changing their behavior, habits, attitudes and perceptions. But that kind of change is difficult, time-consuming and needs constant attention. Common goals, clear direction, appropriate motivation and a good measure of patience are required for long-term change. Leader communicators are a key ingredient to the process. Only they can carry on the daily dialogue employees crave to learn and understand what is happening and changing around them.

Lesson 6: Watch your language

Do you speak the same language as the members of your organization? If you've been spending much time with a consultant, chances are you don't. Consultants make a lot of their money by taking tried and true principles that have enduring value and out- fitting them in a new wardrobe of words. Unfortunately, these words inhibit, rather than enhance, good communication. What's more, if you are a leader and have picked up a consultant's dialect, what you say to your people may well be Greek to them. Your newly acquired dialect will distance you from your people and, if you persist in using it, could even chew away at your credibility.

Speak English. Write English. Keep it straight. Keep it simple. Be clear and be concise. Use words to express yourself not to impress others.

Workplace paradigm . . . reengineering . . . congruency . . . strategic [insert anything here] . . . maximizing performance . . . cultural transformation . . . de-recruitment process . . . and the list can go on and on.

What do these words and phrases make you think about? More importantly, how do they make you feel? Are they friendly, warm, inviting? Do you readily relate to them? Do you relate to them at all? To most people, they are distant and cold. It is tiring just to read them. They have no personality. They are stuffy. They turn people off. They cannot inspire.

The language we use says a lot about us. The language we use in our organizations says a lot about what kind of places they are. Companies caught up in massive culture change have a tendency to introduce massive amounts of jargon into the corporate vocabu- lary. People struggling with thinking about their work differently are only hampered in that process if they have to learn a new lan- guage at the same time.

Unless you are a chemist, new concepts and ideas do not often need new words to explain them. In fact, new ideas are most pow- erfully explained using old words. Don't let consultants lead you off the beaten language path. Stay away from jargon and you will more likely avoid creating a class of cultural elitists—people (often leaders) who talk to each other in a secret code of words which have meaning to only a few.

Changing times are stressful times. And in times of stress, people want information straight and unadorned. The use of jargon creates more suspicion and skepticism than it does confidence and commitment. Stay away from it.

Lesson 7: Communication is not a Swiss Army knife

It can't do everything. As necessary as good communication is to the stability and success of organizations, it can't solve every problem and overcome every obstacle. To be effective and believable, communication about culture change must go hand in hand with actions that bring meaning and life to the words. The adage is true: "What you do speaks so loudly in my ears that I can't hear what you say." Example is still one of the best professors around.

Lesson 8: Trust your professionals

Finally, the last lesson. If you have a medium to large organization, you likely have one or more organizational communication professionals on your staff. Use them and trust them. They should be involved in developing and implementing plans, setting strategy, formulating messages and coordinating your communication efforts.

Most of the good ones understand now that they cannot and should not be the principal communicators in their organizations. That responsibility rests squarely on the shoulders of leaders, formal and informal. But they can organize, facilitate and coordinate the communication work that goes on in their companies. They can counsel, recommend and support. They can create tools and systems to improve the communication process. They can analyze, monitor, gather feedback and make improvements. They are master mechanics for perhaps the most crucial process in the organization.

Conclusion

Information can be like cool refreshing water that quenches the thirst of weary travelers within our organizations. Information, like water, has the capacity to rejuvenate and re-energize, to soothe lips parched by the heat of change and stress. Members of many of today's organizations must cope with unreliable delivery systems and even rationing when what they actually need is more information channeled to the right places at the right time.

Margaret Wheatley in her groundbreaking book *Leadership and the New Science,* calls information "the creative energy of the universe."

> Why is there such an epidemic of "poor communications" within organizations? In every one I've worked in, employees have ranked it right at the top of major issues. Indeed, its appearance on those lists in the past years became so predictable that I grew somewhat numb to it. Poor communication was a superficial diagnosis, I thought, that covered up other, more specific issues.

> Over the years, I developed a conditioned response to "communication problems" the minute they were brought up. I disregarded the category. I started pushing people to "get beyond" that catch-all phrase, to "give me more concrete examples" of communication failures. I believed I was en route to the "real" issues that would have nothing to do with communication.

> Now I know I was wrong. My frustration with pat phrases didn't arise from people's lack of clarity about what was bothering them. They were right. They *were* suffering from information problems.

If you think of information as thirst-quenching water, then you can visualize an organizational communication system as a vast web of water pipes bringing fresh and vital information to every member of the organization. The pipes are designed to carry ample supplies of water to every location. Outlets in various forms ranging from fountains to faucets to hydrants give people access to the amount of life-giving water they want and need daily. And there is a master plan that governs the growth and development of the system to meet the needs of the organization.

Like any system, this one needs maintenance and continuous improvement. Are there leaks or other breakdowns which need correcting? Where does the system need to expand to meet the demand? Do the pipelines themselves need to be enlarged? Do people need more drinking fountains, more access? Are there people drowning in too much water? Are there old pipes, no longer in use, that can be cleared away? In addition to these systemic concerns there are content considerations. Is the water clean and clear? Is it free from pollutants? Is it being delivered at the right temperature, pressure and volume? Is the water being tested regularly to ensure quality standards are met? And, finally, how do those who are drinking the water feel about the system and its ability to deliver what they want and need? These are all questions organizations must ask themselves about their communication systems and processes and the life-giving information they provide to their members.

A certain amount of culture shock among the members of changing organizations is inevitable. But whether that shock resuscitates and gets the heart beating again, or whether it sends the organization into a deeper coma is largely dependent upon the quality of communications within the organization and the commitment of its leaders to be communicators.

(Author's note: Many thanks to Joe Williams of Joe Williams Communications, Inc., Bartlesville, OK, for some of the examples and information used in this article.)

Chapter Fifteen

Vision to Action: The Role of Communications

June T. Johnston and Cynthia Larson-Schwartz

The utilities industry is currently facing the most sweeping federal energy legislation in almost two decades. The Energy Policy Act of 1992 (EPAct) set forth a long-term vision for the nation's electric services industry: the mechanisms for marketing energy services will allow consumers choices between competing generation service providers, and replace the long-standing cost-of-service regulation with performance-based regulation.

This does not mean that the federal legislation has set forth strict steps that all governmental entities must adhere to. Rather, Congress has given states and regions the latitude to develop and implement specific policies and programs in order to make the mission of EPAct a reality. This means that each state will have the same objectives as set forth in EPAct, but will go through separate processes of determining policies that will support and fit in with the climate and needs of their particular state.

The state of California is leading the nation in offering solutions to electricity deregulation. California has been particularly slow in experiencing an upturn in the economy, and by enacting the correct legislation in an aggressive fashion, the concept of retail competition could not only give the state the economic boost it needs but also provide long-term protection against economic deterioration.

California's almost $800 billion economy depends heavily on high-quality and competitively-priced electric service; currently, California's investor-owned utilities charge some of the highest prices in the nation. This fact alone adds another justification for businesses to leave California in order to lower their cost of business and also contributes to the economic burden of already struggling companies.

Utilities and other generation services providers will be forced to offer customer-oriented energy solutions that are competitively priced and provide high levels of customer service. Consumers will no longer be locked into a monopoly franchise and energy service providers will need to create new ways of doing business in order to survive. Developing new skills that are critical to truly compete in this new marketplace is a big challenge for those investor-owned utilities that have flourished in a noncompetitive environment for many decades.

In order to successfully position companies that are being thrust into a new world of competitive marketing, a complete cultural transformation must occur. The way that a company operates will always determine the culture that the employees believe in. When that very belief undergoes modification, or in the case of the utilities is completely redefined, employees will naturally perceive it as threatening. When old rules and values are in a stage of uncertainty, employees will have a tendency to experience feelings of insecurity and vulnerability which in turn sabotage the company's goals. Companies cannot operate within this environment of undermined employee morale for very long without reaching a point of nonrecovery.

Employees throughout all levels of an organization must believe in the company, understand the new direction and understand the benefits to the company and the individual. Companies that have successfully achieved this type of transition have had an explicit (and workable) strategy, and have been able to clearly articulate that strategy to their workforce and customers. People need to feel safe in a changing environment and trust in the leaders and the strategy in order to support it. Without that trust and belief, productivity will charge backwards, and the original need for the cultural change may not matter because the company may no longer be in business.

Cultural change is manifested by communicating and supporting different priorities and doing things differently. One major pitfall is that although some moves such as restructuring and plant closings. can be implemented quickly, it takes time to change the thinking of a large company. If the people do not share a common vision of the outcome of change and the benefits to them, the stress and insecurity they feel will kill the efforts. New action can be viewed as negative if employees feel that they are not part of a coherent, clearly defined and articulated long range plan. Intervention communication is crucial, but even a well-crafted and proactive memorandum from the CEO or a formal speech given at a company meeting will only meet the surface definition of communicating "to inform" but does little to ensure the type of communication that motivates people to believe and take action during a long period of chaos.

The type of communication necessary to prepare employees to handle change and to willingly become an active part of the process is not a single event. It is a continuous process that requires a well prepared strategy creating a consistent message along with identifying the different audiences, taking each of their unique needs into account, and the benefits to everyone for their contribution. Most importantly, it must be communicated consistently, regularly and passionately.

The cultural change will happen only if it is owned by those people who do the work of the company, and it is the job of company executives, managers and supervisors to ensure that the employees integrate the new visions into their own worklives. In his book, *Managing for the Future*, Peter F. Drucker writes "The foundation of effective leadership is thinking through the organization's mission, defining it and establishing it, clearly and visibly. The leader sets the goals, sets the priorities, and sets and maintains the standards." However, in implementing the standards, the leader who cannot effectively communicate changes cannot expect results.

It is very common for companies undergoing cultural transformations to ignore or misunderstand the value of the role of effective communications throughout the organizational chain. After all, what is most important is the survival of the organization in the new game: if the right decisions are made at the top and that information is disseminated to the rest of the company in ways that worked in the past, logic dictates that success should not be far behind, provided that the strategy is sound. It becomes very easy to set the communications aspect as a low priority, or to be blind to its importance, especially when the company has had a history of employee loyalty and past industry success.

Communicating for Belief and Action

Some companies do realize the importance of staying close to the employees as they move through a transitional period. It is not unusual for corporations to spend large amounts of time and money on "reaching" the people so that everyone understands where the company is headed, the reasoning behind certain decisions, and how those decisions might affect the company and the employees. The communication effort might take the form of special newsletters, memos, and information packages. Forms of "live" communications might feature the CEO and/or top executives in various formats: leading town hall meetings, teleconferences, videotapes, involvement in small roundtable discussions, and distribution of voicemail messages.

Written communication has always been important in the businessplace. It is common for the greatest efforts at the top to be focused on the final "approved" word to describe the new order of things. Undoubtedly to exchange facts, data and details, written communication is much more effective than speaking. When a company is undergoing changes, people need documentation about the new payroll system, insurance carrier, or other processes that will impact their lives. There is security in documents: once it is written, it seems more official and permanent.

On the other hand, if the goal of the message is to influence, to persuade, or to get a point across, then it has to be spoken. As Bert Decker, communications expert, explains to us in his best-selling book, You've Got to be Believed to be Heard, "The spoken word and the written word are not just different ways of communicating. Speaking and writing are polar opposites when it comes to communicating. Writing is like a monaural recording: the message comes through on only one channel. Speaking, however, is like a multichannel superstereo in which there are not just two but dozens of channels simultaneously feeding information into our brains. The speaker's posture, expression, energy level, eye contact, inflection, intonation, volume, and actions are just a few of the many cues that accompany and modify the words of the message.

Written communication goes directly to the cerebral cortex, the highly developed reasoning and analytical portion of the brain. Spoken communication carries energy, feeling, passion, and goes right to the emotional centers of the brain . . . It is this emotional side that we have to reach if we want to motivate and persuade people . . ."

"In the spoken medium . . . what you say must be believed in order to have impact. No message, regardless of how eloquently stated, brilliantly defended, and painstakingly documented it may be, is able to penetrate a wall of distrust, apprehension, or indifference. If you want your listener to be persuaded and motivated, he or she must believe your message. And for your message to be believed, you must be believable."

Effective Spoken Communication

A spoken message is made up of only three components: the verbal, the vocal, and the visual. A few years ago, Professor Albert Mehrabian of UCLA conducted a landmark study on the relationships between the "Three V's" of spoken communication. He measured the effect that each of these three components has on the believability of a speaker's message. The verbal element is the message itself—the words you say. Most people tend to concentrate only on the verbal element, mistakenly assuming this to be the message, when in fact it is only part of the message. The second part of the message is the vocal element—the intonation, projection, and resonance of one's voice as it carries the words.

The third part is the visual element—what people see—the motion and expression of a person's body and face as he or she speaks.

Professor Mehrabian's research found that the degree of consistency (or inconsistency) between these three elements is the factor that determines the believability of the spoken message. The more these three factors harmonize with each other, the more believable the speaker.

When these three components contradict each other, an inconsistent message is transmitted, and the verbal content is virtually smothered by the vocal and visual components. Professor Mehrabian's research shows that when a message is inconsistent, 55% of the believability of the of the message is communicated through the visual element. The vocal is 38%, and the verbal component, or the words themselves, is 7%.

When companies are undergoing a transformation, there is no more important time to ensure that all communication is planned to foster employee commitment to help reach the organizational goals. When the message has to do with a corporate change that requires the employees' buy in, it is critical that the attention and preparation spent on the spoken, or the human-to-human communication of the message, be at least what is spent on the "official version" of the words.

What Counts in Spoken Communication

Most people have not been taught what really counts in spoken communication. Ninety percent of our time in business is spent "communicating," but what is truly understood and taken action on is a different matter. The key ingredient to communicating effectively is believability. No matter what is said, it will not make much difference to the listener unless the speaker is credible and believed. Action is unlikely without belief and agreement.

Earlier, examples were cited on how companies will try to reach the employees through spoken communications: The CEO and/or top executives may speak to the employees employing various formats: leading town hall meetings, teleconferences, videotapes, involving themselves in small roundtable discussions, and distributing voice-mail messages. In each situation, unless the speaker is natural and credible, the employees could perceive the executive's attempts at "connecting" to be contrived, boring and/or manipulative.

How then does the speaker use the visual elements to enhance rather than to inhibit a message?

Eye communication is the number one skill. It ranks first because it has the greatest impact in both one-on-one communications and large group communications. When the speaker's eyes meet the eyes of another person, he or she makes an emotional connection. When one fails to make that connection, it matters very little what is said.

Posture and movement is next. A person's posture makes a powerful first impression about his or her competence, rank, position and self-assurance. Posture enhances or betrays credibility. Good upright posture communicates confidence; poor upper body posture often conveys low self-esteem. Even if one feels confident and self-assured, poor posture will convey a lack of poise and confidence to the listener.

Tradition says that a person should always be rooted to one spot when speaking. Tradition is wrong. To make emotional contact with the audience, the speaker needs to convey excitement, enthusiasm and confidence. This means that the speaker must move. Motion is visual and energetic. How can one expect to move people to action while standing still? Movement adds energy and variety to the message and imbues the speaker with an aura of confidence. This is truly important when persuading people to a new vision.

Gestures and facial expressions speak louder than words. There are few things that do more for effective communication than open gestures and warm open smiles. Gestures and smiles reveal the speaker's inner state and propel the message with energy and emotional force.

Energy and humor are also important in making a connection with the listener. The best asset that a speaker has is energy. It is a dynamic quality that anyone can use to reach and persuade a listener. Spoken without energy, the most eloquent and profound words will be instantly forgotten. Humor can be a powerful tool for packing positive energy into communication. Telling jokes however, should be avoided. Too few speakers can pull it off gracefully. Instead, when a speaker relates himself or herself to the audience as a part of the human comedy, they humanize themselves, and thus connect with their listeners. Humanization is the biggest conduit to trust.

As Peter F. Drucker wrote in *Managing for the Future*, "The final requirement of effective leadership is to earn trust. Otherwise there won't be any followers—and the only definition of a leader is someone who has followers. To trust a leader, it is not necessary to like him. Nor is it necessary to agree with him. Trust is the conviction that the leader means what he says."

Who is responsible for successfully communicating the cultural changes? Many would answer that it is the role of the executive staff: the CEO and the senior level executives. It is actually the responsibility of every person in the organization who manages or supervises people. However, it is the CEO's responsibility to provide a communications plan in order to create a consistent message, move it through the organization, and be able to deliver it so that it motivates employees and customers to positive action.

All managers must be able to deliver a tangible image that represents a vibrant, engaging, and specific description of what it will be like when the mission is achieved. The image should provoke emotion and generate excitement. It should transform the mission from words into pictures and convey the mission so that people carry around a clear, compelling image in their minds. The vivid description brings the mission to life. It is the ability to paint a picture with words, and is essential for making the mission tangible in people's minds and vividly describing the end-goal. Without this picture, the people cannot bring the mission to reality.

The Communications Strategy

Missions, visions, and business plans are only words until the doers of the organization bring them alive by including the meaning of the words into their doing. It is usually our habit to start and end with the words and leave the real "communication" to chance. This is probably why communication, or the disappointment in its results, has for years been frustrating the group efforts of all humans working for a common purpose.

The idea that the outcomes of important communication efforts can be proactively managed is easily accepted but rarely acted upon. As with reaching any goal, the real power is not in the goal itself, but in the planning and the action taken on the plan. Important messages can include cultural change, corporate vision, company repositioning, reorganizations or product announcements. All of these business issues require a communication strategy created at the executive levels, with the participation of decision makers from each area involved.

What steps should the CEO take to provide and implement a communications plan?

Develop the message. The message itself and consensus on the message must be obtained at the at the executive level. Ownership begins at the top. An example of a corporate message in the new world of the deregulated utility and ensuing price wars might be differentiation from the competition by providing superior customer service and knowing exactly how it will be accomplished.

Put the message into easily understandable words that anyone will understand. Fully develop a few key points and have back-up information to support those points. In order to be clear about a message, the key points must remain consistent, and anyone within the organization should be able to articulate them.

Identify the different audiences who will receive the message. Usually there is a communication chain within an organization from the top executives to the managers, down to the employees and then to the customers. Each audience has its own needs and prejudices that must be taken into account in the plan to reach them. What is their point of view about the subject? Understanding the different needs of each audience and anticipating their reaction will help to determine the best way to motivate them to take action. As the message is communicated from audience to audience, it is important to maintain the integrity and consistency of the message no matter who the audience is. Too often within a corporation, the original message from the top becomes diluted by the time it reaches the people who truly implement it, resulting in complete disconnect.

Identify and clearly specify the action for each audience to take on the message. The action steps may vary between audiences depending on their role in communicating it farther or implementing it in the work place. What do you want them to do?

Be able to clearly articulate the benefits of the desired action to each audience. Implied benefits rarely motivate. The positive outcomes must be described over and over and personalized to have meaning to the listener.

Determine the most effective methods of delivering the message to motivate each audience for the desired action. Who should deliver it? When? How often? Formal or informal? These details may vary depending upon the audience, their point of view, and the desired action.

Deliver the message in a format that will allow each audience to take action immediately. If the people in this audience have responsibility to communicate the message to yet another group of people, such as customers, don't force them to reword it. Provide them with the tools, presentations, and words that they can apply to the action you want them to take. Make an effort to *humanize* the message. Boring is not memorable. Interest building tools such as color visuals, humor, and analogies for easier retention can bring your ideas to life.

Prepare your delivery systems. There are key individuals who themselves will be the delivery systems for your message: executives, managers, supervisors, PR, salespeople and anyone who will be an internal and external spokesperson for the organization. Make a conscious investment of time and money in the development of their personal communication skills so they will be confident and believable.

Winning the Race: Planning and Preparation

Divestiture in the telecommunications industry in the early 1980's has forced companies to live through landmark changes over the past ten years. The traditionally monopolistic telephone companies have had to radically alter their business structure. Deregulation in the utilities industry will have a similar impact on energy service providers.

Employees continue to be redeployed to other areas at the telephone companies in order to respond to the competitive marketplace that divestiture created. This means that all employees must incorporate a new mindset into their worklives: the challenge is to move quickly from reactive to proactive, from customer response to customer care, and provide a differentiator in a commodities market.

Companies such as AT&T have provided communications skills training to help employees meet their new challenges. Communications skills training has helped employees meet their company's new mission in a variety of areas: engineers have had to become persuasive consultants to non-technical audiences, salespeople who previously had been order-takers have become solutions-oriented consultants, and managers have had to become motivators in a constantly changing business climate. A communications strategy helps people develop new skills and infuse them with confidence and completely change the way they communicate internally within the company and externally with current and potential clients. The utilities industry has an outstanding opportunity to put successful strategies into action today that many telecommunications companies have learned in hindsight.

California is in the forefront of offering solutions to electricity deregulation. One large electric utilities company, Southern California

Edison, has taken steps to ensure that their people are able to respond in the changing industry. They realize that doing business by simply responding to the current client base will no longer provide a foundation for success. Southern California Edison has provided communications skills training in various areas of the company to change the behavior of their employees to ready them for new ways of interaction. Engineers who are utilities subject experts are learning methods of communicating extremely technical information to non-technical audiences without alienating them. Executives are learning how to present information to influence and motive peers and employees to new ideas in the dawn of deregulation.

It is this type of a communications plan that will enable all companies undergoing a massive cultural change to communicate the new vision and ensure that it is achieved. A 1994 survey conducted by the Council of Communication Management showed that in the 70 companies that were polled, 64% of employees "don't believe what management says," 61% of employees believe that they "aren't well-informed of company plans," and 54% of the employees believe that they "don't get decisions explained well." The belief that clear communications with employees and customers is happening or improving is often only a perception that top executives have, because the reality as reflected in the survey is often quite different.

The race has barely begun, but the winners are already being determined by the preparation that is occurring today to differentiate their people in what will be a commodities market. A well-prepared communications strategy is critical to achieving faster and successful cultural change. This strategy can positively change the attitudes of the people who will make the difference, and competitively position companies and individual careers in an industry of change and opportunity.

Part Six:
Strategic Approaches to
Cultural Change

Chapter Sixteen

It's the Strategy, Stupid!

Dr. Cherry McPherson and Scott A. Jacobson

Bill Clinton learned a valuable lesson during the presidential campaign of 1992. That lesson—keep a single, clear focus on the major campaign issue. The budget, of course. And that was hard to do, especially when the media questioned his marital fidelity, his draft status, his political experience. Yet whenever Clinton refocused to the budget, people listened.

Whether you support Bill Clinton or not, you, too, can learn a valuable lesson from his campaign strategy. And that lesson is to identify what is significant, what really makes a difference, and then keep your focus clearly on that issue.

Successful leaders in competitive corporations have already mastered this lesson. These leaders understand that strategy is basically about directing people's energy and commitment towards those decisions and actions that, when consistently applied, produce bottom line results for the organization.

Organization viability is tied to a clear strategy consistently applied. But strategy alone is not enough. And that is where corporate culture becomes essential.

So What Is Corporate Culture?

People who live and work in organizations know how to "go along and get along." Through months and years of employment, they learn the unwritten "do's" and "don'ts" of organizational life. One newly hired human resources professional in a California utility decided to meet with a line vice president about an important issue. So she called and set up an appointment. When her manager learned about her actions, he quickly called her into his office. "Around here, " he explained, "employees don't talk to vice presidents. If you have something to communicate, I'll take it up." So this young woman quickly learned an organizational norm: communication goes up through the chain of command.

These unwritten rules of acceptable conduct are the norms . . . the normal behavior . . . that govern how one must act to be accepted within an organization's society. As such, they are neon signs that tell you about the organization's culture.

Virtually all types of organizations take on characteristics that are unique to themselves. They develop norms and mores that dramatically or subtly define themselves and set themselves apart from other comparable organizations.

For example, one large utility prides itself upon its size in the industry. Promotional materials, advertisements, and even requests for proposals tout its size and number of employees. Conversations with managers and key professionals invariably will include some mention of the utility's position in the industry *vis a vis* its size. Why do you see this consistent pattern? These ways of behaving and interacting are based upon a system of shared values and beliefs. In this particular utility, there is a shared belief that "bigger is better."

So an organization's culture is essentially a set of shared beliefs and values that govern how people act. This is particularly important because how people act determines the viability and survival of a company.

A good example is Coors Ceramicon, a division of Coors Brewery. During prohibition, the ceramics company actually kept Coors in business. As beer sales soared and different bottling techniques developed in the decades following prohibition, the need for the ceramics company declined. In a position common to many companies, Ceramicon found its economic viability of paramount concern to its parent company.

So after developing a clear strategy, Ceramicon focused on developing a performance culture. Joe Warren, President of Ceramicon, understood that the performance of the company depended upon the performance of each and every worker. And more important,

Warren understood that management as traffic cop simply doesn't work. So he implemented a culture where employees routinely provide performance feedback not only to each other, but also to members of management.

A turning point involved one front line employee. This young man habitually allowed his performance to slip. Management would bring him in and confront his performance problems. The young man promised to clean up his act. And he did. For a few weeks or months. Then he slipped back into the old ways. Understanding that this pattern could no longer be tolerated, the plant manager pulled the young man in and again confronted the problem. This time there was a discussion about leaving Ceramicon.

At the next all personnel meeting, this young man stood up in front of the entire work force. And he asked his peers why no one had confronted him about his performance before. Some said they were afraid to. He made it clear that he intended to change—and that he expected others to confront him if they saw his performance slip.

That is culture change. And it is a change where people stopped old patterns and developed new ones. It happens when people re-place old values and beliefs with new ones. At Ceramicon, people understood that performance feedback is not only necessary but actually is beneficial to individuals as well as to the company.

A Symbiotic Relationship

What is the relationship between organizational strategy and cul-ture? An excellent metaphor for this relationship is lichen. Lichen is composed of alga and fungus. The alga provides energy through photosynthesis, while the fungus contributes water and carbon di-oxide. The two co-exist as lichen. In the same way, strategy and culture co-exist in organizations. The two grow alongside one an-other and support one another.

Given the appropriate environment, alga and fungus can live inde-pendently. At this point, the metaphor falls apart. For organizations will always exhibit strategy and culture, even if these arise without careful planning.

Consider any company. At its earliest point, an idea was born. This idea—business machines—led to a business enterprize. Often the idea was the strategy. As the business grew, a culture grew within it. "Do it the IBM way." As times change, the strategy often requires change. But the culture may prevent people from seeing clearly. How can you change if your culture tells you to do it "our way?" So the culture itself may stifle and choke necessary new life. And the entire company may suffer.

So culture develops in support of strategy. Once in place, strategy and culture are in a symbiotic relationship. To survive, a company needs both a viable strategy and a supportive culture. What are the contributions of each?

Setting Direction

Strategy is primarily a direction-setting tool. Everyone within an organization needs a clear and compelling sense of direction. Members need to know what the future holds and how their organization will go about carving out its place in that future.

A few years ago, we had the opportunity to interview a number of employees representing diverse areas of Florida Power and Light. Each person we talked with quickly mentioned FP&L's quest...to be the best managed utility in the United States and to be recognized for it. This short phrase focuses attention to daily management of the utility and provides a clear, recognizable target. The target cannot be reached unless every employee manages his or her work in the best possible way. So a direction, a way to go, has been successfully communicated.

Very often strategy is confused with a strategic planning function within an organization. This can be disastrous, particularly if a staff group of strategic planners are the guardians of the strategy. Jack Welch recognized this problem at General Electric and reacted by abolishing the central strategic planning function. At GE, strategic planners tended to be interested in precision and predictability rather than in fast-paced change. And by relegating strategic planning to planners, operational managers were removed from hands-on involvement and lacked the intimate understanding that comes from working through strategic issues.[1]

This does not at all mean that GE is not strategically directed nor strategically managed. Welch is noted for his candor in communicating strategic priorities. But it does indicate that strategy is not a set of activities.

Four Parts to Strategy

As a direction-setting tool, an organization's strategy is encapsulated in its vision, values, mission, and specific success factors or critical success indicators that undergird the business plan.

A vision statement paints a portrait of the long range future of a company. It tells why the company exists and how its existence benefits employees, customers, and society at large. It describes an important contribution that the organization and its members make. It is something worth striving towards.

At its heart, an organization is a web of relationships among people, whether they are called managers, employees, suppliers, customers, regulators, families, or communities. It is through the connections and interactions of these people that an organization comes to life. So the vision statement describes the nature of these interactions. It tells how people will act towards one another and towards the societies in which they live and work.

One hospital expresses some of these interactions in this passage:

> The children are the center of St. Mary's. Around this core grows a committed staff with a renewed spirit of working together as a team. Our genuine concern for children and

---

[1]

Tichy, Noel and Sherman, Stratford. *Control Your Destiny Or Someone Else Will.* New York: Doubleday, 1993.

for each other makes our work less of a chore and more of an expression of the best that dwells within us.

Values spell out in very specific detail how the organization will govern its actions both internally and in the public arena. For example, one newspaper selected "community" as a value:

We will be the catalyst for improvement in the quality of life in the diverse communities we serve by means of more relevant news, editorials and community involvement.

The definition describes what the newspaper and its employees will do to improve quality of life in the communities they serve. These values are not innocuous, "apple pie and motherhood" mores like honesty and hard work. Instead, business values specify how people and organizations agree to interact. They specify behaviors that describe what effective members will do as part of the organization's culture.

One high tech firm identified "Customer Satisfaction" as a primary value:

Our objective is to meet or exceed all reasonable customer expectations.

➡ We focus on predictable output, superior quality and world class capability.

➡ We value dialogue with our customers that achieves a mutual understanding of business requirements and manufacturing capabilities.

➡ We strive to eliminate all gaps between the customer's expectations and our capabilities.

➡ We form partnerships with our key customers.

This definition very clearly lays out performance expectations for the organization's members. This value is not a "nice to do"; it is a way of doing business.

An organization's vision and values are integrally linked. While the major theme of the vision is the company's purpose, the values chronicle how organizational members will interact as they accomplish the vision.

The **mission** governs a shorter-time horizon. A mission statement tells what an organization will do within the next three to five years towards realizing the vision. It is more specific than the vision and describes measurable accomplishments.

An organization's mission and its **critical success indicators** undergird the business plan. Critical success indicators answer the question, "What are the business results that will lead to success for your company?"

Typical critical success indicators include factors like cost management, shareholder value, customer satisfaction, safety, or employee morale. These factors have very specific numeric values set by executive management to indicate success or failure in achieving the business plan. From year to year, the relative priority among these factors shifts to reflect business needs. For example, many organizations now stress either cost management or shareholder value as the single most important critical success indicator. These companies see economic viability as their survival issue. Other organizations have mastered these challenges and now emphasize factors like growth or innovation.

Once critical success indicators (CSIs) are set, all employees direct their action and attention toward the achievement of the CSIs. Of course, critical success indicators are not isolated goals or objectives arbitrarily set by management. They are the elements that, if achieved, enable the organization to achieve its mission and live out its values. People need to understand where the organization is headed and what the bases are for decisions. Achieving the organization's strategy—its vision, values, mission, and critical success indicators—is the job of all members, from the front line employee to the CEO.

It's a Matter of Culture

But even a clear and compelling strategy is not enough. Organizations that will thrive into the next millennium pay equal attention to the development of a high performing culture.

Remember that corporate culture is a set of values and beliefs shared by an organization's members. People quickly learn to adapt to a culture in order to be accepted and to survive. As they behave in ways consistent with dominant values and beliefs, they begin to take these on as their own. And soon actions become habits, and then habits become routine and invisible.

People no longer question "the way we do things around here." An often heard response to "why?" is "because that's the way we've always done it." When you hear this reply, you are hearing an ingrained response within a culture that does not value creativity nor invention.

But what difference does this make? If an organization has succeeded over the years with a strong corporate culture, isn't the old culture good enough for the years ahead?

That depends on the strategy. If a company continues with strategy intact, the existing culture will likely continue to serve the organization well. But if there are changes in the strategy, then the culture needs reassessment.

Let's look at the utility industry as an example. Utilities historically provided a stable work environment with good pay. People who signed on expected to give a good day's work in exchange for lifetime employment. The company was often part of a family tradition, boasting two to three generations of loyal employees. Within the ranks, most people did a good job. There were some slackers, but generally people got the job done.

When there was a crisis—the lines were down, there was a major storm—you could count on crews to come in and get service restored. When costs increased, customers paid more. It was all settled in a rate case.

What are some of the beliefs embedded in this scenario?

"You are entitled to a job."

"The company will take care of you."

"We don't have to worry about our costs."

"In times of crisis, we go the extra mile."

But times have changed. Utilities can no longer merely pass costs along to the customer. As competition heats up, utilities are looking for survival strategies. Very often these new strategies result in changing how work is done—through downsizing, mergers, reengineering, reorganizations. As new strategies are implemented, new cultures must also be developed. These new cultures often include different beliefs:

"You are responsible for your career."

"The company will help you develop your skills while you are here."

"We must reduce our costs to remain competitive."

And some beliefs stay the same:

"In times of crisis, we go the extra mile."

Think about the disconnects when strategy changes but culture does not. If the strategy requires self-responsibility but the culture supports dependency on the company, how will initiative emerge? If the strategy demands cutting costs but the culture supports using whatever resources are required to do the job, what happens to the financial plan? If the strategy results in loss of jobs but the culture promises lifetime employment, who will manage employee reactions?

As business environments change, companies change strategies. And smart companies develop cultures that support the strategy. Many do not.

Customer service was discovered as a major strategy by one southwestern utility. While company employees prided themselves on providing the best in customer service, usually their actions translated into doing what employees thought was best. Giving the customer options or asking for their preferences was a novel idea.

Bright young managers led a major initiative to promote a new service ethic based on meeting or exceeding customer expectations. Part of the strategy involved empowerment. Everyone—management through front line—was empowered to make on the spot decisions to improve service and meet customer expectations.

Large numbers of managers and employees sat engrossed in training programs designed to get the message across. Most people were enthused about the possibility of improving service. Some crusty crew members weren't about to change . . . they already provided the best possible service. But all in all, the strategy looked as if it just might take off.

Then the crucible of empowerment raised its head. Even managers questioned whether the company really wanted them to take risks and make decisions on their own. Actually, all those policies and procedures existed for a darn good reason. Making mistakes had never been a career enhancing move.

Managers and employees knew the old culture by heart. As they explained, "Around here, you can do anything you want, as long as you want, as long as you're right." After a great deal of cajoling, managers admitted that the new culture was different. You could now make one mistake, but not two.

How can employees act in empowered ways if they are not supported when they make mistakes? This situation illustrates the strong effects of an existing culture. In order to fulfill the strategy, there must be a change in the "normal" ways of doing business. And this means that the beliefs giving rise to typical behaviors must change. In this instance, people had to change their beliefs about making mistakes and about what would transpire should mistakes arise. Of course, the biggest change must occur within management, where the knee-jerk reaction is to punish mistakes.

When companies get to this point, the weight of the old ways often proves too strong. People do not take the touted new ways seriously, for existing patterns are too strong to overcome. So when an organization sets out to change culture, the efforts must be monotonous, continuous, and habitual.

If changing corporate culture is so difficult, are there any keys to success? Award winning Arizona Public Service provides a good example of cultural transformation.

Culture Thrives in Arizona

Like most utilities, Arizona Public Service was boggled by a stability oriented, risk aversive culture. Yet O. Mark DeMichele, President and CEO, knew that his company must respond, and respond rapidly, to a changing utility environment. When he took the helm at APS, DeMichele knew that APS would cease to be a viable company without becoming more cost competitive. And this could only happen through cost reductions. So he took the first step alone—he forced a downsizing resulting in a 30% work force layoff with a $104 million savings.

The cost of this bold move was a resentful and grudging work force. People at all levels, including DeMichele's middle management team and front line supervision, refused to acknowledge any need for change. And DeMichele knew he had only taken the first step. Even more drastic changes would be required to move APS back into a position of leadership. So the basic challenge was to create an environment that facilitates the most difficult change of all—a change of mind. If people could change their minds about the need to change, then comes the opportunity to take the next step—to commit to the actions necessary to make the company successful.

DeMichele turned to strategic change consultant Wayne Widdis of Focused Change International. DeMichele recounted a clear and compelling vision for APS—to become one of the top five investor-owned utilities by 1995. Since APS ranked in the bottom quartile on some measures, this vision seemed impossible even to some of DeMichele's executive team. But he was committed. Together, DeMichele and Widdis agreed that success meant culture change tied to a comprehensively detailed strategic plan supporting DeMichele's "Top 5 by 95" vision.

So executive leaders spelled out an aggressive corporate strategic plan that called for the utility to become one of the top five investor-owned utilities in the United States by 1995. Achieving this strategy would indeed require a massive change in corporate culture. The desired corporate culture was defined by a set of values including factors like learning from mistakes, strategic risk and experimentation, challenging assumptions, personal accountability, and cultural diversity. The first step was to get people to understand that company leaders were serious. Behaving in ways consistent with the new culture was not optional; it was a condition of continued employment.

Widdis introduced a comprehensive cultural change strategy along with a new vocabulary. Consultants are notorious for introducing foreign terms to describe simple ideas, much to the dismay of corporate communication specialists. For example, instead of feedback we use "performance enhancement confrontation." But the vocabulary is part of the change strategy. Widdis used terms like mission, critical success indicators, and anchoring plan that initially left people confused. But the terms got people's attention and even gave them something else to complain about. When people complained, Widdis and his strategic change team had something concrete to talk about. The new ways of doing business at APS, or the culture, to be precise.

What was the cultural change strategy at APS? There were four major components:

➠ a boring and relentless attention to organizational strategy and mission,

➠ an uncompromising focus on managing performance,

➠ making culture itself a critical success indicator as a measure of corporate performance, and

➠ a detailed cultural anchoring plan along with the creation of a strategic change management function.

Boring and Relentless Attention to Strategy

Strategy gives direction to employees. In the early stages, direction is communicated through a constant and consistent focus on the mission and key results. But people didn't even know what a mission was. So a first step included the introduction of the Focus simulations.

Focus became an initiation rite for managers and employees. Managers are sequestered in a hotel for five days with food, water, and a mission statement. Front line workers leave movement-oriented work days to squirm in company training facilities for a short three days that seem like a lifetime. But the message is the same—mission, mission, mission.

In the job of Chief Executive Officer of Focus, Widdis begins with endless repetition of the mission, values, and critical success factors of the simulated organization. He asks people to rate their understanding of the mission. Those brave enough to admit that they don't understand the mission wind up having breakfast, lunch, and dinner with Wayne. "The Focus mission is based on the APS mission. If people don't understand the Focus mission, they probably don't understand the APS mission either," says Widdis. His intent is to have all members of the Focus organization understand that each person, regardless of position or title, has one job. That job is to fulfill the mission, values, and critical success factors. There is nothing else.

By making people see the importance of the strategy in the simulated Focus organization, Widdis prepares people to go back to APS and likewise develop a single-minded focus towards their corporate strategy. You could say that they have a renewed sense of direction.

When DeMichele introduced the phrase "Top 5 by 95," people initially snickered and wondered who he was trying to fool. But their new understanding about strategy coupled with DeMichele's missionary zeal quickly convinced people to pay attention. This man was serious about making APS a leader in the field. And as he continued to exhort, cajole, and prickle, people began to believe that maybe, just maybe, Top 5 by 95 was more than blowing smoke.

DeMichele had people's attention. They knew about the results, about direction. But how would they get there? In a Focus for front line employees, one burly line hand resisted the notion of changing his own ways to make APS Top 5. Session upon session saw no change. Finally, he capitulated. " OK," he said, "I'll do it. Just give me the play book." The play book? "Yeah, somewhere DeMichele has it all figured out. Just tell me what you want me to do, and I'll do it."

But there wasn't any play book. DeMichele and his team knew where they needed to go, but they needed everyone's help in figuring out how to get there. And how—the process—is clearly the domain of culture. The APS values spelled it out . . . through teamwork, continuous improvement, creativity, flexibility, risk taking, and experimentation. The key value underlying it all was performance.

"Performance is the prime measure of each employee's value. . . . We will be accountable for meeting or exceeding agreed-upon targets. Rewards will be commensurate with performance."

Uncompromising Focus on Performance

Easy to say, hard to do. And that is why an uncompromising focus on managing performance was the second plank in Widdis' culture strategy. Like most companies, APS tolerated non-performance. When people were not doing their share, front line employees looked the other way. Supervisors and even managers were hesitant to give performance feedback. No one enjoys giving bad news. And feedback was synonymous with bad news. If you don't tell people how they are doing—the good and bad news—you are not managing performance. On target or off, people perform as they will.

This situation had to change. So Widdis introduced a comprehensive performance management strategy that included a system, some tools, and lots of confrontation. At first, managers were comfortable. The Performance Enhancement Process looked just like a performance appraisal process complete with new forms and a new training program. Business as usual was right around the corner. They were not counting on DeMichele.

DeMichele was clear—performance management meant managers at all levels spending time with direct reports focusing behavior towards the strategy. It did not mean filling out forms. "Quite frankly, I don't really care whether someone signs a PEP form or not...as long as the discussion takes place." DeMichele knew that what mattered was on-going performance feedback and confrontation of non-performance. Starting at the top. With him. DeMichele set out an ambitious plan that cascaded throughout the organization. The plan? To manage performance and spend the majority of one's time with people. The PEP system was simply a tool to structure performance management. "In a culture that manages performance, " says Widdis, "you can throw the system out. You don't need it any more."

But in the beginning, managers at all levels needed a lot of structure. It was the worst of situations. Not only did managers not confront performance, they did not acknowledge their own behavior. They mistook skills for will. By knowing how to give performance feedback—they had taken several company training programs over the years—and by completing annual appraisal forms, they thought they were managing performance. But they lacked the disciplined will to provide on-going feedback and coaching on a routine basis.

The Performance Enhancement Process focused manager's attention toward the desired corporate culture: one based on performance. If performance was the measure of each employee's value, than it was the manager's job to help people perform. This meant spending time with all employees—stars, good soldiers, and sluggards. It meant helping employees understand two things: their individual strategic targets and the new APS performance culture. The job was to produce results, and non-performance would no longer be tolerated.

It sounds so simple, so easy, so natural. But many, if not most, companies fail to manage performance. The market hasn't required it. Take a look at your own organization. What percentage of time do managers and supervisors spend focusing employees' work toward specific targets? How often do people at all levels provide performance feedback to each other? To what extent do employees feel both responsible and accountable for their actions? A consistent reality is that people in most organizations do not manage performance . . . theirs or anyone else's.

One of the most powerful cultural interventions was the Performance Enhancement Process (PEP). Simply put, PEP translated APS' strategic plan into 7000 individual performance plans directly related to the accomplishment of APS' mission and goals. With a sense of direction from the strategy and with specific performance accountabilities through PEP, people were positioned to create a new corporate culture.

Measuring Success

The third plank in the cultural change strategy occurred at the executive level. Widdis challenged APS leaders to make culture itself a critical success indicator of corporate performance. He explained that the existing culture could not get the company to Top 5 by '95. Cultural beliefs like these were ingrained:

"No mistake, however small, will go unpunished."

"Managers and supervisors have all the answers."

"When there's a question, policies and procedures tell us what to do."

"We can't change because the regulators won't allow us to."

"We're a monopoly . . . people have to buy their power from us."

Executives worked at defining the type of corporate culture that supported Top 5 by '95. They debated over the meaning of strategic values like service, cost management, safety, and teamwork. Then they set numeric targets that indicated an acceptable performance level for culture change.

The strategic values became the basis for a culture audit. All employees responded to a written survey that listed statements describing what people would be doing if they were performing congruently with the company's strategic values. In corporate surveys, people often respond with what they think management wants to hear. So leaders at all levels stressed the importance of rating the survey items as accurately as possible. They pointed out that the results would form a baseline for future improvement actions.

As employees completed the survey, they acquired some new information. They learned how company executives expected them to work within the organizational context. While some of this information may be consistent with the espoused (stated but not necessarily actualized) values of the existing culture, most of the values are defined in new ways. These values are operating principles for everyone in the company. An example is in cost management:

> We are committed to operating our company more efficiently through disciplined cost management at every level.

> This will result in stable prices, improved competitiveness and profitability.

The first culture audit occurs immediately following values specification. Its purpose is to provide baseline data for internal benchmarking. Company executives then take two steps.

First, they select specific areas for improvement. In the APS situation, one value consistently ranked low. That value was positive confrontation. DeMichele himself mandated the installation of a process called PEC—Performance Enhancement Confrontation—to address this gap.

233

What is the purpose of PEC? To give managers and supervisors a clear message: positive confrontation is your job. The old APS culture reinforced a reluctance to give on-going feedback about job performance. Many employees reported hearing performance feedback once yearly: at the time of the annual performance review. The PEC process reviews feedback skills and gives managers a clear performance target: to confront specific individuals within one week of their participation in the PEC program.

The second action officers took was a series of face-to-face meetings with all employees throughout the company. Officers like Executive Vice President Shirley Richard met with people at all levels to discuss both the strategy and the values. Wherever Richard was, she consistently asked people about their understanding of the values. She queried employees to find out what they thought some of the problems were in the company's culture and what ideas they had for improving things.

Richard stressed the importance of behaving congruently with the values. When employees asked what she intended to do about low scores on the culture audit, she threw the problem back to the ranks. While leaders set the direction, they cannot create a high performing culture alone. It is the responsibility of every employee to take actions and make changes so that the entire work force lives out the new values. You would often hear Richard quoting Hillel: " If not now, when? If not you, who?" Everyone owned the new culture, not just the officers.

By making culture change a critical success indicator, the executives at APS raised culture consciousness. Although invisible, culture became a driving force in organizational thinking and planning. Each year, the culture audit is administered. Results are immediately fed back to employees so that they can devise specific strategies to close the gaps between current and desired performance.

Anchoring A New Culture
The fourth and final plank in APS' culture strategy saw the development of an anchoring plan. New ways of doing business need to

be firmly ingrained in people's consciousness. Then consistent decisions and actions will follow. This requires the same amount of thinking and planning as does any other strategic area. If left untended, culture will not change.

APS' cultural anchoring plan includes factors such as the Focus simulations, PEP (Performance Enhancement Process), on-going strategic planning, communication, leadership practices, recognition and rewards, and measurement and monitoring. In addition to these generic categories, very specific projects were enumerated. One project involved the introduction of best practices studies as a strategy for organizational learning and improvement. The first best practices study examined the following question:

> How do successful companies create and anchor a continuous improvement culture?

A team of front line supervisors and employees, including union representation, visited organizations like Federal Express, McDonnell Douglas, Florida Power and Light, and General Electric. They hoped to discover specific actions taken by these companies to create cultures that prized continuous improvement. The study team presented their findings back to a group of 100 APS managers in a two day conference. During the conference, small teams of participants took the best practices information and created very specific projects to move APS toward a continuous improvement culture.

As additional projects like this one were integrated into the cultural anchoring plan, APS leaders began to realize that whatever happened within the company affected the culture. This is a basic systems principle: every action affects everything else within the system. An emergent need was the tracking of company actions for cultural impact. This led to the creation of the Strategic Change Management Department.

Headed by a director who reports to an executive vice president, the Strategic Change Management Department seeks to integrate all company actions in support of the strategy and culture. The Strategic Change Management Department also facilitates the change process and implements the cultural anchoring plan across all areas of the company.

Reengineering provides an example of the integration process. As part of the strategic planning process, the officers targeted streamlining work processes and improving work efficiency as necessary steps in APS' future. A consulting firm was hired to lead the reengineering effort at APS. The consultant's model is based on principles and assumptions that are at times incongruous with the new APS culture. The Strategic Change Management Department became a major player in determining the impact of reengineering on the culture and then developing strategies to mitigate negative impacts. Quick examples include providing support to those employees experiencing job displacement and developing strategies to assist individuals and teams as they become increasingly strategically self-managed.

The culture change work of DeMichele, APS leaders, and front line employees is part of a two-year strategic change transition that cut more than $44 million from APS' annual operating budgets, reduced its customer utility costs by 10%, and generated a 96% customer satisfaction rating among customers who have contacted the APS Customer Service Center. These changes enabled APS to give customers a 2.2% rate decrease. This is proof that ways of doing business at APS have dramatically changed and have yielded benefits for consumers.

In the Spring of 1993, APS won the coveted Edison Award—the electric utility's highest honor. Awarded through a vote of peer member utilities, Arizona Public Service has been singled out for its cultural transformation process.

The development of a high performing culture at APS is a continuing story. DeMichele strongly asserts that change is the future at APS. So he requires flexibility, innovation, and speed from all who choose to remain part of APS. The company continues to evolve, and so must the culture.

Six Steps to Culture Change

The APS story exemplifies six necessary steps to achieve strategically directed culture change. When implemented in a sequential process, we find that it is indeed possible to change corporate culture.

1. Define business values that lead to the desired corporate culture. Then operationalize these values with specific behaviors required from all people at all levels and in all jobs, from officers to front line employees. This first step occurs as part of the corporate strategic planning process. Corporate leaders act as stewards in defining how the company and its people will responsibly interact with each other and with those whom they serve.

2. Identify corporate culture as a critical success indicator and set an overall measure of acceptable performance. Strategic planning sets direction; strategic values define culture. Since culture is intangible and typically taken for granted, many employees fail to see culture development as an important process. Corporate leaders make culture change a priority when they set a specific culture change measure and hold everyone responsible for accomplishing it. This measure should be tied to gain sharing in those companies with a gain sharing program.

3. Audit the existing culture against strategic values. Discover how well the existing culture matches the desired future state. Using defined strategic values as the basis, develop a cultural auditing tool to be completed by all organizational members. Collect and analyze the data to determine the current culture. This process enables you to identify major gaps requiring resolution.

4. Set specific improvement targets that will enable you to meet the cultural critical success indicator. Based on initial audit results, corporate leaders identify key priority areas. These are areas with low scores on the audit or critical areas that can prevent success if not remedied. For each priority area, set a numeric target that indicates acceptable improvement.

237

One company observed increasing safety violations resulting in injuries and even death. Safety was therefore identified as a priority value requiring additional attention. An individual's safety target was zero reportable incidents on a daily basis.

5. Develop specific culture change projects to close the gap between the current and desired future state. Within each improvement area, actions must be taken to move towards desired performance. Change projects include specific plans and actions within a targeted area. Common improvement areas include leadership practices, training, communication, rewards and recognition, safety, and performance management. By delegating the development of change projects to multi-level teams, leaders enlist all members in the culture change process.

6. Continue the cultural audit on an annual basis. After implementing culture improvement projects, its is essential to again take the pulse of the organization. How are we doing? To find out, re-administer the culture audit. Then go through the process listed in Steps 4 and 5 to continue crafting your culture.

Imagining that you cannot change culture makes as much sense as saying that you cannot set organizational strategy. What is undeniably true is that culture evolves with all groups, whether families, business organizations, or nations. Those who want to shape the future will accept the challenge of creating cultures that are beneficial, healthy, and supportive for all members.

Living on the Edge

An organization is essentially a living system. A common warning voiced by many organization theorists calls attention to the average life span of a business organization: 40 years. Why do these organizations experience such relatively short life spans when compared to other institutions? We believe that one factor stems from leaders who fear change. These are the leaders who have worked hard, accommodated old cultures, and now hope to hold their companies together until they retire.

We are learning that entropy—or decay—is not the only future for living systems. Indeed, self-organizing systems are able to exchange energy with their environments and evolve towards increasing levels of complexity. How?

By living on the edge in states far from equilibrium. By exporting wastes and importing energy. By developing states that enable self-renewal. We believe that leaders who understand these basic systems principles, like GE's Welch and APS' DeMichele, themselves have the energy to strategically direct change. They live out on the edge of turbulence without ever looking backwards. Recognizing that the status quo only degenerates, they instead look to continuously rebuild and re-energize their organizations. A state of constant, vibrant change where an organization openly interacts with its environment is the only safe place to be. They fear neither the unknown nor the future.

These leaders are the guardians of our future. They understand and use both strategy and culture to reorganize their companies to even higher levels of complexity.

Continue the Dance

We have looked at the relationship between strategy and culture. Like the ancient Chinese symbols of the feminine yin and the masculine yang, they move in a continuous dance seeking a dynamic balance.

Strategies are like living creatures. They are born into a new and sometimes hostile environment. Often they are not fully developed. They need support, nurturing, and sustenance as they mature.

Included within strategy is a set of values that specify how a company will do business. Values define what is acceptable and not acceptable within the business environment. These values are the critical DNA between strategy and culture.

Strategic values outline the kind of internal environment that the strategy needs for support. By assimilating these values, culture becomes an outgrowth of strategy that soon takes on a life of its own.

Culture takes values and creates conformance and congruency. As people begin to act consistently with the new values and new beliefs, then an environment is created that enables the strategy to flourish.

But a culture that reaches equilibrium will die, as will its strategy. For an organization to live, its strategy and culture must be in a continuous dance of co-evolution. As strategy and culture evolve, the organization renews itself and becomes increasingly viable. This is the secret that true leaders know.

Chapter Seventeen

Will the Fittest Survive?

Donna Welsh-Johnson

Top performing utilities may not fare well in the years ahead unless they gear themselves now for competition, deregulation, and technological advancement. Prudent strategic planning and management will play a large role in determining survival of the fittest.

Review of current literature provides countless examples of how the most capital intensive industry in the U.S., the electric utility industry, has dramatically changed over the past two decades and continues to undergo enormous structural changes as a result of competition, threat of deregulation, and technology advancement. Further, because the electric supply industry has experienced excess capacity in recent years, many observers wonder if market forces might do a more efficient job of regulating utility activities than the present regulated environment. Suggestions range from loosening FERC's review of wholesale rates (to permit any prices that fall within a broad zone of reasonableness) to suggestions that all economic regulation of privately-owned utilities be eliminated, and that the utility system be vertically disintegrated.[1]

In response to these structural changes and market forces, top performing utility management are focusing their operational strategy on a profit/loss basis by establishing marketing objectives and policies that are consistent with their financial capabilities and limitations. Moreover, the former collegial atmosphere *amongst* utilities is eroding as utilities acknowledge that neighboring utilities are, when competing for expanded customer bases and new markets, just as much a competitor as a neighboring independent power producer (IPP) or nonutility generator (NUG). Hence, in

---

[1] *Structural Reform in Electric Power: A Framework for Analysis*, H. Quirmbach and J. P. Action. Rand Corporation, August 1987.

management's response to competitor behavior, the astute are prudently practicing both short-term and long-term strategic planning and management. In other words, the "fittest" utility managements are not asking, *"How will next year be different,"* but rather, *"What must we do differently next year to get us closer to our strategic intent?"*

Arming Yourself for Strategic Planning

Strategic planning is, in many respects, not dissimilar to military strategy as both business and military organizations "engaged" in such planning seek to exploit their own strengths and capitalize on their competitor's weaknesses. Business or military success, however, rarely hinges on accident or heuristics, but rather on attention to detail and a keen awareness of the operating environment and conditions. Of course, a fundamental difference between military and business strategy is that business strategy is formulated and implemented based on *competition*; military strategy is based upon *conflict*. Another difference, of course, is that the military accepts "losses" as justified and necessary to win a skirmish or battle, whereas business can be less forgiving.

One of the many problems experienced by utility management to date in both the formulation and implementation of strategic plans has been perpetuated by the "strategists" themselves. Strategists from the major business schools arm their clients with concepts like segmentation, the value chain, competitor benchmarking, outsourcing, horizontal and vertical integration, concentric versus conglomerate diversification, strategic grouping and mapping, and mobility barriers. And while all these concepts have merit and are not to be discounted, all too frequently we get caught up on concepts rather than on the *process* of strategic planning itself.

Another problem acknowledged by management is their response that although strategic planning is billed as a way of becoming more future-oriented, their strategic plans reveal more about today's problems than tomorrow's opportunities.

242

Understanding the Strategic Management Process

Once there were two company presidents who competed in the same industry. These two presidents decided to go on a camping trip to discuss a possible merger. While hiking deep into the woods, they suddenly came upon a grizzly bear that rose up on its hind legs and snarled. Instantly, the first president, having planned ahead, took off his knapsack and put on a pair of jogging shoes. The second president said, "Hey, you can't outrun that bear." The first president responded, "Maybe I can't outrun that bear, but I can surely outrun you!

And this is managing strategically . . .

Clearly, effective strategic planning is difficult. For some, it is one-third art, one-third science, one-third guesswork. To others, it is an objective, logical, systematic approach for making major decisions in an organization. It attempts to organize qualitative and quantitative information in a way that allows effective decisions to be made under conditions of uncertainty.[2]

Given the fact the utility industry is regulated and, in many respects, just emerging into the competitive arena, it is suggested that strategic options available to the industry are, at this juncture, typically more limited and should be focused on more fundamental forms of strategy. In other words, *identifying and improving their core business competency.*

Strategy Formulation

Figure 1 provides an effective and practical business strategy for a utility to follow to attain competitive advantages. Within this model, the planning process is segregated into three phases: formulation, implementation, and evaluation. All three phases occur

---

[2] Fred David, Strategic Management. (New York: Macmillan Publishing Co.) 1993.

Figure 1
Utility Business Strategy for Attaining Competitive Advantage

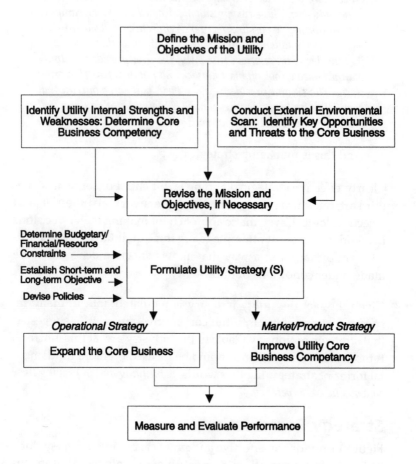

at three hierarchical levels in a large organization: corporate, divisional or strategic business unit, and functional.

Strategy formulation includes developing a business mission, identifying an organization's external opportunities and threats, determining internal strengths and weaknesses (core business competency), establishing long-term objectives, generating alternative strategies and contingencies, and choosing particular strategies to pursue. It also includes deciding what new businesses to enter and what businesses to abandon, determining budgetary, financial, and other resource constraints, assessing regulatory constraints and the political environment, developing a clear understanding of the risks and consequences, and choosing whether to expand or diversify operations.

Step 1: Define the Utility's Mission and Objectives

Formulation of a strategy involves several, methodical steps. Although it is not to be interpreted as a rigid linear process to be effective, it does require an orderly sequence of logical steps. It starts with a most basic yet highly important step—that of defining "What is our business?" and "What is it we do best?" Nothing may seem simpler or more obvious than to know what a utility's business is. However, "What is our business?" is almost always a difficult question and the right answer is usually anything but obvious. Even statements that appear simplistic such as, "We want to be your utility or power supplier of choice," are complex in terms of attainment. In any case, the answer to this question is the first responsibility of strategists. Only strategists can make sure that this question receives the attention it deserves and that the answer makes sense and enables the business to plot its course and set its objectives.[3]

Step 2: Identify the Utility's Strengths and Weaknesses

Identification of what is termed here as the "core business competency" is often linked, in strategic terms, with conducting the "internal environmental scan." To identify a utility's core business competency, it should identify and assess it's internal strengths and/or weaknesses and define it's **distinctive competencies.** All core business activities should be viewed as a value chain or constellation, coupled with the idea that they can be accomplished in a superior fashion. **Building competitive advantages involves**

---

[3] Peter Drucker, *Management: Tasks, Responsibilities, and Practices* (New York: Harper & Row, 1974), p. 61.

taking advantage of distinctive competencies. When the external environment is in a state of flux, the firm's own resources and capabilities may be a much more stable basis on which to define its identity. Hence, *a definition of a business in terms of what it is capable of doing may offer a more durable basis for strategy than a definition based upon the needs which the business seeks to satisfy.*[4]

As a result of effectively assessing core business competency, utilities now have the opportunity to establish marketing objectives and policies that are consistent with their financial capabilities and limitations. Further, the process may bring management to the realization that it is counter-productive to place too great an emphasis on one function at the expense of others.

Step 3:   Conduct an External Environment Scan: Identify Key Threats to the Utility's Core Business

Like it or not, several once-termed industry "trends" are now a reality. Notably,

➠   rivalry amongst utilities is intensifying and will most likely continue due to regulation enhancing open access;

➠   the realm of utility customers that are "captive" is eroding as large individual customers or groups of smaller customers find it possible to integrate backwards into the power supply chain by acquiring alternative or in-house generating capability;

➠   technology, economics, lack of clear product differentiation and declining regulatory barriers, among a host of other factors, are all working to quickly and definitively crumble any existing barriers to entry into the work of electric utility companies. These new players (IPPs, NUGs etc.), not yet bound by any significant regulatory obligation or burdened by huge corporate overheads, bring a different, leaner market and

---

[4]   Robert Grant, "The Resource-Based Theory of Competitive Advantage: Implications for Strategy Formulation." California Management Review (Spring 1991): p. 116.

profit focus to the power supply arena, squeezing utility margins further;

➡ the emergence of super-regional utilities, as exist in banking, may lead to the creation of economies of scale that do not currently exist. This would give operating units of such companies competitive advantages over large, but single-territory utilities;

➡ increasing regulatory pressures will add to the utilities' declining control over power supply decisions;

➡ demand-side management (DSM) and other load conservation measures is projected to become a utilities' single most important means for thwarting the needs of increased generating capacity;

➡ access to environmentally clean, reliable and economical sources will become strategically important.[5]

Strategy Implementation

Strategic implementation requires the utility to establish annual goals and objectives, devise and/or modify existing policies, inform and educate employees to stimulate motivation, and most importantly, allocate resources consistent with budgetary goals, constraints or limitations. Too often, the strategic management process falters from not ensuring such checks and balances are established within the feedback process. Implementation of the strategy formula, consistent with budgetary goals, will include developing a strategy-supportive culture, creating an effective organizational structure, redirecting marketing efforts, preparing budgets at the functional level, developing and utilizing information systems, and motivating individuals to act. This phase is usually considered to be the most difficult in strategic management since adaptation to any change is a significant undertaking often hinging on timing and organizational dynamics.

---

[5] See *Electric Utility Strategies and the Emerging Industry Structure—Parts 1 and 2*, The Electricity Journal, November and December, 1991 by Seetaram Motupalli. Motupalli applies Michael Porter's popular "five forces model" in an attempt to map the industry forces driving profitability.

In most organizations, the transition from strategy formulation to strategy implementation requires a shift in responsibility from strategists to divisional and functional managers. For this reason, it is critical that divisional and functional managers be involved to the extent possible in strategy formulation activities.

Step 1: Improve the Core Business Competency

Subsequent to identifying "what it is we do best," is *"how can we fine tune or improve our core business to achieve distinctive and competitive advantages?"* Implementing operational strategies that seek to fine-tune and improve efficiencies allows a utility to reach corporate performance objectives. These objectives are achieved through gains in functional efficiency and effectiveness.

Singularly adopting an operational strategy as the sole corporate strategy, however, is not without risks for a utility. For instance, it can be asked with conviction if merely employing an *operational strategy* will adequately protect a utility from strategic risks, such as a substantial reduction in load demand. The argument can also be waged that operational strategies have not been fully successful in the past as utilities have required rate relief to offset expenses. **For operational strategies to be successful, utilities must re-think their way of doing business, or conversely, re-engineer the business.**

The following measures are suggested to the utility industry as a means to improve its core business competency. It is strongly put forth that implementation of some, if not all, of these measures are essential if utilities are to position themselves financially, and ameliorate their core business.

Restructure and Re-think about the Way You do Business

⮕ operate all aspects of the utility value chain from a business perspective rather than from a technical perspective. This is rule number 1.[6]

---

[6] Bill Saporito, "Companies that Compete Best," *Fortune* (22 May 1989).

In a recent article, six characteristics were given that describe the most competitive companies in America: (1) market share matters; the 90th share point isn't as important as the 91st, and nothing is more dangerous than falling to 89; (2) understand and remember precisely what business you are in; (3) whether it's broken or not, fix it—make it better, not just products, but the whole company if necessary; (4) innovate or evaporate; particularly in technology-driven business, nothing quite recedes like success; (5) acquisition is essential to growth; the most successful purchases are in niches that add a technology or a related market; (6) people make a difference; tired of hearing it? Too bad; (7) there is no substitute for quality and no greater threat than failing to be cost competitive; these are complementary concepts, not mutually exclusive ones.

➡ if so indicated, restructure to a flatter organization with greater flexible boundaries. This includes downsizing or "right-sizing" in certain business units;

➡ recruit from outside the industry. This is vital for added perspective and will assist utility managers with shedding the existing "regulatory and/or nuclear mentality." Additionally, acquire personnel with more non-traditional utility skills i.e., power marketing; new business management; management information technology.

➡ recognize and manage to the recognition that "a dollar is a dollar" despite its accounting classification as capital or operations and management. Utilities traditionally have operated on a "cost-plus" basis because of their regulated and protected returns. As this increasingly erodes, utilities must encourage experimentation and risk-taking, and their reward systems should match these objectives;[7]

➡ transition to a customer and service value-based culture. (This is considered by some to be the most difficult transition for utilities.)

---

[7]
See M. Russo, N. Floyd, and M. Fester, "Adding On: How to Make Diversification Work", *Public Utilities Fortnightly*, February 15, 1993.

Tie Performance Goals to the Devised Strategy
Establish a direct tie between the strategic goals of the utility and performance incentives. This will seek to ensure that the organization is actively working to achieve its strategic goals.

Marketing—Get Used to the Idea That Customers Are Not Captive
Fully understand your customer base. This means better fulfilling the customers' needs, **identifying market segments that can contribute more to profit margin**, and, identifying characteristics or opportunities for new product or service bundles.

Recognize that Marketing and Selling Are Two Different Entities
Marketing is a strategic activity; selling is more tactical. Selling concentrates on revenue generation; marketing is concerned with profitable customer acquisition and retention.[8]

Improve Your Operations Management
In a climate where supply options proliferate and demand growth is uncertain, utilities will be forced to manage their production to be low-cost providers. Basically, this means reassessing the product cost to product value relationship.

Re-evaluate Your Capital Allocation Process
Studies conducted on companies as a whole (utility and non-utility), show it is not unusual for companies to spend capital inappropriately in terms of misallocating or wasting 20 to 40 percent of capital budget; concentrating 80 percent of capital spending on less than 40 percent of costs; erroneously concentrating on solving yesterday's problems rather than those of the day; and focusing their allocation process predominately on incremental solutions. *As a result, the capital budget, for many companies, is often little more than a random collection of high-return projects that make no contribution to competitive or operations strategy.*

---

[8] Motupalli, *op cit*. See specifically Part II of Motupalli's article for more in-depth discussion of these issues.

Given today's competitive environment, utility analysis and capital allocation methods must be expanded to take into account a number of key financial considerations, including,

1. Linking investment criteria to strategic objectives,

2. Expanding the utility's generating options,

3. Plant life extension and revitalizations, and

4. Re-examination of cost/benefit of stringent equipment design and reliability criteria i.e., the marginal benefit versus costs of going from 99% reliability to 97%.

Establish Formal Strategy and Competitive Intelligence/Analysis Groups

Good competitive intelligence in business is one of the keys to success. Utilities need to establish effective competitive intelligence programs that (1) provide a general understanding of the "business" of the industry and its competitors; (2) identify areas in which competitors are vulnerable and assess the impact strategic actions will have on competitors; and (3) identify potential moves that a competitor might make that would endanger a utility's market share.[9]

The increasing emphasis on competitive intelligence in the U.S. is evidenced by more and more corporations acknowledging this function on their organizational charts under job titles such as Director—Strategic Planning, Competitive Strategy Manager, Director of Competitive Assessment. Responsibilities associated with this position must include planning, collecting and analyzing financial and other trend data, dissemination of intelligence to key senior management on a timely basis, quantitative analysis (regression, econometrics, etc.) of the data, researching special

---

[9] John Prescott and Daniel Smith, "The Largest Survey of 'Leading Edge' Competitor Intelligence Managers." *Planning Review* Vol. 17, No. 3, (May-June 1989), p. 6 - 13.

issues, and recognizing that information is important and determining its appropriate recipient.

Separate Strategic and Business Planning Activities

Make a distinction between strategic and business planning; the former deals mainly with strategy formulation and the latter with resource allocation. As both are parts of an ongoing management activity, they are interrelated. The business plan is developed with strategic scenarios in mind.

Step 2: Expanding or Diversifying the Utility's Core Business

Another strategic means available to industries as a whole for increasing or expanding their core is through diversification. The results to-date for the utility industry have spurred healthy debate over whether utilities are suited to meeting the rigors of competitive ventures[10] or who should accrue most of the benefits achieved—i.e., the rate payer or the stockholders?

The intent, of course, of diversifying through either mergers or acquisitions (M&A) is to provide the utility with better market leverage, while improving shareholder return-on investment (ROI) and associated reduction of risk levels with present markets.

While advice from management consultants suggests that a firm or utility should not stray far from its basic areas of competence, diversification is still an appropriate and often successful strategy if planned and managed well, particularly if primary market growth is at risk.

Advice for Utilities Considering Diversification

Utilities planning to diversify are having increasing difficulty in finding the right mix of ventures for their unregulated portfolio.

---

[10] M. Russo, N. Floyd, and M. Fester, "Adding On: How to Make Diversification Work," *Public Utilities Fortnightly*, February 15, 1993.

Therefore, any diversification strategy must be a calculated assessment of risk and reward of the new venture. These must include:

➠ an analysis of the company's strategic thrusts;

➠ evaluation of the attractiveness of proposed business segments. This should include targeting related industries and those businesses where activities complement and focus on their core skills and technologies such as DSM;

➠ analysis of the cost of ingression—i.e., the cost of entering the business cannot be so high that it capitalizes future returns;

➠ determination of the organizational structure subsequent to the merger or acquisition;

➠ assessment of the regulatory oversight of diversification actions;

➠ assessment of the probable impact on stock prices for both corporate parent and acquisition; and,

➠ assessment of traditional financial targets, forecasted income, and cash flows for the overall diversification effort. In other words, the proposed merger and acquisition (M&A) should offer the potential for continued profitability, or else why invest?

Strategy Evaluation

The strategic management process as defined above for a utility results in decisions that can be significant, having long-lasting consequences. Erroneous strategic decisions can have serious repercussions, and can be exceedingly difficult (if not impossible) to reverse. Therefore, most strategists agree, that strategy evaluation is vital to a firm's well-being: timely evaluations can alert management to problems or potential problems before a situation becomes critical. Evaluating the success of a strategy entails (1) examining the underlying bases of the strategy; (2) comparing expected results with actual results, (i.e., plan the work/work the plan), and (3) taking corrective actions to ensure that performance conforms to plans.

Characteristics of an Effective Evaluation System

Effective strategy evaluation should meet several basic requirements to be effective. Among these requirements are:

➡ evaluation activities should be economical—too much information can be just as bad as too little information, and too many controls can do more harm than good;

➡ they should provide managers with useful information about tasks over which they have control and influence;

➡ they should provide timely information: the "timeliness" however needs to be determined on a case by case basis to prevent dysfunctionality;

➡ it should be designed to provide a true picture of what is happening. (For example, in a severe economic downturn, productivity and profitability ratios may drop alarmingly, while employees and managers are actually working harder); and,

➡ the process should never supplant common sense and partnership.

The "fittest" companies managing strategically treat facts as friends and controls as liberating. These companies not only survive but thrive in troubled waters because their strategy evaluation and control systems are sound, their risk is contained, and they know themselves and the competitive situation inside and out. They see information where others see only data. They covet anything that removes decision-making from the realm of mere opinion. Successful companies recognize that an organization with no sense of direction and no coherent strategy precipitates its own demise.

Chapter Eighteen

Changing to Meet the Competition: A Corporate Survival Guide for Electric Utilities

William G. Gang

We cannot foretell the future, but we can anticipate it, and we can prepare ourselves to make intelligent choices from the alternatives the future is likely to offer. In examining the paths to future success, utility executives and planners are realizing that conducting business as they have in the past is the path to failure. After several generations of developing a culture that responds to the stimuli of a regulated monopolistic environment, utility management now faces a new challenge—**competition.** The marketplace has changed, and the utility must now change to survive. In this respect, most utilities are at a new frontier.

There are three forces that impact a company's ability to achieve its desired results in the marketplace: (1) the company's own planning and execution efforts, (2) the impact of "uncontrollables", such as regulators, the economy, interest rates, or legislation, and (3) the actions of strategic allies and competitors. Until recently, utility executives have not had to consider competition seriously in their planning efforts. Now the world has changed. In the last ten years, cost pressures on utilities have continued to increase. Public utility commissions have been reluctant to grant rate increases, and we have seen a degradation of as much as five percentage points in utilities' authorized rates of return. The National Energy Policy Act of 1992 has superimposed competition upon this scene. Competitive pressures from neighboring utilities, Independent Power Producers (IPPs), and other Non-Utility Generators (NUGs) are forcing utilities to seek a new paradigm. Utilities cannot sit idly by and say "I own the wires." This is what AT&T said. Only when they lost a significant portion of their base business, did AT&T recognize the seriousness of competition. They are now engaged in a very expensive "winback" effort directed at former customers.

Operation in a regulated environment is fundamentally different from operation in a free and competitive market. A regulator does not want to put you out of business; a competitor does. If a regulator drove a regulated entity from business, the regulator would have nothing to do. A competitor, on the other hand, can drive a company from business and take the customers of the vanquished firm for itself.

So what can utility management do to plan for competition? One alternative is to conduct business as usual. As mentioned, this approach will lead to the ultimate demise of the company, probably with power generation going "down the tube" first. Failure to adequately consider the possible actions of a competitor is acting like the military commander who complained, " We didn't win, because the enemy shot back." There are, however, a number of planning actions a utility can take to provide for its own success in this new competitive environment.

1. Implement "Swot" in the Strategic Plan

In the unregulated commercial world, the purpose of a strategic plan is to secure and maintain a sustainable competitive advantage. Adopting this as a planning purpose is step one for the utility executive. With this in mind, an analysis of STRENGTHS, WEAKNESSES, OPPORTUNITIES, and THREATS should be an integral part of the front end of the utility strategic plan. If a strategic plan begins with words about culture and values, and then proceeds directly into a discussion of goals and objectives, it is inadequate. The following questions must be considered:

➡ STRENGTHS—What strengths do I have in the marketplace relative to my competition? How can I bring these to bear at a decisive point in time?

➡ WEAKNESSES—What weaknesses do I have in the marketplace where a competitor can hurt me? How can I strengthen these or make them seem unimportant to my customers and my potential customers?

256

➠ OPPORTUNITIES—What are the short- and long-term opportunities available in the marketplace? How do I best position myself to take advantage of these?

➠ THREATS—What are the short- and long-term threats presented by my competitors and by uncontrollables? How can I neutralize or accommodate these threats?

These questions are basic. Much more detailed planning formats should be used for their consideration in the appropriate parts of the strategic plan. Competitive information is most important in two places in the strategic plan. It is used in assessing the external forces bearing on the company (the opportunities and threats), and it is used as input during the selection of strategic alternatives. The major point here is that most utilities do not consider the above questions adequately, if they consider them at all.

2. Try Wargaming

Wargaming is the development and testing of alternative strategies through competitive simulation. The key here is to test proposed strategies, actions or plans against what a competitor **could** do (not what you think he **will** do) and to develop contingency plans to provide for uncontrollable events that **could** happen (not what you think **will** happen).

In the play of a wargame, personnel from the utility are divided into teams representing the company and each of its competitors. The teams deliberate separately on strategies and actions to be taken to address a market or a number of markets. The teams then present their deliberations in plenary sessions, and umpires compare the strategies, decide on successes and failures, and award market share increases and decreases accordingly. Subsequent iterations of play are used to respond to competitors' strategies or to respond to postulated changes in "uncontrollable" conditions. At the completion of simulations, all players regroup to review the strategies decided upon along with key lessons learned from the play. They also summarize additional data and information needed to complete plans, and develop action plans.

In wargaming, the utility teams do not just develop more effective plans to defeat the competition. They also develop the ability to think competitively, unfettered by long-standing corporate constraints and precedents. Wargaming has been successfully used by the telecommunications industry in preparation for competition. What tended to happen was that the "home team" followed its business-as-usual conservative habits during the initial iteration of play. The employees playing the roles of competitors, however, went straight for the throat, and developed successful (and often brutal) strategies in the first round of play. During subsequent iterations of strategy development, the "way it was" went out the window as utility players sought a new paradigm for their business. All players learned to appreciate the serious need for new thinking in dealing with competition.

By providing a testing link between planning and action, wargaming helps to improve the probability of strategic victory of the company and it supports improved long term planning efforts. In summary, the advantages of this useful tool are that it:

➡ Provides insight into what **could** happen,

➡ Identifies opportunities for exploitation,

➡ Identifies obstacles and threats,

➡ Helps build an understanding of risk,

➡ Increases the strategic, operational and tactical knowledge of management, and

➡ Identifies needed planning information.

Wargaming can be used at all levels of planning: strategic, operational and tactical. It can help managers understand the long term threat of a competitor. It can be used to launch a new product or service. It can be used to develop a plan for attracting a company to locate in a utility's service territory. The keys to successful wargaming are extensive prior planning and choice of a knowledgeable facilitator.

Electric utility executives are in the initial stages of developing wargaming as a competitive tool. While some are contemplating its use and others are committed to it, none have adopted it vigorously yet. However, the interest is growing, showing a pattern similar to wargaming development in the telecommunications utilities, where it is now a common planning tool.

An example from telecommunications is useful to illustrate the advantages of wargaming a strategy prior to implementation. A certain telecommunications manufacturer, who wishes to remain unnamed, wargamed different strategies of resource allocation to research and development. Billions of dollars and multi-year development projects were involved, so the cost of error could have been high. The company wanted to know how to best allocate its research and development (R&D) resources to become a leading global supplier. The initial conservative strategy wargamed was to allocate roughly equal amounts to several product groups, depending on the size of the total budget to be sufficient to drive all products forward. It wasn't. Their serious global competitors had deeper pockets, and used these funds to increase market share in every sector. In the next simulation, the company redistributed the R&D funding to slightly fewer products, with the same result. The firm finally converged on the successful strategy of focusing on a few products with a high probability of success, while concentrating on certain regional markets where it already held a competitive advantage in these product lines.

Chief among the lessons learned from the wargame were:

⇒ A new way of thinking had to be adopted before success was possible, and

⇒ A financially disastrous strategy was avoided by wargaming prior to implementation.

3. Develop and Use Competitive Intelligence

Now that your neighbor is a potential competitor, what is he doing? Are you watching him? If he is sharp, he is watching you. At the annual conference of the Society of Competitive Intelligence Professionals last year in Los Angeles, there were only eight U.S. electric utilities present. They were Arizona Public Service, Detroit Edison, Duke Power, Florida Power & Light, Louisville Gas & Electric, Salt River Project, Southwestern Public Service, and Tennessee Valley Authority. This number has to increase in the future, and indeed it did at the recent conference in Boston, but it is still indicative of the utility industry's presently perceived need for competitive intelligence. In the past, utilities simply have not seen the need for it. As a result, data of competitive importance currently resides in pockets all over a utility. The company probably has no systematic approach to gathering these data and processing them into information that can be analyzed and applied as intelligence.

Historically, utility planning was largely an internal process. Driven by the budget, planners utilized internal performance data to form plans and to take action. More forward thinking utilities began to include customer data and information as well as industry events and issues in their planning process. Now, with competition on the scene, utility executives must consider a systematic approach to competitive intelligence and competitive analysis.

Utilities must develop a competitive intelligence system that has the capability to collect, analyze and disseminate competitive data and information. It is a fundamental part of understanding the threats and opportunities referred to in the previous planning section above. Such a system will help Florida Power Corporation understand Tampa Energy's facility for picking off lucrative wholesale customers; it will help TVA understand whether or not the city of Memphis is seriously considering buying electricity from Arkansas Power & Light; and it will help Northern States Power understand the ability of a broker to lure away the contract to supply power to six municipalities.

A key to establishing and maintaining a competitive intelligence system is deciding what information is needed. Most utilities today do not clearly understand what they need to know. A good place to start in developing these essential elements of information is to compile a competitive overview and then, as required, a competitive profile on each firm believed to be a potential competitor. The difference between these two documents is depth. The profile is an in-depth strategic portrait of a confirmed competitor. The overview is developed from a greater altitude, and is useful in familiarizing oneself with a firm's "personality" and in deciding whether or not the firm is, or could become, a serious competitor. In developing these documents, the utility can recognize the information it lacks and can assign tasks to remedy this situation. The systematic and routine accomplishment of these tasks is the basis of a competitive intelligence system.

In starting a competitive intelligence system, some utilities are considering a novel "shadow competitor" approach. The shadow competitor is a utility employee whose job it is to become the company expert who "gets inside the head" of a competitor utility. His responsibilities and functions are to:

- Establish and maintain the competitive profile,

- Collect data and information on the competitor and convert it into intelligence,

- Disseminate the intelligence appropriately,

- Respond to requests for intelligence on the competitor he shadows, and

- Play the role of his competitor in any wargaming.

It is important to realize that some cultural change is necessary in a utility before employees and even management will appreciate the need for competitive intelligence. First of all, utilities do not generally have trained competitive intelligence analysts on their payroll. A competent analyst should have both intelligence experience and industry knowledge. Use of an internal personnel asset for this function requires training. In hiring from the outside, the experienced analyst must be brought up to speed on the industry. Utilities are currently taking both approaches. Also, utility personnel other than the analyst should not be expected to contribute instantly to support a new competitive intelligence system. An example of failure in this respect is instructive.

A western utility hired a consultant to assist in the establishment of a competitive intelligence system. The consultant came from the oil industry where the need for competitive intelligence had been culturally ingrained for years. The system developed by the utility and the consultant depended on a database that in turn depended on the voluntary contribution of data and information by utility employees. The system received only three entries in the initial four weeks of operation, not a startling success by any measure. This difficulty may be avoided by:

➟ Starting slowly with dedicated personnel gathering information on a few competitors,

➟ Internally publicizing your efforts, and

➟ Automating only when a manual system proves workable.

A number of utilities are developing competitive intelligence capability with these factors in mind. The Tennessee Valley Authority is developing an intelligence network. Arizona Public Service has a small contingent whose job it is to gather and analyze competitive information. One of this group is an intelligence analyst recently hired from the aerospace industry. San Diego Gas & Electric (SDG&E) has recently established a Strategic Planning and Projects Division. Integral to that division is the establishment of a "desk" concept similar to that used in the U.S. State Department. There are "desks" to gather and analyze data on IPPs, other utilities, and changes in uncontrollables that may influence SDG&E's ability to attain its desired results. Baltimore Gas & Electric, which had data collection fragmented about the company, has decided to centralize the function and orient it toward competitive intelligence. Last October, Sierra Pacific Power completed an assessment of their position in the Western States Coordinating Council (WSCC) to understand their competitive position in the region, and to provide management with intelligence input to the strategic decision making process. Central & South West, the Dallas-based utility holding company, is reported to keep competitive information files on over twenty utilities in nine states bordering their service area. Their intent is to be in the forefront of utility merger activity. The list of examples continues to grow as utilities recast their activities to meet the competitive threat.

4. Plan to Reduce O&M Costs

Regardless of pricing strategies adopted in the planning process, one fact is abundantly clear. If a utility is not a low-cost producer in its geographic region, it is at risk. Not only are revenue and market share at risk, but so is sustained credit quality. Therefore, the utility preparing for competitive operation must reduce its cost structure as much as possible. Capital budgets are probably already closely monitored, as is appropriate. Now operation and maintenance (O&M) costs should also be prudently addressed. Since sixty to seventy percent of O&M costs are personnel related, a review of staffing levels at operating sites and at headquarters is the critical opportunity for cost reduction.

Any staffing analysis done at a utility has to be viewed as prudent by both regulators and shareholders. As these two groups often hold conflicting goals, a staffing analysis that satisfies both parties and reduces cost is not easily accomplished. One methodology that has achieved acceptance by regulators and investors alike is benchmarking. That is, a utility compares its staffing and organizations with those of other well-performing utilities, and makes organizational changes and staff reductions where appropriate. Regardless of the methodology used, the following parameters should be examined in any staffing analysis:

➡ Utility and contractor staffing levels,

➡ Layers of management,

➡ Spans of control,

➡ Functional responsibilities, and

➡ Interface relationships.

Comparing one utility with another offers cost reduction opportunities through gains in efficiency. That is, any economies achieved are a result of answering the question, "Am I doing things right?" This avenue for cost reduction should be exploited, and quickly, but it is only one step in preparing for competitive operation. Operating effectiveness needs to be addressed at the same time. Effectiveness improvements are found in answers to the question, "Am I doing the right things?" For example, it will be difficult for a utility subject to cost-based rate of return regulation to secure a competitive advantage over a "lean and mean" IPP without using every strategic and tactical tool at its disposal, including effective planning, wargaming, gathering intelligence, and reducing O&M costs.

As part of their preparation for competition, a number of utilities have addressed the staffing question or are in the process of doing so. Pacific Gas & Electric, for instance, has implemented an early retirement program, and has recently examined staffing in its Steam Generation Department as part of a company-wide program. Centerior has completed a staffing review of its fossil operations, as well as a separate review of staffing at the Davis Besse and Perry Nuclear Power Plants. Florida Power Corporation has completed a review of staffing at their Crystal River 3 nuclear plant. These are but a few of those taking similar measures as the electric utility community seeks to ready itself for competition.

Understanding competition and instituting the changes required to meet it are fundamental to utility success in the future. The four suggestions above are key steps a utility can take to ensure its competitive success. Some utilities are taking these and other actions to secure the future, but there is much to be done. The question is, WHAT ARE YOU DOING?

Chapter Nineteen

Strategic Transformation: The New Game

Joe D. Doyle, John R. Childress, and Jim Ondrus

At this point in time, no one can be certain of what the future holds for electric utilities. Only one thing is certain, change is imminent. In their semi-annual analysis of deregulated industries, entitled "Predictable Patterns," Venture Associates, Inc., outlined the possible future for electric utilities based on their assessment of the evolution of other formerly regulated businesses such as airlines, railroads and the regional phone companies. Given the insight provided by this and other studies, one would hope that electric utilities could make a graceful transition into the "competitive arena" via the experiences of other industries. Intellectually, this is a simple concept and appears to have a simplistic answer. And, the competitive threat is not new. It has been used as an impetus for organizational change efforts for several years now. However, most electric utilities are still not confident that they are positioned to handle the "new game." One reason is that most utilities have no strategy in place for coping with this future and, with the exception of recent events in California, the future has not arrived.

The past pattern of behavior of regulated companies was to wait for the regulating body to essentially "pre-determine" their strategies via regulation. Obviously, companies in competitive environments must chart their own strategies and become adept to change. The primary reason that many electric utilities find strategy formulation and organizational change difficult is because of their corporate culture. In the words of Winston Churchill, "first we shape our institutions and then they shape us."

In order for a company to optimize its performance, the strategy of the company must be matched by a set of organizational routines and structures which support that strategy. Once the strategy is initiated and the organization has structured itself to implement the strategy, people know (ideally) to behave in a manner which

265

supports the strategy and structure. The collective behaviors become habits, which in turn result in the culture. This alignment of strategy—structure—culture (Figure 1) creates a highly effective organization where the collective energies of all employees are channeled towards common goals.

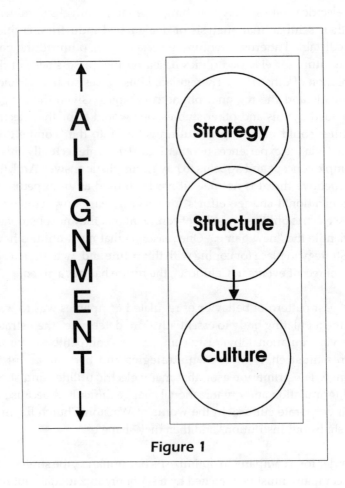

Figure 1

This chapter will discuss the alignment process and the management of change in the electric utilities industry. In addition, lessons learned by one of the regional telephone companies, following the divestiture of AT&T, will be used to illustrate efforts to align strategy, structure and culture.

Organizational Alignment

Within the U.S. industry, it is easy to see examples of organizational alignment. While Wal-Mart pursues the mass merchandising discount strategy, Nordstrom, also financially successful, serves the retail industry with a strategy revolving around full-line apparel stores and greater attention to service. Both Wal-Mart and Nordstrom are large, nation-wide organizations that have been able to evolve strong cultures that are in alignment with their respective strategies and structures (see Figure 2).

Indeed, many industry observers agree that it is the strength of the Wal-Mart and Nordstrom cultures (which are very different, yet equally strong) that make both organizations able to implement plans better than their competitors, who also pursue similar strategies, but with less aligned or cohesive corporate cultures, yet each organization is aligned and therefore highly productive in achieving its objectives.

The classic, hierarchical, military-style culture of many electric utilities has evolved in response to the regulatory environment. Now here's the problem. Behaviors after time become unconscious, automatic and comfortable. Anyone who has ever tried to quit smoking or to lose weight knows how difficult it is to change your habits and behaviors. It's as if you are "frozen" in a pattern that is difficult to break. Therefore, in order to change for the future, the first phase involves "unfreezing" the corporate culture in order to create an environment where the organization can plan for competition and uncertainty (Figure 3).

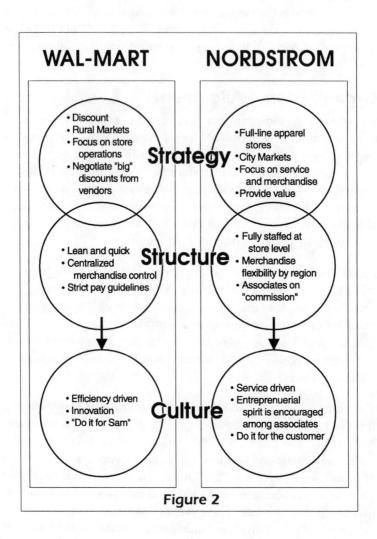

Figure 2

Phase 1: The "Unfreezing"

Figure 3

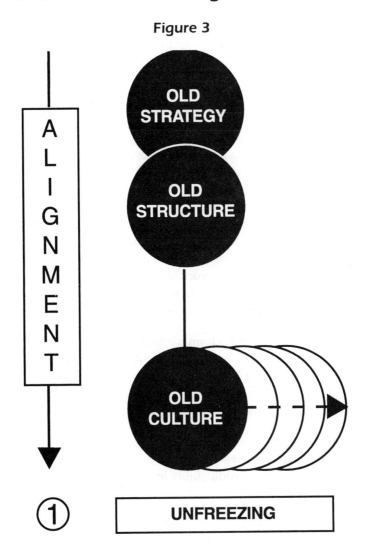

From our experience, in order to "unfreeze" the culture, it is important to first work at increasing willingness to change to a high level (commitment, compassion, sense of urgency), then put in place the necessary skills (capabilities).

To unfreeze an ingrained culture, organizations need to understand the cultural inhibitors to change (Figure 4), and:

➠ Identify cultural strengths and barriers—define the gap—in relation to company strategy and competitive advantage.

➠ Establish a set of high performance values and behaviors that can be used to define the new culture desired.

➠ Make sure that any ongoing initiatives such as Total Quality or Customer Service are seen as key elements of the culture change process.

➠ Traditional training and academic processes are ineffective when dealing with corporate culture. Learning new cultural norms must take place from the "inside out" as compared to the "outside in." Unless management and employees re-examine their old beliefs and work habits, and then are able to gain insights into new and more effective organizational values, norms and behaviors, cultural shifts will not take place.

➠ The senior management team is both the role model and the initial change agent for a culture shift. The culture change process must provide the senior team with a positive experience of the new cultural norms and behaviors desired. In addition, the senior team must become the role models of the new culture.

➠ Culture-change seminars for employees must be developed to provide a significant positive emotional experience that creates an openness and accountability for the culture change process.

➠ A "critical mass" of employees, starting with the senior management team and encompassing at least 40% of the organization, is necessary before the culture-change process will really take hold.

➠ Openness, trust, positive feedback, and coaching are the key pillars during the culture change process.

➠ Revise company policies and human resource systems to better reinforce and match the new cultural norms desired.

Figure 4

Typical Cultural Inhibitors to Change

Hierarchical leadership

Turf-building and pyramid structures

Opportunism and lack of principals

Hidden agendas, dishonesty and lack of openness

Distrust and fear

Short-term and strictly bottom-line driven

Task-oriented and internally focused

"Can't be done" attitude

Blame and making excuses

Union/Management problems

Lack of trust

Insufficient training

Hold onto the past and resisting change

Strict rules and rigid policies

Win/Lose games

Trying to develop the skills (capability) of change without a high level of willingness is in most cases a waste of time, effort and money. The unfreezing process must proceed in four steps:

Step 1: Build Commitment and Sense of Urgency among the Senior Team

All members of the Senior Team must display their willingness to lead and implement change through a high level of commitment, passion, and sense of urgency. In many ways, this group must become a team that both together and individually are viewed by the company as truly committed to culture change.

Step 2: Learn the Skills of Culture Change

Once a "team" consciousness is developed among the senior managers, and a higher degree of willingness is achieved, the next step is to learn the skills of leadership and culture change so they can become highly effective change agents.

Step 3: Understanding the Need and Building a Sense of Urgency in all Employees

With a properly designed culture change process, and the active leadership of the senior management team, the entire employee base must come to understand the "need for change" and build a desire and sense of urgency about being involved in a culture shift.

In some instances, if there is no real imminent financial or perceived business threat to push the company into change, then employees must be led into a new culture by a powerful and compelling vision of an enhanced and empowered work environment. People need to be educated and clearly understand that if the culture does not change, then in a few short years the company could be significantly at risk because of the rapidly changing energy industry and highly competitive market place.

Step 4: Everyone is Accountable to Make It Happen

In this step of the process, all employees learn not only the tools of change, but how to put them to use via "Action Teams," etc. to build the new Performance-Driven culture.

The unfreezing process should continue to all levels within the organization, especially since almost everyone will be impacted by the changes. More importantly, the change management and leadership skills will prove to be an invaluable asset in later phases as you draw on the wisdom of the organization in order to achieve the vision.

The next barrier that must be overcome deals with stability and certainty. The old game was stable and predictable to a great extent.

Predictions of the future (if made at all) were usually extrapolations of the past. Anyone who has managed a business in a truly competitive market can tell you of the pitfalls of relying on the past to predict the future. Competitors seem to always find a way to break the rules. In this day of accelerated information technology and rapid socio-economic change, the reliability of the past as a predictor of the future is diminishing at an increasing rate. In order to deal with this uncertainty, electric utilities must have the ability to "suspend disbelief" and allow themselves to "dream" of the future using the techniques of scenario building (Figure 5). This is only possible if the culture has been unfrozen and is ready to break the current paradigms.

Phase 2: "Dreaming"—Building Scenarios

The utility business used to be a very "certain" business in the eyes of customers, employees and financial markets. Today, and in the foreseeable future, it is a very uncertain business, especially for electric utilities. One tool which can help organizations deal with uncertainty is *scenario building*.

Scenarios are stories about the future. They are a set of integrated perceptions within which various predictions can be tested. By creating a story instead of an outcome, an entire context is created within which decision pathways can be determined. If done properly, decisions may manifest themselves which might not have even been apparent otherwise.

The reasons scenarios work can be illustrated by examining your childhood. Think back to how your parents used simple stories to help you learn. By telling a child a story, a relatively abstract concept could be brought to life by simply stimulating his/her imagination. As a child experiences the story, he/she begins to place him/herself in the situation at hand. Consequently, he/she begins to naturally envision a response. The learning takes place as the story is completed and he/she compares "his/her ending" with the story. Think of trying to explain the virtues conveyed in "the little boy who cried wolf" to a child (or anyone for that matter) without using a story.

Figure 5

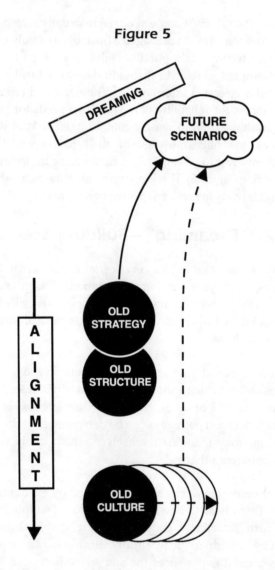

Strategy scenarios play the same role. Since peoples' decision processes are usually driven by unconscious systems of beliefs or mindsets, the first step is to raise the awareness of the mindset by articulating it. As strategy stories of the future are constructed and companies are allowed to envision their future, they are allowed to examine their collective beliefs and gain insight.

The process is quite simple. First, the key socio-economic drivers of the company's markets are identified. Then, the senior team of the company collaborates to construct a few fundamentally different views of the future. A simple approach is to consider three different views. One pessimistic, one optimistic and one status quo. Business stories are then constructed around these views using various techniques including imagery and multi-media systems. The senior team then interprets these views collectively and projects the company's response. The most likely "dream" is then chosen from which the plan for the future can be derived. More importantly, if these "dreams" are constructed as a group effort of the senior team, a shared set of perceptions and responses are developed.

This is valuable not only in building consensus as to the destiny of the company, but in helping the company respond to an unanticipated future. For instance, an electric utility might construct one future where electric vehicles are cheaply made and in high demand (optimistic). The next step is to determine the company's general place in this future and discuss what the company's strategy would be. Would they be manufacturing cars or other products, or would they only be providers of energy? A different scenario may be one in which electricity truly becomes a commodity and utilities become brokers, leaving the product to a few, major companies. A third scenario may be that mergers and acquisitions create a few, large regional utilities, with no need for local organizations. Whatever the scenario finally chosen, by thinking through numerous different scenarios, the company is more able to respond to the situation. The real value then of the scenario is a better decision-making process, not as a method to predict the future. It is a tool to help us cope with the uncertain future once it has arrived.

Phase 3: Vision and Strategy

Many utilities have already dreamed of the post-regulatory world. As a result some implicit strategies exist individually within those who have ventured into the future. These strategies manifest themselves in discussions, meetings and even publications. Rarely

275

however do these dreams receive the institutional attention they merit. The norm is still explicit strategies which continue the patterns of the past, in denial of the pending changes. Ideally, various dreams of the future would be formally discussed by the executive leadership of the company, who would then decide on one adopted dream, the vision. This vision would then become the driving force for the strategy (Figure 6).

Figure 6

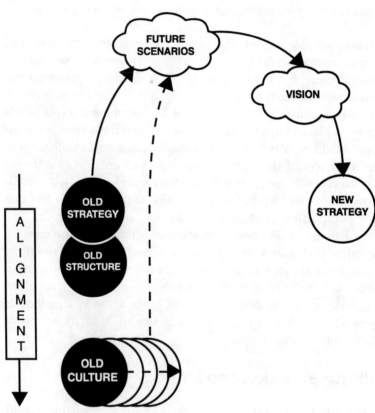

Common Vision and a Clear Sense of Direction

Where there is no vision, the people will perish.

Proverbs 29:18

In many ways, a shared vision and clear sense of direction represent "magnetic north" for employees within an organization. It represents the idealized picture of what the company and its people can become. A vision is much more than just information or objectives; a vision evokes strong feelings! It is the feeling and the picture of the future that tends to infect employees with high energy and commitment.

Simply stated, a vision is a clear picture of the future as we would like it to be. A statement of "who we are," "where we are going," and "why it's important to us" that appeals to the more noble, cause-oriented elements within all human beings, and as such captures the imagination, unleashes creative energies, and uplifts the spirit of individuals throughout the organization.

Like "magnetic north," the vision acts as a beacon that draws the organization forward and allows it to face difficult times with energy and optimism. Vision pulls employees into a "new way of life" and significantly narrows the gap between plans on paper and implementation in the marketplace.

Many companies make the common mistake of equating a vision with a mission statement. In a sense, they believe that goal setting and strategic planning are the same as visioning! While a mission and strategy spells out the "How To's" in a company's quest for competitive advantage, a vision is the "Why To's" that tend to motivate people to give their best with enthusiasm and commitment. People don't get emotional about a business mission, but a vision can ignite the latent potential in all of us!

The usefulness of a vision statement that is clear and powerful is easily seen in those companies that are facing change, either as a result of internal growth or from increased competition in their industry. Whether the organization is growing, "right-sizing," or making strategy changes as a result of competitive pressures, a clear and compelling vision will provide a clear beacon to follow during what otherwise can be a confusing and emotionally charged period of change for everyone in the organization.

Perhaps the best known example of a powerful vision is the Constitution of the United States of America. Reading the opening words cannot help but evoke a string of strong feelings that are as compelling now as they were in colonial times:

> We the people of the United States, in order to form a more perfect union, establish Justice, ensure domestic Tranquility, provide for the common defense, promote the general Welfare, and secure the Blessings of Liberty to ourselves and our Prosperity, do ordain and establish this Constitution for the United States of America.

The Constitution of the United States of America
September 17, 1787

Another powerful vision that redoubled the commitment and resolve of an entire nation was the emotional commitment unleashed by Winston Churchill's famous "Blood, Toil, Tears and Sweat" speech in the House of Commons on May 13, 1940, and followed a few weeks later by his "We Shall Never Surrender" speech. These and other visual pictures were filled with emotion, optimism, and noble cause that galvanized the commitment of a nation and its people to not only survival, but victory in spite of recent setbacks in the war with Hitler.

On a national level, another example of the power of a shared vision and clear sense of direction occurred in the late 1960's when Dr. Martin Luther King took the words of our constitution and put them into a verbal picture filled with emotion and appealing to the highest instincts of people. In his famous, "I have a dream . . ." speech on the mall in Washington, D.C., before the largest crowd ever assembled for a civil rights demonstration, the picture of a country where men of all races, creeds and colors could sit down to a table in brotherhood galvanized both blacks and whites to finally come to grips with the issue of civil rights for all Americans. So powerful was that vision that common, ordinary people became heroes and role models through their actions in accordance with this new vision for America. Numerous acts of non-violent protest, often with considerable jeopardy to those involved, were spawned by this clear and compelling vision of the future.

A powerful and compelling vision causes action! Just as John Fitzgerald Kennedy used the vision of a "man on the moon within the decade" to unleash the creativity of the nation to conquer the obstacles of manned space flight, so numerous businesses, even whole industries, have been built by the inspiring power of a vision.

The automobile industry, virtually non-existent at the beginning of the 20th Century, was pulled into being by the vision of Henry Ford to "provide safe, reliable transportation for the common man!" The modern telecommunications industry, which touches every part of our business and personal lives, gathered strength from the vision of Theodore Vail for a phone in every home and a commitment to "Universal Service, end to end!" The photography industry is now a world-wide, multi-billion dollar business, but its founding organization, the Eastman Kodak Company "began with the vision of one man who saw a way to meet a very human need: The need to picture, share, and preserve the times, people, places, and events of our lives!"

In the absence of a shared vision and a clear sense of direction, individuals easily become confused, insecure, and often are filled with negative interpretations of company actions and changes. Such a situation occurred immediately after the breakup of AT&T. Following the breakup, a corporate survey asked 6,000 employees to share their thoughts and feelings surrounding various aspects of the divestiture and the new organization. The findings reveal somewhat of an identity crisis for the AT&T employees, the sentiment being:

> I knew the old Bell System, its mission, its operation, its people, its culture. And I knew my niche in it. In that

knowledge, I had identity and confidence about my company and myself. Now I work for a new company, one-fourth its former size, with only a partial history and no track record. With the loss of our mission, universal service, and the fragmentation of the very business of providing telephone service I find myself asking, 'Who are we? Who am I?'

Tunstall, 1985, p. 152

An organization without a shared vision and clear sense of direction finds itself frequently in a "reactive" mode, with crisis management seeming to be the most often used style of management. An organization without clear direction often exhibits characteristic symptoms:

➡ Frequent reorganizations with little positive effect.

➡ Money and time spent on "technology upgrades" with the belief that better technology will solve our performance problems.

➡ Excessive blaming and finger pointing, especially between senior managers and their departments.

➡ Squabbles over departmental budgets with each area trying to provide for its own agenda.

➡ Loss of numerous, talented, long-term employees who complain about a directionless company.

Clearly, a Shared Vision and Clear Direction are the basic foundation pillars for organizational change.

A New Strategy

After the vision has been articulated, the next step is to mold the new corporate strategy that will provide the framework and game plan for achieving the vision. Strategy can be defined in various ways:

The determination of the long-term goals and objectives of an enterprise, and the adoption of courses of action and the allocation of resources necessary for carrying out these goals.

Alfred Chandler,
*Strategy and Structure: Chapters in
the History of American Industrial Enterprise*

A strategy is the pattern or plan that integrates an organization's major goals, policies and action sequences into a cohesive whole. A well-formulated strategy helps to marshal and allocate an organization's resources into a unique and viable posture based upon its relative internal competencies and shortcomings, anticipated changes in the environment and contingent moves by intelligent opponents.

James Brian Quinn,
Strategies for Change: Logical Incrementalism

Strategy is the pattern of objectives, purposes or goals and the major policies and plans for achieving these goals, stated in such a way as to define what business the company is in or is to be in and the kind of company it is or is to be.

Kenneth Andrews,
The Concept of Corporate Strategy

A simplistic view of the "old" strategy in utilities was how to recover costs in the base rate. A new premise, driven by competition and increasing pressure from stakeholders, is to earn a rate of return over the cost of capital. One simple strategy could then be to increase the long term profitability of the corporation.

In order to formulate the strategy, the external opportunities and threats must be compared with the internal core competencies of the company. The first step is to use the vision to derive specific business that the company desires to compete in. Next, an internal analysis should be conducted that includes not only an assessment of the corporate culture, but the strengths and challenges. The net result should be the identification of the core competencies of the company and the areas where competitive advantage can be established and sustained.

Once the core competencies have been identified, an external analysis should be conducted that evaluates the opportunities and threats that exist in the market. Competitors are a relatively new aspect to be considered in formulating utility strategy. In the electric utility business, competitors include:

➡ Neighboring utilities that once shared information and sometimes resources.

➡ IPP's and other new generators.

➡ Demand side management and other technologies that reduce demand.

The size of the market and segmentation and the barriers to entry are undergoing rapid change in the utility business. As a result, companies need to carefully focus on the critical determinants of competitive advantage, the key success factors of the industry.

Figure 7 illustrates a formal method of determining key success factors. And a discussion about probing for key success factors is presented.

Finally, the companies competencies are compared with the key success factors in order to determine the actions that must be taken in order to achieve competitive advantage and profitability. This strategy must identify specific organizational goals and objectives which can be translated into "core strategies" and be assigned to specific organizations or process teams.

Phase 4: Shifting the Structure— Reengineering

The reference to process strategy is a result of a major shift in organizational thinking to reorganizing companies around the core processes that serve customers instead of the functions that drive internal operations. However, most organizations have not achieved the dramatic shift of their organizations and routines required to accommodate process strategies. Therefore, a major change in these structural elements is usually required.

Figure 7

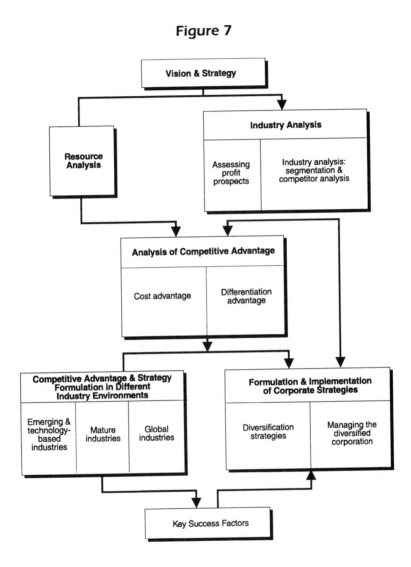

Probing for Key Success Factors

As a consultant faced with an unfamiliar business or industry, I make a point of first asking the specialists in the business, "What is the secret of success in this industry?" Needless to say, I seldom get an immediate answer, and so I pursue the inquiry by asking other questions from a variety of angles in order to establish as quickly as possible some reasonable hypotheses as to key factors for success. In the course of these interviews it usually becomes quite obvious what analyses will be required in order to prove or disprove these hypotheses. By first identifying the probable key factors for success and then screening them by proof or disproof, it is often possible for the strategist to penetrate very quickly to the core of the problem.

Traveling in the United States last year, I found myself on one occasion sitting on a plane next to a director of one of the biggest lumber companies in the country. Thinking I might learn something useful in the course of the five hour flight, I asked him "What are the key factors for success in the lumber industry?" To my surprise, his reply was immediate: "Owning large forests and maximizing the yield from them."

The first of those key factors is a relatively simple matter: the purchase of forest land. But his second point required further explanation. Accordingly, my next question was: "What variable or variables do you control in order to maximize the yield from a given tract?" He replied: "The rate of tree growth is the key variable. As a rule, two factors promote growth: The amount of sunshine and the amount of water."

Impressed that this director knew how to work out a key factor strategy for his business, I offered my own contribution: "Then under the opposite conditions, where there is plenty of water but too little sunshine—for example, around the lower reaches of the Columbia River, the key factors should be fertilizers to speed up the growth and the choice of tree varieties that don't need so much sunshine." I spent the rest of the long flight very profitably hearing from him in detail how each of these factors was being applied.

Source: Kenichi Ohmae, *The Mind of the Strategist* (McGraw-Hill/Penguin Books, 1982)

The technique that is most often associated to this re-alignment is process reengineering (Figure 8).

Figure 8

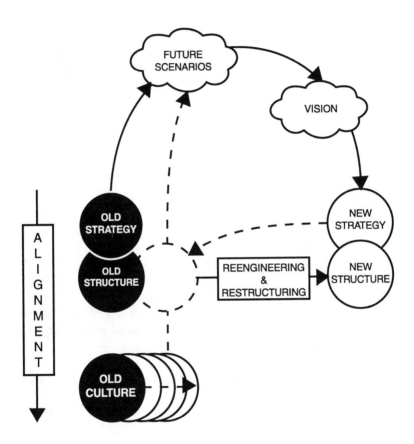

Figure 9 illustrates a utilities transition from a functional to process orientation.

The same "outside the box" thinking of the future used to dream and construct future scenarios is also imperative of the process improvements that must be made in order to implement the strategy.

285

Figure 9

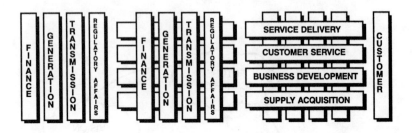

The unfrozen culture will again be crucial in order to delay the kind of breakthrough thinking required to surface "sacred cows" and break comfortable routines. The goal is to create quantum process improvement and alignment to the new strategy.

The first step is to draw and engage the senior management team in determining the key processes. The vision and strategic analysis should provide the framework for identifying the key processes. The senior team must endorse these processes and be the source of "process champions." The next step is to build cross-functional process teams which are tasked with the following:

➧ Mapping existing organizational routines and/or processes.

➧ Developing models for the "ideal" process using benchmarking and other analytics.

➧ Use interactive facilitation and process reengineering techniques to manipulate the existing process maps and analytics, completely shattering existing models in some cases.

➧ Institutionalize the new processes and routines by using information technology or other tools.

➧ Re-organize people and resources around the new processes.

286

The new structure should now be aligned to the new strategy and its derivative processes. However, the culture is still in a state of flux induced by the "unfreezing." In order to complete the organizational transition, the culture must be shifted or "fit" to the strategy and structure, achieving alignment. (Figure 10)

Figure 10

Reengineering
Requires a Shift

From ➡ To

Functional Departments	Process Teams
Hierarchichal Structures	Flat Structure
Discrete Tasks	Multi-dimensional Work
Follow Directions	Do What's Right
Management	Leadership
Supervising	Coaching
Training	Education
Activity-Based Compensation	Results-Based Compensation
Vertical Advancement	Horizontal Broadening
Policy-Driven	Customer-Driven

Phase 5: Fitting the Culture

The last phase involves moving the old, "unfrozen" culture into alignment with the new strategy and structure (Figure 11). A new set of organizational beliefs and behaviors that are critical to the new strategy and processes must be identified. The entire organization, starting with the senior team, must be aligned to these "strategic beliefs and behaviors." Two key mechanisms can be used to build this alignment. One is a 360 degree feedback mechanism, which is valuable not only for assessing personal and organizational status with regard to the "new cultural behaviors," but which can also be used to measure the culture shift.

No one would argue that building a strong organizational culture can enhance the success of aligning an organization towards its vision, mission, values and business goals. Much documentation in books, research and articles have cited this for over the past twenty years. What is more difficult to tell is how well an organization's culture is progressing toward these goals of alignment. How do you measure an organization's progress on such subjective measures as values, core beliefs and behaviors?

The Value of Having a Tool to Measure Culture

1. Provide a baseline of the organization's behavior relative to the core beliefs and values of the culture and provide a method of more objectively measuring this cultural performance over time. It will provide feedback on how the organization is doing making the core beliefs and values a reality in day-to-day activities at the company.

2. Send a clear message to the entire organization that living the core beliefs and values of the culture is one of the most important things everyone needs to do, from senior level through non-management level. This assessment process enables the leaders to measure and pay attention to the culture—your greatest cultural lever in making change.

Figure 11

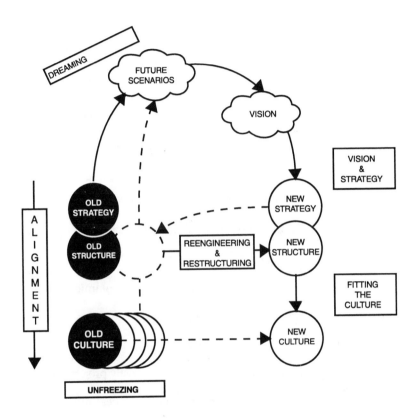

3. Provide the opportunity for everyone to develop personalized action plans based on the report's feedback and receive continuous coaching on their performance relative to living the core beliefs and values. This strengthens the message of continued self-improvement for all participants utilizing the assessment tool.

4. Provide the organization feedback as to its cultural performance in which they can effectively measure how well they are

meeting the cultural aspects of its strategy and use the company-wide data to develop action plans for personal organization improvement.

With core beliefs and values being a new set of organizationally shared values, people will want to see the "score." Alignment will occur by everyone knowing what core beliefs are and knowing how they individually measure up to those beliefs. The company will also be able to jointly work on common areas that generally all score lower so that individuals will be able to work as a team in further developing alignment to their organization's core beliefs.

Without a real focus on realigning the culture, it's as if the old culture anchors the organization, preventing it from moving forward.

Signs of a corporate culture out of alignment include:

➠ frequent reorganizations, but the same problems persist;

➠ unwillingness to take risks, or make long term commitments;

➠ resistance to new ways of doing things;

➠ lack of accountability; spending time blaming or finding fault;

➠ power plays and poor teamwork, causing costly project delays;

➠ mistrust between management and employees; and

➠ lack of clear vision or direction, people are "confused about where we're going.

A Case Study

"Ma Bell doesn't live here anymore."

Charles L. Brown, Chairman, AT&T

Let's look at the Bell Telephone system, an organization whose culture had been ideally suited to meet its strategic goals, and which was later forced to respond to a dramatically changing business environment.

For more than half a century, "universal service, end-to-end" was the Bell System's corporate vision and they were very good at it! As the components of their business evolved—financial policies, technology, pricing philosophy, product and market strategies and organizational design—all served to support this pervasive mission. Overall, the Bell System's strategies were driven by regulatory and technological considerations. Financial policies were geared toward dividends, with a high debt structure and heavy external financing. Bell Laboratories, insulated in the regulated environment, was able to focus on basic research and technological opportunity, without worrying about consumer preferences. Pricing philosophies were such that everyone could afford a phone. Market strategies served monolithic markets with standardized product offerings. The corporate structure was large and centralized, organized by function.

The cultural attributes that developed from this organization included a "regulatory mindset," consensus orientation and a bias toward staff analysis. The reward system fostered lifetime careers, with a slow and steady progression and a strong focus on hierarchy. Other characteristics included dedication to customer service, group accountability, standardized procedures, and formal communications.

W. Brooke Tunstall, an AT&T vice president who was closely involved in the divestiture planning, provides an inside view of the cultural dynamics at AT&T in his book "Disconnecting Parties":

> All these [cultural] attributes evolved to directly support one superordinate goal, universal service. In fact, everything related to the culture was affected by this goal; the kind of people hired, their shared value systems, the infrastructure of processes to run the business. All were committed to the unchanging objective of providing high-quality service at affordable prices to everyone in the United States. Rarely, in fact, had corporate mission and corporate culture been so ideally matched.

> Tunstall, 1985, p. 146.

291

In the immediate years before the January 1984 divestiture, the Bell System's business environment experienced a dramatic change, as it began the shift from a monopolistic, regulated environment to a competitive, deregulated one. After divestiture, the new business units responded with numerous changes that were fundamentally different from the way things were previously done. A new strategic orientation would be driven by market opportunities and financial needs. Financial strategies would be geared to meet Earnings Per Share growth, with a lower debt structure. Research and design efforts would shift toward the application of technology to customer needs. Markets would be segmented, with customized offerings. Finally, the organization would be restructured into smaller, more decentralized businesses to better support the market and customer driven philosophy.

Following the breakup, a corporate survey asked 6,000 employees to share their thoughts and feelings surrounding various aspects of the divestiture and the new organization. The findings reveal somewhat of an identity crisis for the AT&T employees.

It's easy to imagine the tension as employees struggle (even today) to meet the demands of the new organization, as the culture which had previously worked so well is now out of alignment with the new strategy.

One major challenge faced by the senior leaders within AT&T and the seven Regional Bell Operating Companies is establishing and promoting new cultural elements, while keeping the best of the old. The culture must shift from a consensus to a risk orientation; from a regulatory to a competitive mindset. Deliberation must give way to action. Employees can no longer expect lifetime careers with steady promotions; instead they must adapt to a meritocracy, where rewards are based on individual performance.

The "Baby Bells", which have been the most aggressive at pursuing strategies for the new competitive telecommunications environment, are currently posting excellent returns and solid stock performance. It is no secret, however, that the majority of these Earnings Per Share gains have come from cost cutting, retirement incentives and restructuring, not necessarily increases in productivity or operating performance. With employee morale at low levels, it remains to be seen whether or not the leaders of these organizations can shift from the old "Bell culture" of entitlement, lifetime employment, and job security to create a work environment of empowerment, trust, accountability and sense of urgency, all of which are elements in a high performance, competitive culture that is much more in alignment with their new competitive strategies.

Summary

Utilities have evolved through years of conditioning and adaptation to a somewhat benign but complex regulatory environment. These changes have shaped and reshaped organizations. Now the utilities industry must make a quantum leap, a re-evolution, into a more dynamic and competitive environment ripe with predators. The process of transforming them from being regulatory-driven, to market-driven will not be an easy transition. The key is focusing on the invisible element, the culture. Once the culture is made more visible and "pliable," building scenarios, devising new strategies, and reengineering processes become easier and more effective. The new culture can then be sculptured and aligned to the core processes. This will ensure the greatest chance of achieving sustainable competitive advantage.

The following two pages contain forecasts for the 1990s. Businesses that want to be competitive may want to keep international, technological, work, socioeconomic, and life-style trends in mind.

Towards the new millennium: a summary of forecasts for the 1990's.

The International Environment

➤ Increasing imbalance of population—between 1950 and 2025 the OECD countries proportion of world population will have fallen from 23 to 12 percent and Europe will account for 3 percent of the world population.

➤ Widening gaps in living standards between developed and developing countries—1.5 billion people in "absolute poverty" (income less than $300 per year) by 2000.

➤ Between 1980 and 2020 the number of people over 60 years old in Japan will increase from 15.0 m. to 34.7 m., in USA from 35.8 m. to 66.9 m., in USSR from 34.7 m. to 69.3 m, in China from 73.6 m. to 238.9 m.

➤ Explosive and anarchic development of Third World megapolises— Mexico City will have 30 million inhabitants by 2000.

➤ Lack of international leadership, USA and USSR economically weak; Japan unwilling to accept increasing international role.

➤ Worldwide environmental problems including: inadequacies of water supplies in developed as well as under-developed countries; climatic changes; pollution problems notably problems of acid rain, waste disposal and nuclear accidents.

➤ Monetary instability with strong fluctuations in exchange rates.

➤ Rapid economic growth during the 1990's.

Technology and Work Patterns

➤ Increased automation, shift to smaller-scale production, mass production, mass production of variety.

➤ Manufacturing jobs requiring higher skills, but growth in service sector mainly providing low-skill jobs.

➤ Major breakthroughs in biotechnology; diversificationof energy sources through fusion, coal gasification, geopressure; application of superconductivity; new composite materials.

Socioeconomic Trends

➡ Development of a dual economy—a formal economy and an informal economy.

➡ Declining effectiveness of state-provided services speeds privatization of the provision of collective goods and services (health, education, environment, culture). Nevertheless, the growing problems of healthcare for the elderly poses an increasing economic drag.

➡ Emergence of new inequalities in material living standards, security and social status.

➡ Democratic processes increasingly influenced by institutionalized pressure groups and increased power of the old ("The grey panthers").

➡ Increasing leadership role of women in private and public sectors.

Life-styles and Living

➡ Trends towards global uniformity matched by heterogeneity and differentiation of life-styles and a resurgence of cultural nationalism.

➡ Increased insecurity reflected in regeneration of the family unit.

➡ Search for new forms of fulfillment—family, children, group life, associations, networks of solidarity and exchange.

➡ Continued urbanization, with rejuvenation of city centers and increased social segregation in urban areas.

Source: Michael Godet (Conservatoire National des Artes et Metiers), "Into the next decade: major trends and uncertainties of the 1990's," Futures Vol 20 (1988), pp. 410-23. Huhes de Jouvenel (futuribles International), "Europe at the dawn of the third millennium: a synthesis of the main trends, "Futures Vol 20, October 1988, pp. 506-18; John Naisbitt and Patricia Aburdene, Magatrends 2000, (William Morrow & Company, New York, 1990).

Part Seven:
Outside Views

Chapter Twenty

A New Vision of Leadership

Michele Darling

If I wanted to cite a badly led corporation, I could think of no better example than Springfield Nuclear Power. Springfield Nuclear is best known for its most famous employee, the bumbling every-man Homer Simpson of Television's hit animated show, *The Simpsons*. But the reedy, slit-eyed CEO, C. Montgomery Burns, is the perfect caricature of the bad, old corporate leader. Burns, as those of you who are Simpsons' fans already know, is autocratic, covetous of money and power, contemptuous and flint-hearted.

His employee Homer is capable of indulging in petty malfeasance or precipitating a meltdown. Whatever the feckless Simpson does, however, C. Montgomery Burns can be counted on to respond with the sensitivity of Attila the Hun and the deviousness of a Borgia. He knows who number one is and how to look out for him.

The cartoon Mr. Burns has no perfect parallel in real life. The caricature is only interesting because it's a stereotype of the classic notion of what a big corporate boss is supposed to be like. And perhaps to a greater extent than we image, old stereotypes condition our thinking about leadership and what we think a leader ought to be.

It's easy to slip into. Modern corporations can face a daunting array of problems at any given time. Changing markets for products and services, competitive pressures, regulatory issues, labor problems, trade pacts—the list is endless. Wouldn't it be comforting to think that there was an all-seeing eye in the executive suite? A decisive, autocratic, knowledgeable and courageous leader? Someone who, as one former prime minister told us, realizes that a leader must be a leader?

I don't think so. The leadership profile I've just described is no longer effective. That's because our concept of what constitutes appropriate and effective corporate leadership is always changing. It is always being redefined. Let me give you a couple of examples.

Only a decade ago, we didn't automatically assume that CEOs would be aggressive corporate image builders or public spokes-people. Lee Iacocca of Chrysler showed us what CEOs could do in this regard. Others as diverse as George Cohon of McDonald's and Conrad Black of Hollinger have followed, refining the art of visible leadership.

In the early 80s, business leaders weren't routinely expected to be corporate visionaries. Leaders like Xerox Corporation CEO David Kearns, who set corporate direction with a clearly expressed vision, stood out among their peers. Today, most major corporations, including my own, have visions and statements of purpose that set their behavior.

Business realities are changing all the time. And as they do, corporate leadership—what the boss is doing, and ought to be seen to be doing—evolves and improves as well. What I'm writing about are some of the directions in which it has been evolving.

I'm going to suggest that we are heading toward a kind of business leadership that, in certain respects, is quite unlike the traditional form we've known. It's different from what most of us are used to and will require changes in our attitudes and actions, whether we're CEOs, managers or line employees.

A new reality has grown up around us and we have to reckon with it.

By the time I'm finished we'll be contemplating corporate leaders who are radically different from the fictional C. Montgomery Burns. If the trends I'm going to be talking about prevail, the best person to run Springfield Nuclear will turn out to be caring rather than caustic, generous with information rather than secretive. This person will be a mentor who will encourage, guide and support rather than bark orders.

We are already moving in this direction. Internationally respected CEOs such as Yotaro Kobayashi of Japan's Fuji-Xerox or Paul

O'Neil at Alcoa have been described as charismatic leaders, people with the ability to inspire in the traditional sense. But they are also renowned for their skills in motivating employees with coaching, training and moral support.

Corporate leaders reserve the right to make decisions, but they're also interested in democratizing their companies and getting increased employee involvement. Corporate structures are still more often than not hierarchical, but leaders are more aware than ever of the needs and feelings of their subordinates. There's a decided willingness to communicate and consult. There's systematic delegation of responsibility to lower levels of management.

These developments are expressed in many different ways. Management theorist Peter Drucker has likened the corporation to a symphony orchestra with the CEO/leader as conductor. In more practical terms, companies such as Heinz and Colgate-Palmolive do everything from reducing the middle layers of corporate management, thus freeing up communication between the CEO and line managers, to having different parts of the company treat each other as if they were independent suppliers. There is no one magic method, only a host of initiatives.

All these changes reflect the new realities that large corporations face. One person can no longer effectively control a large, multifaceted corporate enterprise. I don't care how many hours a leader works, how much management by walking around the leader may do, how intelligent or financially adept that person is. It is simply impossible to pull all the strands together on one desk.

Why is this so? To start with, we are in a period of increasingly rapid change in business. Take the financial services industry as an example. In the past year, we have had to deal with external issues including legislative changes that have further eroded the competitive barriers in the industry. We have faced public scrutiny over specific segments of our business such as credit cares.

And we've had to ponder the potential impact of Canada's participation in a North American Free Trade Agreement. Those are just a few of the items our corporate leaders have to contemplate in addition to day-to-day competitive pressures.

I don't think the financial services industry is unique in this. The degree and pace of change seems greater in all businesses. And as this happens, corporations are becoming more and more accountable—to customers, shareholders, suppliers, regulators, fiscally-strapped governments and, increasingly, the general public.

If you doubt what I'm saying, ask yourself any or all of the following questions. How have you experienced more intense competition in recent years? How have you felt your competitive position has been eroded since the last recession? Do you feel your employees are more demanding than they used to be and, as a corollary, do you find it harder than ever to find the right kind of employees with the right skills? Have you noticed that your customers are more demanding and prone to dictating the terms of your business relationship?

In this kind of challenging environment, unresponsive leadership runs the risk of failure. On the other hand, the right kind of leadership can make a huge difference; it can turn established thinking upside down. In this respect, I think of the great supermarket object lesson of the 1980s. The major producers of foods and household goods, the Procter and Gamble's and General Mills' of the world, used to dictate terms to the stores that stocked their products. You always knew that Tide and Wheaties would get good display and shelf space.

That is, until David Nichol of Loblaws came along. He proved with the development of the "President's Choice" product line that you could turn house brands into formidable national brands and completely upset a traditional supplier/customer relationship. It is not an isolated example.

The evolution of corporate leadership is also being influenced by changes in society. One way we see this happening is in the employee population. Society has become less rigid and more democratic. People question the status quo, sometimes to an extraordinary degree. We see this in family life, schools and universities, religious life and government. It is only logical that this trend should affect business.

Employees today are far less inclined to accept corporate bureaucracy and authoritarian management, than their parents were. The word "career" used to suggest lifetime employment with one company. Now we understand it to mean that an individual seeks betterment, in challenging work and improved living standards, wherever possible.

Internally, we can see this in the ambition people show to move into different areas of the corporation. And if we can't accommodate them, we know there's a reasonable chance that they'll seek satisfaction somewhere else.

You hear a lot in this country about the skills shortage and how it's luring us as we attempt to compete in global markets. What we sometimes ignore is the fact that employees very often have great skills and are highly motivated to use them. They want to make a contribution; they want to be recognized and rewarded.

How many times have you heard business leaders say their greatest resource is their people? It sounds trite, but it's true. One of the most compelling tasks for the evolving corporate leadership I've been talking about is to harness the enormous resource represented by employees.

How well are we doing at this and the other tasks of leadership? In many respects I think we're doing very well. In the past few years business leaders have to an unprecedented extent been rethinking what their companies do and how they operate. Abroad, there are some well chronicled examples such as General Electric Corporation chairman Jack Welch or Drake Business School CEO May Ann Lawlor. Here in Canada we can point to people such as IPSCO CEO Roger Phillips. All of them have shown leadership by helping their companies—their employees—adjust to new realities.

My own company, Canadian Imperial Bank of Commerce (CIBC), has spent a great deal of time and effort in recent years redefining what we do. We've tried to isolate the values that drive us and the things we want to achieve.

Our values—commitment to stewardship, respect for individuals, encouragement of initiative and creativity, the quest for excellence—are the clear and simple refined outpourings of arduous self-examination. So is our basic purpose—to be the leading performer in all our product areas.

Like all those authorities and books that we have been delighted with in recent times, I'm telling you that CIBC and other corporations are reinventing themselves to cope with new realities. And at the center of it all is the need for a vision, a sense of purpose and direction.

This affects the way we look at corporate leadership. I believe that the new realities we face, the pace of change and the uncertainty of life in general requires that leaders increasingly be visionaries who are capable of directing, encouraging and coaching others.

Peter Senge of the MIT Sloan School of Management put it very well in an article for the *Sloan Management Review*. He described what he called "learning organizations," companies that grow and prosper over the long term by adapting and regenerating themselves in the face of change. In these kinds of companies, he said, the role of the leader is no longer that of the charismatic decision-maker.

"Leaders are designers, teachers and stewards," he wrote. "These roles require new skills: the ability to build shared vision, to bring to the surface and challenge prevailing mental models, and to foster more systematic patterns of thinking. In short, leaders in learning organizations are responsible for building organizations where people are continually expanding their capabilities to shape their future—that is, leaders are responsible for learning."

Senge provides evidence that this style works. His best example recalls how Johnson & Johnson responded when one of its key products, Tylenol, was tampered with in 1982. The company referred to the credo developed by its founder 40 years before, a firmly implanted vision that starts with the assertion that "service to the customers comes first," and withdrew all stocks of the product from the market. The move was costly, but effective, and eventually Tylenol reclaimed its dominant place as a headache remedy.

Leadership that seeks to take a simple vision and then teach, nurture and shape a company is a challenging, demanding and exciting concept that ultimately brings success. Companies like Johnson & Johnson have known this for a long time; now many more realize it. It shows just how far we've come along the evolutionary cycle.

Implicit in this style of leadership are a number of things. As I've said, information is not to be hoarded, but communicated freely. People at all levels of an organization are to be looked at not merely as employees with specific work-related functions, but as well rounded human beings who are the sum of their parts.

And as someone whose company is engaged in a major effort to improve service, I can tell you that this style of leadership changes our notions of who supports who. As our Service/Quality campaign has taught us, it isn't the bottom of the organization that supports the top, but rather the other way around. The customer doesn't deal with the chairman or an executive vice president, but with loan officers and tellers.

This brings us to another of those truths about leadership. Power doesn't accrue to those who hoard it. Real power is obtained only by those who give it away. Or, as Colgate-Palmolive CEO Reuben Mark once put it: "You consolidate and build power by empowering others."

When leaders ignore these truths, when they attempt to be aloof or dictatorial, it's noticed. Consider a management practices survey that was done about a year ago in the U.S. by *Industry Week* magazine. In essence, it showed that as you move down through the

ranks of many business organizations, confidence in top managements' leadership ability deteriorates.

Decrying this tendency, *Industry Week* concluded: "Today, top executives are being called upon to behave as leaders—to set direction, establish goals and strategy, and help their workforces see
clearly how they can contribute to improvements in quality and
productivity."

This survey's findings seem consistent with what I see happening
in business and society as a whole. People crave strong leadership;
all you need to do to realize this is read the newspaper or listen to
radio phone-in shows or talk to your friends. Nobody out there
knows how to lead, we seem to be telling each other.

I think this attitude overstates the case. We live in an age where
problems can sometimes be more imagined than real. This is the
era of the scare headline and the superficial analysis and a lot of
the information we get is foreboding.

I also think, however, that we have to try to deal with people's
fears and clarify their uneasy perceptions. And I happen to believe
that leadership that shares information and knowledge, real
knowledge, and brings more people into the folds of events, is a
very good way to do it.

We've come a long way with our evolving idea of leadership. I
found a good indication of this in a recent book by the American
journalist Sally Helgesen. Helgesen went back to the work of management scientist Henry Mintzberg in the late 1960s and re-exam-
ined the profile he had assembled of top business leaders.

The pattern won't surprise you. Mintzberg's executive leaders
worked at an unrelenting pace through their days. They felt dis-
rupted by the unexpected. They made little or no time for non-
work activities. They were highly absorbed in the day-to-day
matter of their jobs and had little time for reflection. They kept
information to themselves.

By way of comparison, Helgesen looked at some of today's top executives and made some interesting discoveries. She found that they tend to work at a steady pace and schedule breaks in their day. They see interruptions as an important part of their job because they feel a need to be accessible and caring about the activities of people around them. They make time for non-work activities.

They focus on what Helgesen calls "the ecology of leadership," seeing management as a continuum with long range implications. They see dimensions of their lives beyond their jobs. They share information.

There were other differences, not to mention some interesting similarities Helgesen's executive leaders had with their historically distant counterparts, but the point is this. Generally speaking, the style of leadership has evolved considerably.

I have to put in an important qualifier here. The corporate leaders that Mintzberg studied were all men. The leaders Helgesen profiled were women. That's another measurement of how leadership has evolved. Roughly 20 years ago, the notion of a female CEO was a foreign one. But not any more, as we see more women assuming the top role.

You could conceivably make a case that women are intrinsically better suited to the style of corporate leadership that we practice today than men are. After all, women are supposed to be naturally more consultative, more caring, more liable to share power.

It will be a long while before we have any hard proof that women will make a difference in the realm of leadership. In my bank, women now constitute 14 percent of senior management. Five years ago, women held down perhaps three or four percent of those jobs so that's an impressive gain.

Indeed, there are more women generally in the management ranks at CIBC. And while it's too soon to be conclusive, there are indications that the most effective teams in our organization are those where there is a balance between men and women.

That's a positive sign, but we would like to have more senior women because it's simply good business—it widens the pool of talent available to us and it better reflects our customer base. Our chairman has set a goal of having women in one-third of all senior jobs.

In the end, though, such corrective actions aren't necessarily about leadership. Certainly, the qualities of leadership that I've been talking about have no reference to gender, race or creed.

Most of the references I've made have been to companies led by men. The development of less rigid hierarchies, the improved communication and consultation, increased delegation and the nurturing of employees' abilities and feelings—all have come in companies run by men. But they could have just as easily been companies led by women or minorities. Nobody, to my knowledge, has cornered the market on leadership ability.

Chapter Twenty-One

A Rating Agency Perspective

Susan Abbott

Securities analysis as applied by Moody's Investor's Service is aimed at providing the investing community with an independent opinion as to the ability of an issuer of fixed income securities to pay its obligations in a timely manner. This activity is an art, not a science, and requires a good deal of judgment regarding the probability of any given set of circumstances coming to bear on the future of an issuer. There are a variety of approaches taken by the agency in formulating its opinions, and a large number of components to an analysis. This paper describes one approach to fixed income securities analysis. It explores how the evolution in an industry from monopoly status to a competitive environment affects the critical elements of securities analysis including a shift of emphasis toward assessing management capability, and corporate culture.

Industry Overview

Electric utility companies, like telephone, and gas companies before them, are going through the wrenching changes that accompany the evolution from protected monopoly to market driven competitor. The accelerating globalization of trade and the slower economic growth of the U.S., Europe, and Japan have placed a much higher degree of competitive pressure on U.S. manufacturers. Consequently, industry in the United States is demanding lower electricity prices (especially where energy is a significant element in the production process) in an effort to lower costs to enable it to compete with global rivals. This market-driven need for lower energy prices is an important factor behind the movement to restructure and de-regulate the electric utility industry. To date, the most significant change in structure and regulation is contained in the National Energy Policy Act of 1992. That act, however, is basically a reflection of many fundamental changes that have already taken place in the industry. Moody's expects that the rate of change will accelerate over the next five years, driven primarily by economic forces. Those forces will put financial pressure on utilities and will threaten their credit quality. The degree to which those threats erode financial flexibility will depend on a company's relative cost position, its customer profile, its supply and demand position, the region in which it operates, its transmission capability, and the relative efficiency of transmission capabilities of surrounding utilities. Competitive pressures will lead to declining average credit quality for the industry and an increase in merger activity as utilities strive for greater efficiency and more defensible territories. The ultimate outcome will be heavily influenced by management's responses to these challenges.

The U.S. utility industry began to restructure in earnest in 1978 with the passage of the Public Utility Regulatory Policies Act (PURPA). In amending the Federal Powers Act, PURPA had a multiplicity of goals, including the promotion of energy conservation, the efficient use of electric utility resources, and the development of independent power projects defined as "qualifying facilities" (QFs). Many of the provisions of PURPA essentially provided for the development of broad rate structures that gave customers more choice, and reflected the cost of service. These provisions thus set the stage for greater pricing flexibility and more choice for the electric customer. As the world economy continues to become more competitive, the pressures brought by the industrial customer on rates charged by U.S. utilities are continuing to effect change in an industry where utilities had traditionally provided all the power at prices determined on a regulated rate of return basis. Now, power supply is increasingly available from a variety of alternative sources, and pricing is being defined more and more by what the market is willing to bear. Consequently, the ability to deliver competitively priced services will be dependent on a company's ability to focus on cost and customer satisfaction. The skills needed to accomplish this goal are very different from those needed to successfully run a regulated, cost of service based business.

The issues with which electric utilities are now dealing center around, first, their ability to maintain current large commercial and industrial customers through competitive pricing and service, and secondly, their pursuit of growth opportunities outside their own service territories. The National Energy Policy Act of 1992 officially opened up transmission to parties outside the traditional utility industry. The pressure on rates from industrial customers persists, new competitors continue to enter the generation business and major changes in the method of regulation of the U.S. electric utility industry are inevitable. In addition, activities being pursued outside the boundaries of the United States by certain utilities in the belief that better returns are available there add risk to these companies' profiles. In the long run, the confluence of these momentous changes is likely to lead to considerable pressure on the creditworthiness of U.S. electric utilities. In order to maintain a reasonable level of financial flexibility in a more competitive environment, a utility must offer superior service at the lowest possible price, and make wise investments that will earn a return commensurate with the risk profile of that activity. In order to succeed in a more competitive marketplace, utility managements will need to focus on creating value for all stakeholders; shareholders, bondholders, and customers alike. In addition, developing a new corporate culture that will encourage and empower all employees to participate in the successful redefinition of corporate objectives is essential if a company is to prosper in the new environment.

As industrial customers of electric utilities have choices and continue to demand lower electricity prices, and regulators respond with a new set of rules which allows for freer competition, electric utilities must change their focus in order to compete successfully. The ability to succeed in a monopolistic environment requires a set of skills that enables utilities to drive to a successful outcome of rate cases and other regulatory activities. The ability to negotiate with legislators and other politicians is key. Concern for consumers centered on the question of whether the level of satisfaction, or dissatisfaction would affect the company's relationship with the regulators.

Now, industrial customers have choices in the forms of self or cogeneration. And provisions in the National Energy Policy Act of

1992, although prohibiting retail wheeling from being ordered by federal regulators, have left the idea and the activity in the hands of state regulators and legislators. Michigan will be experimenting with limited retail wheeling, and California has outlined a plan to provide all customers choice by 2002. We are sure other states will be watching with great interest as these programs move forward. Retail wheeling legislation has not been passed in any other states, but even before the California and Michigan plans were announced, the threat of such revolutionary shifts in this historically protected industry resulted in dramatic changes.

The industry has responded to the demands of its industrial users by shifting its focus from the regulatory arena to its customers. The term "ratepayer" has been supplanted by the word "customer," indicating a shift away from a pattern of building a plant, putting it in rate base, raising rates, building a plant, putting it in rate base, raising rates . . . . Since the customer is no longer captive, and individual utilities are concerned that a larger universe of competitors will some day be vying for their customers, managements of electric utilities have found it necessary to reevaluate the critical success factors in their industry, and realign their management practices to succeed in a different environment.

Moody's overriding concern is whether any given management has the skills necessary to accomplish a very different set of goals than it possessed during most if its career. Identifying the critical success factors in a new environment is difficult enough. But organizing and motivating an entire work force that has operated on a different set of parameters for many years is an overwhelming task. Assessing the level of skill of a given management now requires the application of the kind of industrial analysis which takes into account free markets and competitive pressures. Although retail wheeling, and truly free competition is not yet a reality, it is on the way; and prudent analysts assume that it is here now. Likewise, decisions made by utility managements that adopt a "no regrets" strategy are more likely to lead to success in an environment of change than if they try to estimate the likelihood, timing or degree of more open competition.

As competition escalates, the need to keep prices down, or be able to reduce them overshadows the traditional relationship with the regulator. In addition, interest rates, on which allowed returns are determined, have dropped dramatically. As a result, were a utility to request a change in its prices to capture costs not currently reflected, regulators may lower the allowed returns to reflect the change in interest rates. Therefore, utilities are attempting to "recover" new costs by decreasing existing costs without having to risk a commission order to reduce the allowed return on equity. For a "cost of service" industry, this mindset is, indeed, difficult. It is not enough for management to understand the challenges ahead. Whole cultures must change. Work patterns must be examined for redundancies and inefficiencies. Cost must be driven out of the business at every opportunity. The only way this is going to happen is if all employees of the company are motivated and empowered to find ways to provide a reliable service that meets customers' needs at an acceptable price. Cutting costs is difficult for an industry that has such large sums of capital invested in production plant, and it therefore takes some imagination. It is not enough to cut staff. Eliminating positions without changing the way work gets done permits those eliminated positions to creep back into the system over time. Unless work patterns are changed, success will be elusive. In addition, empowering people requires that they have a larger picture of the business, what makes it work, and what part the individual plays in creating success. This too, is a daunting task for management. It must shift the power base, and the decision making process within the company to lower levels where the people who actually do the work can effect the most change.

Management and organizational skill in a changing competitive environment is an important determinant for success. However, an examination of more fundamental factors must be made to determine what point the company is starting from. We have defined Moody's mission, and described an analytical construct used to explore the creditworthiness of any given utility. We will also describe how the focus of our analysis has shifted in order to take into consideration the escalation of competition in the electric utility industry.

Important Factors in Rating Agency Analysis

In order to assess the potential for success or failure of any enterprise in this more competitive electric utility industry, analysts must look at the critical factors which influence the outcome of any given corporate strategy. In this section, we will examine the purpose of the analysis, and the structure of the analytical activity in order to better understand how Moody's assesses electric utilities.

Moody's Mission

The function that a rating agency performs in the capital markets is to provide accurate, impartial and independent opinions to investors on the ability of issuers to meet their fixed income obligations. Moody's evaluates the measure of protection that a company's sustainable cash flow is likely to provide bondholders. This enables investors to compare fixed income opportunities across borders, and ensures that investors pay the appropriate price for securities based on the credit quality of the issuer. The rating scale is essentially a universal language that indicates to investors the level of creditworthiness they can expect from any company issuing debt in the marketplace. The highest rating available is Aaa. Figure 1 contains the full rating scale from best to worst. Issues rated below Baa3 are judged to have "speculative" elements and their future cannot be considered as well-assured. In other words, there is a greater likelihood that payment of principle and interest on these securities will not be made on a timely basis in both good and bad times.

Analysis of the Electric Utility Industry

The electric utility industry in the United States has historically enjoyed high ratings because of the relatively protected nature of the participants. Companies have benefitted from monopoly status which has almost guaranteed a financial profile good enough to provide for timely payment of interest and principle in almost all cases. In fact, even the few electric utilities that have suffered bankruptcy have paid their obligations on their first mortgage bonds, despite the lack of a legal requirement to do so. Average ratings have fallen over the past decades under pressure

Figure 1
Rating Scale

Investment Grade	Aaa	Prime 1
	Aa1	Prime 1
	Aa2	Prime 1
	Aa3	Prime 1
	A1	Prime 1
	A2	Prime 1 & Prime 2
	A3	Prime 2
	Baa1	Prime 2
	Baa2	Prime 2 & Prime 3
	Baa3	Prime 3
Speculative Grade	Ba1	Not Prime
	Ba2	Not Prime
	Ba3	Not Prime
	B1	Not Prime
	B2	Not Prime
	B3	Not Prime
	Caa	Not Prime
	Ca	Not Prime
	C	Not Prime

of heavy construction requirements and regulatory disallowance of expensive nuclear investments. However, the industry still carries an average rating of A3, a highly respectable level in the mid investment grade range. The following discussion describes various elements that are examined in the determination of a rating.

Analytical Construct

Determining the rating of an electric utility involves a three-pronged approach: a fundamental analysis, a financial analysis, and a strategic position analysis. An examination of any utility from these three points of view allows Moody's to proffer an opinion about the likelihood of timely payment of principal and interest on any fixed income security issued by that utility.

Fundamental Analysis

The fundamental analysis of a company allows the analyst to assess the historical and current position of the company's business. The analyst determines the company's underlying strengths and weaknesses that will determine its ability to generate cash flow sufficient to pay its fixed income obligations on a sustained basis. The key areas of interest are the service territory and the stability of its economic base. Is it reliant on one or two dominant industries? Are the industries all cyclical, or are some less sensitive to the overall economy or counter cyclical? Diversity in an economic base adds stability to revenue flows, allowing for more certainty of cash flow and therefore the utility's ability to cover its fixed obligations.

Customer classifications— residential, commercial, or industrial— help the analyst understand the predictability of revenue generation. Residential customer usage is highly predictable, but is also very weather dependent, especially in climates subject to extremes of heat and cold. Residential usage is also inefficient, in that it creates sharp peak demands in times of extreme weather and at certain times of the day, usually in the early evening. Commercial customers are less predictable, but use a good deal more energy. Industrial customers use the most energy, but their usage tends to rise and fall with economic conditions.

An understanding of the sources of generation, the reserve margin and the generating cost position of the company are extremely important. How the energy that a company sells is generated can change the risk profile of a company, depending on such factors as fuel costs, volatility of fuel cost, reliability of generating plant, and the loss of a particular plant due to accident or malfunction. A nuclear plant, for instance, generates power at a very low incremental cost. However, its capital costs are usually quite high. If the plant is taken out of service for any reason, the company's incremental costs go up, its ability to generate power at low cost is damaged, and possible power replacement and capital costs may rise. In addition, because of the high capital costs, any margin erosion due to loss of power sales from that plant would damage the company's ability to cover its fixed costs.

The reserve margin position of any company can indicate the likelihood that it will be compelled to build new plant, thereby increasing risk as it engages in a construction program and re-enters the regulatory arena. Construction usually requires some raising of capital, sometimes distorting a company's capital structure by adding debt to the balance sheet without commensurate equity. And once a capital program is completed, the company faces the daunting task of requesting permission from state regulators to include the costs of the project in rate base. In the past decade, it has not necessarily followed that because a company believes it has taken the most prudent action to provide power supply to its customers, that regulators agree. Many utilities have suffered write-offs of plant costs as a result of regulatory disallowance of such costs.

Additional issues such as transmission capacity are also key, indicating the ability of the company to send or receive electricity without interruption. The company's propensity toward diversification has been important in the past because of its implications for dilution of the regulatory safety net for the overall enterprise. As utilities become more like traditional competitive industrial companies, diversification will continue to be important, but the analysis of those activities will be focused on whether management understands the new business instead of on how much dilution of the regulatory support system is created from diversified activities.

Finally, but most importantly, the regulatory and political environment, and management capability must be examined. These are issues that are very difficult to categorize, or capture in a single, meaningful description. They are, however, pivotal to the health of any electric utility. Regulatory practices vary from state to state, and a regulator's treatment of utilities varies from company to company within the same state. Regulators are charged with maintaining a balance between ratepayer and shareholder interests, functioning as a substitute for the free market. Regulation in the United States is based on cost of service plus a profit. Historically, analysts have focused on whether the profit allowed was fair in relation to the cost of capital in the marketplace, and on whether the manner in which the companies were permitted to collect their revenues was sufficient to enable them to actually earn the profit allowed. Whether regulators allow utilities to generate sufficient cash flow to cover its obligations can depend on whether regulators believe that the obligations the company has taken on are in the best interest of the ratepayers. If they do not, the company can face write-offs at worst, or just not be able to collect revenues to cover certain disallowed costs. This has a very destructive effect on the utility and can damage its financial flexibility if the disallowance is severe enough.

The management skill needed for success in a regulated environment is the ability to work successfully with regulators and politicians in addition to making sound business decisions. But because the customer base is basically captive, the utility manager has not traditionally focused much on the ratepayer beyond providing reliable service. Management's attention has been on regulation for the past 20 years. The analyst's focus has also been on whether management can successfully negotiate its way around the regulatory arena. Utilities have historically spent a good deal of effort on engineering and regulatory issues, trying to assure reliable service in a manner and at a cost acceptable to the regulators.

From an examination of these issues, an understanding of the company's history and the reasons for its current financial condition can be determined. For instance, many companies that completed nuclear plants after 1978, when the accident at the Three Mile Island nuclear plant took place, suffered cost overruns and completion delays resulting from ever changing NRC requirements. Subsequently regulatory disallowance of some of the costs associated with those plants resulted in lower cash generation in proportion to financial obligations. The companies are supporting assets for which they are not collecting any revenues, reducing the protection of interest and principal payments, and therefore, financial flexibility. Other companies have a history of adversarial relationships with regulators. As a result, their financial flexibility has suffered as regulators are not inclined to give the utility the benefit of the doubt, and come down on the harsher side of any question involving these companies.

Financial Analysis

The next step in an analysis is an examination of the financial statements, to evaluate a company's historical and current financial strength. Financial indicators are different for each company, and it is therefore difficult to describe a set of parameters that adequately define creditworthiness. Each combination of indicators is unique, and describes a different picture. The indicators of greatest importance are cash flow measurements. Cash flow interest coverage, cash flow for construction, and cash flow as a percentage of debt outstanding are especially important. Capital ratios are also important, and are typically adjusted to reflect off-balance-sheet items such as lease payments, and purchased power obligations. An accounting convention used for regulated utilities is an account entitled "allowance for funds used during construction," which is a non-cash account that adds to earnings. It is important to determine the quality of earnings in terms of how much of net income is actually non-cash earnings. Debt service, dividend payments and other financial obligations are paid in real money. Therefore, real money must be available to cover those obligations. If a large portion of earnings is a result of accounting practices, the enterprise is less able to pay its obligations.

A thorough examination of the financial accounts, their footnotes, and anomalies to the accounts will allow the analyst to determine the current financial strength of the company. This is a starting point from which to gain an understanding of future challenges the company faces. The analyst is able to determine whether the company is starting from a position of strength or weakness.

Strategic Position Analysis

The third stage of the analysis is exceedingly important, especially in light of the fundamental changes the industry is facing. The analyst is interested in upcoming challenges, how the company plans to overcome obstacles, and whether financial projections are realistic, attainable, and sustainable.

The issues that have been of most importance historically have included territorial growth, construction plans and resource requirements, regulatory issues, the changing competitive environment, and organizational issues that may hinder achievement of goals. An analysis of a company's strategic plan assesses whether management has appropriately recognized the issues facing it, how it plans to deal with those issues, and whether organizational and managements skill are sufficient. It is also important to assess how aggressive the plans are, how realistic the expected outcomes, and what the impediments to success may be. In that process, an analysis of financial projections is done, including an understanding of the assumptions that have been made, how dependent success is on regulatory activity, and whether there is any cushion in the projections for the unexpected. A review of management's track record is also important. Some managements have been very accurate in their past projections. Others have a tendency to overestimate their likely success, leading the analyst to take a more skeptical view of the company's ability to meet goals.

Analysis of a Newly Competitive Industry

Fundamental, financial, and strategic position analyses are vital to assessing credit quality of any industry. These components don't change because of the introduction of competition to an industry. But the emphasis does shift. A rating analyst is still interested in growth in the service territory, but instead of seeing growth as being, on balance, positive, the risk associated with providing for that growth becomes more important. Historically, high levels of growth presented a utility with the challenge of providing for greater demand by building new generating plant on which it would earn a profit under traditional rate of return regulation. The concern has shifted over the past two decades to whether regulators will allow the company to include all of the costs of new construction projects in rates once the project is completed. In a competitive environment, growth represents not just the need to provide additional capacity, but also represents an attractive opportunity to competitors. Choices that a utility must make now are somewhat different. Instead of focusing largely on the engineering questions surrounding new capacity additions, electric utility managements must also consider how additional capital expenditures will affect the company's cost structure. Will they increase the average cost of generation? Will production costs increase to a point that is above that of a neighboring utility which might then want to try and attract your customers? Will they make the company less competitive in the wholesale market, or, in the event of retail competition, less competitive with retail customers? Will increasing demand attract independent power producers, and if so, does management wish to purchase power from them, and what are the consequences of that decision?

Sources of revenues have taken on a different cast as well. Prior to this period of potential retail competition, getting a third of your revenues from industrial customers was considered not just normal, but desirable. Industrial customers use a lot of energy. In addition, in many jurisdictions, industrial customers subsidize residential customers' rates to a certain extent, keeping residential rates artificially low. Residential ratepayers are also voters. Industrial companies don't vote. Therefore, regulators and politicians were anxious to keep residential rates low whenever possible. Of course, too much industrial concentration has never been good, because the economic difficulties of large customers could present a threat to the utility. That is still true. But now, industrial customers are the ones agitating the most for reduced prices, and are the only customers that have the choices. They can self generate, or co-generate. Therefore, a utility with a large industrial base of customers is not only at risk in the event that economic conditions affect its industrial customer base adversely, but it is also under pressure to reduce its prices to those customers or lose them altogether. Large commercial customers can also be threatened. Residential customers are not yet at risk, although it is not inconceivable that at some point in the future, all customers will have the option to choose an electric provider other than the local utility. But for the time being, having a large industrial base represents the greatest risk in regard to revenue classification.

One of the biggest changes in the past few years involves the issue of cost. The electric utility industry has historically been regulated on the basis of cost plus a rate of return with reliability of service far more important than cost. Utilities were rewarded for, and therefore motivated to, undertake the building of new generating capacity. According to the regulatory scheme, if a company builds a plant that is used and useful, it will be placed in ratebase and customers will pay for it. Other stakeholders will benefit from a return on the capital used to build the plant. Under this system, utility management is concerned with building a plant that works well and working effectively with the regulators to ensure that the plant will be allowed in the rate base, and that shareholders will receive a return. In a more competitive environment, the ability to sell products at a competitive price must be the focus. Companies therefore have to concentrate on keeping costs down, rather than getting costs included in rate base. Instead, creation of stakeholder value takes on paramount importance.

In a competitive environment, management decisions surrounding new generating capacity will need to change as well. Large central station plants with generating capacities of 800 megawatts to 1200 megawatts represent an idea whose time has passed. Not only has demand growth slowed to 1-2% per year in many parts of the country, making large baseload capacity additions unnecessary, but the capital needs for baseload plants are so enormous as to potentially inflate a company's cost structure, and undermine its competitive position. Traditional considerations of diversity of generating sources, purchased power expenses, and the volatility of fuel prices continue to be of concern. Finding ways to satisfy demand reliably at the lowest possible price, enabling the company to minimize costs and maintain or improve its competitive position should be the focus. This requires a shift in organizational mindset. All employees need to be motivated to find more efficient ways to accomplish assigned tasks. This calls for a fuller understanding of how the whole enterprise functions, and a more bottom-up management style. For an industry that has prided itself on first rate operations for 50 or 60 years, with less concern for the cost of service than other, competitive industries have had, the compromises needed in order to minimize costs, satisfy an increasingly restless customer base, and still provide reliable service are an enormous challenge. A commitment to being a low cost, high performance company is required at all levels, from the chairman's suite, to the plant maintenance staff in order to successfully meet these challenges.

An ancillary, but still very important issue in the U.S. electric utility business is that of diversification. As regulators lower allowed returns on equity in response to lower interest rates and cost of capital, and the lack of natural growth in the United States, companies are turning to opportunities outside the U.S. There are many areas in the world where electric systems are being privatized and economic growth far outstrips that of the United States. These situations represent an attractive opportunity for U.S. electric utilities who know how to build generating stations, but don't have the opportunity any longer at home. Although the propensity of a large portion of the industry to take advantage of these circumstances is understandable, the risks of building generating plant, and conducting business in a foreign location is naturally greater than it is at home. Electric utilities know how to build generating plant, but the political, currency, and cultural risk the companies will encounter elsewhere is new to them. The threat of appropriation of the project by an unstable government, the risk of being unable to repatriate earnings, and the difficulties of doing business in an unfamiliar culture make the risk associated with these opportunities of concern.

Regulatory and Political Environment

In an atmosphere of change and uncertainty, the question of what form regulation will take in the future is a critical one. Likewise, the flexibility of the regulator during a period of transition to a more competitive environment is extremely important if a utility is to adjust to a competitive focus. Command and control behavior on the part of the regulators with no willingness to adapt to new circumstances will put a company in a disadvantageous position. Instead of seeking the highest rate of return as one would as a regulated monopoly, in a competitive world a utility must focus on meeting customer needs in both price and service. Without the regulatory flexibility to change the terms of service to a customer, a utility will become unable to meet its customers needs in a timely manner, and in the end, lose that customer to a competing choice. Similarly, regulators are facing choices themselves. They need to ask themselves what kind of regulation is most constructive in a competitive environment. Regardless of whether the regulator is in favor of competition or not, it already exists. If a regulator recognizes that traditional rate of return regulation motivates utilities to make choices, like building new baseload plant, that are not necessarily compatible with that company's competitive position, and is willing to devise new, and more constructive regulatory frameworks, it is likely that a utility will be better able to succeed in a more open marketplace.

The fact that federal regulators do not have the authority to order retail wheeling, and that state regulators are not, by and large, in favor of a quick transition to such an environment may, in and of itself, delay the implementation of widespread retail wheeling. We do believe, however, that retail competition, in whatever form, will continue to reshape this industry, and will require management and regulators to think differently about their roles.

Management

While regulatory response to changes in the industry is important, the response of management is even more pivotal. A formerly collegial industry is dealing, for the first time in 60 years, with incipient competition. There has always been competition in the wholesale market, and in the form of self generation. Co-generation was encouraged by the Public Utilities Regulatory Powers Act in 1978, escalating retail competition. Now, with the possibility of retail wheeling, the industry is facing a potentially dramatic escalation of competition. Utilities must think in terms of customers, instead of ratepayers. They need to focus on developing products

that meet their customers' needs, not just provide reliable generation and transmission. Companies whose monopoly status formerly encouraged them to share information readily now need to
engage in competitive intelligence activities to determine what
other companies are doing without giving away their own plans.
The shift to this completely new way of thinking is the greatest
challenge facing the electric utility industry today. Managers who
have lived their entire professional lives honing the skills needed
to build first class generating plant, and to deal successfully with
regulatory barriers must now turn their attention to reducing and
keeping costs low, finding out what the needs of the customers are,
and satisfying those needs. They must develop profitable new
markets perhaps outside the traditional service territory, balance
costs and quality of service, and most importantly, shift the focus
of the workforce to make it effective, accountable and driven by
competitive fervor. This may require breaking the utility into business units, accountable for their own costs and profitability, training employees to operate successfully in a customer driven
business instead of a regulatorily driven one, "right sizing," and
other relatively disruptive reorganization efforts.

Changing the mindset of an entire workforce is very difficult. People are naturally resistant to change, but they can accept it more
easily if they feel that they are involved in decision making. The
key to successful re-deployment of workers is an acculturation
shift which empowers them by giving them a complete understanding of the challenges ahead, and motivating them both
monetarily and psychically to drive the cost savings and customer
focus from the bottom up. A successful utility will be one that has
encouraged and empowered all its people to help produce profitable, sustainable business in a less predictable, more challenging
environment.

Chapter Twenty-Two

The Need for and Process of Cultural Change: The Observations of Experience

Bruce E. Alspach

> **cul-ture 1.** The totality of socially transmitted behavior patterns, arts, beliefs, institutions, and all other products of human work and thought typical of a population or community at a given time.
>
> *Webster's II New Riverside University Dictionary*

How many times have you heard, "that's not the way we do things here?" What is really being said is, "the culture of our organization has prescribed methods and ways of doing things and if you want to get anything done, you had better learn these ways!"

And generally, a successful company has a functional culture that contributes as much as strategy or people. The stories and examples are endless: a weekly beer and pizza party, the boss's office co-located with the workers, the button down white shirt and dark suit, or the management golf game. What works, works. The issue is what to do when it doesn't work. The answer to that question is easy—change the culture—but first you need to demonstrate that the culture is the culprit.

Culture is not the first thing management generally focuses on when things go wrong. A typical first reaction is to blame the marketplace or economy: "our customers are experiencing . . . " or "the economy is not showing growth. . . " When we see market share erode, it becomes the competitions' fault, "how can they stay in the business when they price below costs?" And when the blame can't be placed externally, the strategy comes into question, "do we have the right product" or "is the pricing plan accurate." Pretty soon, the organization is challenged, ". . . its just too expensive to have all these people" or "we really need to re-engineer the work and improve the . . ." Finally, we attack the leadership, ". . . the manager just can't do it" or ". . .the manager just doesn't get it." And not once did culture get challenged, examined or advocated. Why?

Culture comes slowly to an organization. It is an evolutionary product that is shaped by the actions of every person in the organization. Events perceived as positive get good internal press while events perceived as negative are held up as examples of what not to do—positive and negative reinforcement. Over time, the strategy, people, organization and culture come together. If the result is business failure, then the organization becomes a lost civilization. But if the organization is a success, then the civilization flourishes; its history proudly shared and its way, or culture, boastfully preached. How many times have you heard "do it this way" and you too will be successful! And it works! Great, but over time perhaps results come less frequently or with greater effort. The competition has launched a new initiative and you respond with a new strategy. But wait a second, the strategy implementation requires behaviors a bit different than the accepted way and it doesn't feel right, it doesn't fit—its uncomfortable.

Guess what, it is uncomfortable. It is uncomfortable for you and your team and the organization. It didn't address the behavior patterns, it didn't support the beliefs and institutions. It didn't fit! This is the beginning of the cultural mismatch and you must decide to keep the culture, evolve it gradually or change it radically.

Knowing this, what are the rules to follow when you want to consider, or have made the decision, to change the culture? Well, based on experience, here are some "observations" you can compare notes with:

Culture is Driven by Process
It is never a case of "if it ain't broke, don't fix it"—cultures are neither right nor wrong. Culture is not driven by an objective, it is driven by the process of attaining the objective. The strategy defines the objective; the implementation process defines the culture of the organization. How are meetings held, who can speak up, is there debate or simply consensus? Who can make decisions, how

big, how quick. Are mistakes acceptable or even encouraged? And ultimately, the culture reinforces the process. And that becomes the catch—when the process no longer works, the culture needs to be changed to allow new processes to be introduced.

No Amount of Cultural Matching Can Fix a Bad Strategy

Cultural issues are the latest area of management interest. How many times have you heard, ". . . to redefine the culture of this organization and be more customer focused . . . with shorter product to market cycles . . . "? Those sound a lot more like objectives than behavior. Perhaps what is being said is, " . . . management has allowed itself to become consumed with internal behavior patterns and instead of looking out for the customer, we have been focused on internal institutions that promoted parochial beliefs." If that is really the case, it is doubtful a fundamentally sound strategy exists in the first place.

In all probability, the strategy is infested with parochial interest and beliefs. If performance focused R&D got the business to its current position, but the market is looking for lower cost, don't bet that technology oriented management will yield to the marketing people! That's why "skunk works" blossomed and flourished! They allowed a strategy to be articulated and implemented outside cultural boundaries.

A Good Strategy Can be Ruined by a Cultural Mismatch

Cultural and strategic matching require a well articulated strategy. But when things go wrong, it is often the strategy that gets blamed or scrapped when the culture pulled everything down. That response to the competitive initiative; did it share the same objectives as those pursued in the past? All the objectives? Not just the basics: market share, profitability, growth etc., but how about the unwritten social contracts, or the environmental awareness or the community involvement? Are you going to work your team three times harder and void their little league coaching commitments? Will that slightly premature product introduction blemish your outstanding quality record? Will that new procedure force a customer service person to say, "I'm sorry, I can't help you?" Matching strategy and culture requires consideration of all the objectives.

Strategy Influences Plans, Culture Influences Actions

Failures are too often explained in terms of strategy, market, people and other tangibles. And likewise, cultures are too often described in terms of objectives instead of desired behaviors. And this is where the impact of culture on strategy is so very great. Strategy tells us what we want to do, the path we want to follow. A good strategic plans defines goals and objectives, it speaks to what we want to be versus what we are. It doesn't describe how the people will go out and make it happen. Culture can make or break the strategic outcome. How the people go about implementing the strategy will be decided by the culture. If the strategy is evolutionary and actions established, the business will move right along. But when the strategy is revolutionary and new actions are demanded, attention must be paid to both simultaneously. Luckily, since wholesale changes are not frequent, the organizational culture has time to adapt and evolve. But when it doesn't have time to evolve, watch out!

Successful Cultures Resist Change

A good strategy develops into a good business which develops a strong culture which creates a powerful infrastructure which prevents changing the basic strategy which starts the business into a downward spiral which forces a major realignment of the senior management which brings in a new strategy which may or may not start the cycle all over again. There has got to be a better way!

The senior management must be able to articulate the culture and be prepared to modify it in advance of a strategic change. How does the organization work right now; how does it need to work in the future? How fast is the competition moving, does your organization move as fast? Why not? How many review cycles do you have? What functions are the mythical icons and is success still defined by them?

328

When two organizations get together, say in a merger or a consolidation, it's essential to consider the differing cultures. What's important to each one, what are the hot buttons, what are the fears and concerns. How does each organization process its work; how important are the social (coffee pot) interactions? What behaviors do you want to continue, and which do you want to squelch? Can each side be a winner? What is the informal organization and why do it leaders prevail? The answers to these questions and the actions taken to address them will provide significant rewards.

Perhaps one organization was confrontational, enjoyed open aggressive meetings where facts and opinions were placed on the table. The other consisted of a more gentile group where conflict was studiously avoided and consensus was developed outside the actual meeting. Imagine the first gathering, the frustrations encountered by both organizations. Nothing—at least nothing positive—would transpire. Notice, no one approach is more correct than the other, each has its strengths and weaknesses.

At this point it is up to the leadership to define what behavior is acceptable. Which style will be allowed to dominate—and when.

Culture Allowed to Institutionalize Equals Bureaucracy

When a culture begins to permeate the organization, good intentioned people begin to document and institutionalize the behaviors that have been adopted by the organization. Over time, as the environment changes, the requirements of a progressive organization also begin to evolve. And then the documented behaviors rise up to drag the necessary change down. Remember the stories about reports? The manager who got hundreds of pages of reports and questioned who read them all. Without announcement, the reports were stopped and nary a soul voiced an objection. Such is institutionalized culture. It continues behaviors and rituals performed in the context of what worked yesterday and not what is required today.

When Change is Imminent Consider the Cultural Impact

Nobody likes change. Great efforts are taken to minimize the impact of change. We over-communicate, we give time for mourning (all change is loss), we involve people in the change. And the change is made and we go about our business operating with essentially the same culture as before. And much change can be accommodated within the existing culture, but not all change. This has been preached over and over in the context of quality—it comes from the top; management must demonstrate its commitment to the company wide drive for quality. And the same is true for the less global changes—different cultural models must be adopted that reinforce the desired behaviors. It can be something as simple as shorter, more focused meetings—take away the chairs and coffee pots. And consider the impact of indirect change—the great example here is a layoff, focus on the remaining people and not only those going out the door.

Cultures Can be Changed: Check the Cultural Icons!

As you walk around your business newly sensitized to the behaviors and cultures around you, it's easy to be overwhelmed by the multitude of cultural icons. Office layouts, decorations, business equipment and even doors which are open or closed. One completely innocuous example—dual overhead projectors. A newly arrived GM insisted that presentations be made from dual overhead projectors and that no light be allowed between slides. After that person failed, the second projector was forever retired, a symbol of what not to do. That's probably not how you would want to see your culture changed, but the lesson is there—seize that icon which best typifies what you want changed and make a public example of its retirement. How about the TV commercial from United Airlines where a business owner walks in and says an old friend just called to say good-bye, we lost his business because he didn't see us anymore. Then out come the airline tickets and the closing line is, "I'm off to see an old friend." Powerful stuff. Think that sales organization will embrace personal selling? You bet! And of course, the drama you create is dependent upon the situation. You just need to know what to change.

330

Leadership Requires a Conscious Understanding of the Culture

Cultures will evolve based on perceived success or failure. The proposal format, the business meeting, attire or travel plans—everyday functions of a business but carefully watched to define what is acceptable or unacceptable. And what is acceptable is generally in a narrow range of choices when considered against the possibilities. Repetition of successful themes reinforces what must be done. And soon, style over substance prevails, the path of least resistance becomes the path of choice. Leadership must remain in control of the culture, keep it working in a positive direction by challenging it when it dictates how things get done. What is the objective and what is the behavior? Do I want the same style meeting for a high risk proposal review as I want for a discussion on future strategies?

Look around at the meetings. The presentation styles, the interaction between team members and the decision process. Is it homogenous or is it tailored to the situation? Are the right facts being considered, are the same people asking all the questions? Are things happening fast enough or with enough diligence?

Look beyond the meetings, look at all the person to person interactions within and external to the business. Is the actual behavior equal to the desired behavior? How are customers' questions being answered? How are communications to the employees managed?

There Are Many Ways to Implement Cultural Change

As you consider what needs to be done, think about the impact you want to make. Do you want dramatic change, is it necessary? Then it better be very focused. Do you want an evolution? Then pick around the edges and work towards the core. A physical reality which can be used in both cases comes to mind: a frog tossed into a pot of boiling water has the reflexes to jump out unharmed but a frog placed in a pot of cool water over a burner will be boiled alive. Undesirable behaviors can be terminated with a shock; desirable behaviors can best be incorporated gradually.

Target the Behaviors that Make a Difference and Can be Modified

Remember the eighty/twenty rule? It applies here also. The more you dig into a situation where significant change is necessary, the more change you want to do. Don't. What are the key drivers, where will you get the most bang for your buck. And when you have multiple locations, address the business issues, not the local color—unless that is the problem. And if it is, it may be bigger than you—don't try to instill your nationalistic culture on foreign soil! Instead, look for the independent behaviors and focus on those which can be modified.

Provide the Framework for Cultural Change and Let the People Implement

So now you have identified the new culture, you know what you want to change. It fits the strategy. You want to get it done. Communicate the program. Set the example. Let people follow. Coach them, guide them, let them get comfortable with the new way. Let them experiment. They probably will catch on quicker than you think and make very positive suggestions along the way.

Don't Throw the Baby Out with the Bathwater

Now that you are actively changing the culture, discarding the old and creating the new, you must still provide the vision of where the people are going. You must lead. And in the process of leading, setting the new examples and letting the people define new and better ways, having a say in how things will be done, watch out for one key thing—don't abdicate. Define your role and cultivate it. Create the icons that reinforce society as you perceive it—whatever it may be. Be decisive. Are you the coach or the quarterback of a high performing team? Both positions are necessary and effective yet with very different roles. Lead, know where you are going and what your added value is today and tomorrow.

Summary

Culture is that very important third element in strategy implementation, a peer with programs and people. The best strategy can be a non-starter without any one of the three elements, but culture is one of the hardest to identify, critique and change. Why? Because it doesn't impact our objectives, perhaps going after market share or value pricing. Nor does it impact to whom we have delegated the task. But it does impact our leadership of the organization, it gets right to core of how we conduct business.

And above all, remember this: the culture of an organization is defined by its leadership. Leadership determines the personality and behavior of the organization. Your cultural agenda will only succeed if you "walk the talk." Good luck!

Chapter Twenty-Three

No Ethics, No Change

Mark J. Pastin, Ph. D.

Change has been at the top of the management menu through boom, recession and now recovery. We simply haven't found the right way to organize for today's and tomorrow's economy. Despite a decade of down-sizing, right-sizing and reorganizing, we are not much better at implementing change. One of the reasons we have not improved our ability to change organizations is that we still do not understand the relationships among organizational culture, organizational ethics and change. Very simply, organizational culture is a barrier to adaptive change, while adaptive change is impossible without attention to organizational ethics.

I focus on culture as an impediment to adaptive change for several reasons. While organizational culture qualified as a management fad in the middle 1980s, it has outlasted suspicion as a fad. Today, admitting "I ain't got no culture" is like admitting "I can't read"; you only make those around you think that you have lost interest in management. Organizational culture has struck a resonant chord in just those managers who are not typically taken in by fads. They sense there is something important about whatever it is that constitutes organizational culture. This instinct is sound even if organizational culture is the wrong vehicle for it.

Even though organizational ethics and organizational culture are closely related, the obsession with culture does not extend to ethics. Ethics is seen either as an add-on embellishment or as an adjunct to the organization's legal compliance efforts. But the truth is that ethics is the heart of organizational culture. In fact, if ethics is the heart of organizational culture, then the myths, symbols, rituals, ideologies, and customs—the elements of culture on which the organizational culture movement focuses—are the fat around the heart, strangling it and destroying its vitality.

Ethics is not only the heart of organizational culture, it is also the fulcrum for producing adaptive organizational change. Since ethics is the fulcrum for change, changing an organization without ethics is akin to changing a tire without a jack. The adaptive organization seeks strong ethics and weak culture. This dynamic combination is the key to promoting change that is timely, not chaotic, and supported by key organizational constituencies.

To understand why a strong organizational culture inhibits adaptive change, while strong organizational ethics facilitates adaptive change, we need to look at what organizational culture and organizational ethics really are.

Culture

Let us begin with a quick overview of culture: Marvin Bower defines culture as "the way we do things around here." [1] In other words, culture addresses **how** things are done as much as **what** is done.

The definition I prefer says that culture is all the "historically created designs for living, explicit and implicit, rational, irrational, and nonrational, which exist at any given time as potential guides to the behavior of men." [2] Cultures are conservative, judging the future by the past, and often irrational.

The question the definitions raise is: Why would any organization want a strong culture? A strong culture puts basic beliefs, attitudes, and ways of doing things beyond question. But unquestionables must be questioned for an organization to be quick on its feet, strategic, and capable of adaptive change. Because cultures are rooted in tradition, they reflect what has worked, not what will work. Can anyone doubt that AT&T's problems in adapting to a competitive environment were partly due to its bureaucratic culture? IBM's

---

[1] Bower, M. *The Will to Manage* , New York: McGraw-Hill, 1966, p. 23

[2] Kluckhohm, C., and Kelly, W. "The Concept of Culture." In R. Linton (ed.), *The Science of Man in the World*. New York: Columbia University Press, 1945, p. 97

long struggle to reorient itself has been as much a struggle against its past culture as the marketplace.

Cultures are, by consensus, hard to change. The stronger the culture, the harder it is to change. And most established organizations have strong, if not attractive or "appropriate," cultures. Passenger railroads had strong cultural traditions (poor service, disregard for passengers). Most chose to perish rather than change. The steel industry was afflicted by a strong adversarial and anti-entrepreneurial culture.

Finally, culture is process oriented rather than result oriented. Who cares if the process is right if you do not get the desired results? There is little consolation in knowing you ran the plays right if you lose the game.

In some ways, the recent management fad for re-engineering organizations is an acknowledgment of the failure of strong organizational cultures. But re-engineering suggests that the issue is one of throwing out the bad old ways and finding new better ways. But the problem is really one of focusing on the hows rather than the whats in both the culture and re-engineering ideologies.

If the complaint about organizational cultures is that they change too slowly, the complaint about ethics is that it is changing too fast. ("What happened to the work ethic of integrity, honesty, and hard work?") This is puzzling since the ethics of a person or an organization is no more or less than the basic ground rules by which the person or organization operates. What is the relationship of ethics to culture? Are there strong-ethics, weak-culture companies?

The Ethics-Culture Connection

The ethics of an organization is no more or less than the basic ground rules which determine what actions are acceptable, commendable and approved versus actions that are prohibited, discouraged, and disapproved. One way of putting this is to say that an organization's ethics is the basic **social contract** governing day-to-day actions in the organization. Ethics is closer to the surface of an organizational culture than other components (myths, ideologies, and anesthetics). When an organization enforces its ethics, its ground rules come into view. When the every-man-for-himself ethics of an organization forces out a female executive, she sees one strand of the organization's ethics clearly. When my former boss said, "Pastin, you're too aggressive," I learned that the ethics of my organization said, "Don't make waves."

Ethics has another role. Ethics is the forum in which societies, groups, and organizations argue fundamental changes in their bylaws (ground rules). American society has been torn by ethical debate on abortion. Some segments of society seek a change to a more permissive ethics of abortion. Other segments seek a return to a past ethics (they would be among those who say that ethics changes too quickly). Criticism is as much a part of ethics as enforcement is. You can ignore criticism of your aesthetic ("You call that music?"), your ideology ("You can't be serious about voting for him?"), and even your personality ("You lack drive!"). But if someone criticizes your ethics, take heed.

Ethical criticism is not offered lightly and is not to be taken lightly. If you disregard ethical criticism by the group you belong to, you state your willingness to exit the group. You are saying that you regard the organization so lightly that you do not even care about its ground rules.

For an organization to change and adapt, its culture must *learn*. It must allow challenges to its basic principles in a setting that tolerates some change without threatening to undo the organization. Thus, organizational culture promotes discussion of issues in ethical terms and mandates that these discussions are serious. This is functional in that it provides an opportunity for a culture to change while keeping what is valuable in the culture intact. It is dysfunctional in that it remands vital issues to the court of interminable discussion, out of the line of action. Since the discussion is held in the culture's living room, fundamental change is inhibited. It is like discussing modernism on the steps of the Parthenon.

The moral of the story for managers? *If you want to initiate basic change in your organization, start discussing ethics.*

But do you want to and will it work? The answer is a qualified yes. We shall first look at an organization that initially tried to change its culture without using ethics to do so. (When I say that the organization, Motorola, initially attempted a culture change without using ethics, I mean that Motorola did not look at culture change in ethical terms until it ran into problems.)

Good Deal, Bad Deal

Motorola was one of the first major corporations in the United States to see the advantages of participatory management. The company committed significant resources to creating a company-wide culture of participation. Motorola began by fostering participation at the level of workers and their supervisors. Workers liked it or, at least, accepted it. Once supervisors got used to putting in the time (a lot) required to foster participation, the performance of their units improved. So did the supervisor's compensation. The program stalled at middle management.

What halted the program at middle management? The philosophy "This too will pass" is entrenched at this level. Experienced managers know that other programs have been tried and that one survives by producing results. Motorola's middle managers "knew" this wisdom and acted accordingly.

Unlike the workers' jobs, the middle managers' jobs were unprotected by union contracts or the mimicking of union contracts in nonunion companies. In theory, two compensations make this a fair deal: Middle managers have the opportunity to make more money and rise to higher rank, and they have the freedom and security of being able to move laterally to an equivalent or better position in another company. Motorola's participation program threatened both compensations.

The middle managers continued to be elevated by the numbers. It is almost impossible to quantify good participation. Shouldn't

339

middle managers be able to translate good participation into good numbers? Good participators should not receive two rewards for the same conduct, as they would if good participation and good numbers were separately rewarded.

The problem: Motorola's middle managers were already "stretched out." Time spent on participation would detract from the numbers for the foreseeable future. There was also a sense of hypocrisy. Middle managers were expected to listen to every suggestion offered by line workers. But they felt that they were not equally listened to by those above. They "knew" too that numbers were still the game and, moreover, that top management would not yield one iota of its power to give middle managers more say over top-level decisions.

Surely, you say, the managers who did not like the new culture could leave. Not so easy, even in the most robust of economies. The participation program required that managers concentrate less on their own areas of specialization and become more familiar with other areas. The managers thus moved from area to area, spending more time "learning the company" and less time developing skills related to their training. They became more specialized as Motorolans and less specialized in finance or engineering. This lowered their market value.

Motorola's move to a culture of participation met resistance because of ethics. The relevant concept is fairness. The shift to a participatory culture produced a correlated shift in the implicit contract between the company and its middle managers. The program to change the culture did not reckon with this shift in the implicit contract.

Most cultural changes are thwarted by middle managers. Middle managers are the lubricant in these changes. When an implicit contract is violated in a one-sided way, there is a response. Since middle managers cannot start a protest movement or go on strike, they respond quietly. They slow the program down, talk about its silliness, and create an atmosphere of unworkability. Underhanded but effective. *Whenever an organizational change is*

340

perceived to disadvantage one group, that group will take action or in-action to restore perceived fairness.

Motorola's top management caught this problem in time. Top management realized that one of the firm's ground rules stated that all that really matters are the numbers. So they created ways of quantifying participatory success. They also realized that you cannot have a ground rule emphasizing the value of listening to those beneath you unless you, too, listen. Motorola's top managers now bend over backward to listen to managers and employees at every level.

Motorola's top management restored fairness, and it has worked. Motorola dealt much more effectively with the downturn in the semiconductor industry in the 1980s than many of its U.S. com-petitors, and it has moved successfully into telecommunications and consumer markets.

Change by Contract

Whenever you attempt to change an organization in fundamental ways, you shift the underlying implicit contracts of the organiza-tion—the unstated **social contract** or ethics. Even if the changes are fair, the process is upsetting, since it creates uncertainty about the ground rules by which organization members live. They do not know if the contract shifts will be fair. And we have seen that the changes can be quite unfair to some groups, groups with the power to thwart change.

Looking more closely at social contract ethics reveals a model for achieving organizational change without the pitfalls of culture.

Social contracts are *not* explicitly negotiated. Social contracts are carried by the cultures of the groups, organizations, and society to which we belong. While cultures carry social contracts, there is lit-tle correlation between the strength of the culture and strength of the contract it carries. (Bodies carry brains, but there is little corre-lation between the strength of the body and the strength of the brain.) The social contract is an implicit agreement about the

341

ground rules or ethics of the group. Organizational social contracts establish ground rules relating to rewards, conditions of employment, and performance expectations.

Every organization is a web of implicit contracts. Every time we enter a new organization, we also enter this web of contracts. How do we tell if these contracts are sound? Social contract ethics offers a standard: A contract is sound if the parties to the contract would enter the contract *freely* and *fairly*. Since social contracts are not explicitly negotiated, social contract ethics asks what parties *would* agree to in a hypothetical negotiation. Obviously, there is plenty of room for debate. The only acid test is an actual negotiation. But even if the basic contracts we live by will not be part of an actual negotiation, social contract ethics helps us judge whether contracts will support or thwart organizational change.

A contract has no standing unless the involved parties entered it, or would enter it, freely. *Freely* is open to interpretation. If I hold a gun to your head, you may freely give me $10,000 for one copy of this article. Your agreement was free in that it was not an involuntary reflex, such as twitching with fear. You could have refused and faced the consequences. But no one would criticize you for welching on this agreement.

It is for such reasons that employment by voluntary agreement fell into disrepute. Management used to argue that workers were not entitled to organize unions on the grounds that they were free to either enter into or not enter into an agreement to work for the company. David, however, was in no position to negotiate a fair deal with Goliath. Instead of blaming unfair *application* of employment by agreement and creating legal recourse, employment by agreement became the villain. As always, when a social contract is perceived by one group to be unfair, that group takes action (for better or worse) to restore perceived fairness. Unions were formed.

Social contract ethics addresses this point: Contracts must be both free and *fair*. A contract need not be fair in the sense that everyone fairs equally well under it. A contract allows people to pursue interests cooperatively or competitively, *without expectation that each*

342

party will reap the same rewards. The contract ensures that the involved parties understand the conditions of joint or competitive action and cannot cry foul if the outcome is not what they hoped for.

If you want to find out if the existing contracts in your organization are perceived as unfair, assume the position of the other affected parties and ask how you would view the contract. *If you want to find out if a change you would like to introduce shifts the social contract in ways that will be perceived as unfair, assume the position of the other affected groups and ask how you would view the contract.* There is a minor industry devoted to techniques for win-win negotiations. (Consult your mailbox.) If you grasp the simple turnabout-is-fair-play idea of this paragraph, you know the secret.

Motorola's middle managers initially resisted the participation program because they believed top management would not agree to work under it. The shift in the social contract created advantages for one side and disadvantages for another. This is the problem with many organizational changes. The changes shift the basic contracts by which the firm works. In bureaucratic organizations, even the hint of change breeds resistance. When the change disadvantages those who must implement it, the resistance is effective. Middle managers practice Gandhi's philosophy of passive resistance. If it worked against the British Empire, it will work against the personnel department.

Organization by Social Contract

While the social contract is an ethical concept, it contains a new model for implementing broad-based organizational change with a minimum of resistance and with a high likelihood of success. Like all new organizational forms, once we have the idea, we find organizations that have used it all along. We now look at two companies that used this idea over a period of time to manage change and to adapt.

Cadbury's Anticulture

Suppose you manage a multinational corporation based in Great Britain. You compete in an industry in which labor costs are crucial, labor is unionized, and production technologies are changing rapidly. Your chances of success? Small. These are the exact circumstances under which Cadbury Schweppes has managed strong, sustained success.

Cadbury Schweppes has done so by attending to little more than basic social contracts. Cadbury Schweppes' main products are confections and soft drinks. It is an old company. The Cadbury line of the company started in 1824, when John Cadbury opened a tea-and-coffee shop in Birmingham. Jacob Schweppes founded the Schweppes line in 1783. The present company resulted from a merger of Cadbury and Schweppes in 1969.

You would expect Cadbury Schweppes to have a strong culture. The company has always been run more or less in accordance with Quaker ethics of its Cadbury founders. A visit to corporate headquarters or to manufacturing facilities undercuts this expectation. There are few corporate symbols, none of the bells and whistles characteristic of strong-culture companies, and no need to do things "the Cadbury way."

While Cadbury Schweppes does not have a "strong-culture," it has an evident corporate philosophy. The philosophy is simple: The individual is to be fully respected, and all significant decisions are participatory.

This philosophy explains the lack of a strong culture. The individual is to sacrifice nothing except a commitment to work to the best of his or her abilities at Cadbury Schweppes. The culture of a Cadbury Schweppes operation fits the culture of the community in which it operates.

Cadbury Schweppes pays excruciating attention to basic agreements with managers, employees, suppliers, and customers. While this commitment to fair basic agreements has been expressed in a formal participation program since 1973, it has always been practiced. This manifests itself in countless meetings between top management and every level of manager and employee.

When management meets with employees, employees are given detailed candid information about the financial and operating issues. The thinking of management is offered, and the advice of all employees is sought. Advice is not sought in the suggestion-box mode. Employees are asked directly whether they agree with management and whether they have better ideas.

At one meeting, floor-level union officials chided top management for going to slowly in closing a dated facility and transferring operations to a more modern site requiring fewer employees. The atmosphere at such meetings is businesslike, with friendly banter and hard argument across ranks.

Despite its age, Cadbury Schweppes is an adaptive company. Since it can discuss its problems forthrightly, it can address them realistically. Because the basic contracts are fair, and expected to be fair, managers and employees speak up without fear. Everyone asks everyone hard questions. When managers at various levels are asked to discuss basic changes needed to stay competitive, there is none of the bristling and hedging apparent in virtually every corporation. Instead, forethought, confidence, and willingness to think things through is evident.

Core Investments

Consider now Core Investments, Inc. (fictional name), a small, extraordinarily successful stock brokerage. The company was founded by Roy Katz when he was already top producer in a large house. He objected to team-play hoopla, the necessity to sell a company-dictated product line, and the general lack of freedom. So he started his own firm based on a unique set of agreements.

Katz's agreement with his brokers is clear from the beginning. Their job is to sell successfully by any means they deem appropriate, within the limits of a very high ethics. Loyalty is actually discouraged; brokers are encouraged to find better offers elsewhere. The firm is confident that it is the best and that it can offer you the best deal if you deserve it. The outcome? Every broker is a star—and is paid full market value. If a broker makes it past the first two years, he or she will want to work at Core forever. The reason? The basic contract is fair, clean, and enables each individual to flourish in the way that is best for that individual. No loyalty is asked, brokers are essentially unmanaged, and there is no evaluation since you set your pay through performance. Core violates every rule of the culture-excellence-leadership movement and leads a high-ethics, no-culture, excellent firm.

Core weathered a near tragedy in its early and most vulnerable days. At the time, the company placed a strong emphasis on resource-based investments. Subsequently, many brokers were stung (although not as badly as their clients) when such investments turned bad. But Core had foreseen the problem and changed course in time. It did so because its brokers had argued for the change. They had been intensely critical of Roy Katz, attacking the heart of his investment philosophy. Consequently, the company took a course that was controversial but correct. Core is able to change to meet the rapid changes in its environment because its basic contracts align the interests of its key employees.

Cadbury Schweppes and Core Investments have consistently been able to adapt and change, because they manage the basic ethics ground rules, or social contracts, above all else. Because the agreements are fair, they work. This approach points the way to the future. As more work is done away from the shop floor or desk, management by culture will not work, for it requires a lot of personal contact. But management by fair social contracts requires minimal contact, and a fair deal is what we all seek. Companies that run by fair implicit contract can make abrupt and basic changes that are unthinkable in other organizations. Managers and workers can think outside the box, and the agreement-based firm can adapt quickly and even think the possibility of tragedy through.

Manage Ethics for Change

The lesson is clear. Forget culture and think about fairness. Think about the basic ground rules, or social contract, in your firm. Establish and stand by agreements that are good for you and the firm.

Be sure that you would work under the contract voluntarily. The thinking manager will ask, "If I were to occupy the position of a lower-level manager or employee, would I accept this as a fair basis for work?"

Can you find a fair approach every situation? Of course not. That is why it is so important that the underlying ground rules be sound. If they are, you can quit handing out "atta boys" looking like "atta bozo" and get on with the job of managing change.

Author Biographical Information

Susan D. Abbott currently serves as Associate Director in the Electric, Communications, and Speculative Grade Group of the Corporate Department at Moody's Investors Service, managing a group of analysts who follow electric and water utilities globally. She joined Moody's in June of 1982 as a senior analyst in the Electric Utility Group. In January of 1984, Abbott was named Associate Director in the Industrial Group. Following further assignments as Associate Director in the Financial Institutions Group, and Administrative Services, Abbott served as Associate Director and Vice President, International, in Moody's London office. After returning from London, she joined the electric utility group that she now heads. Prior to joining Moody's, Abbott was a Senior Investment Analyst at Aetna Life and Casualty in Hartford, Connecticut, lending to electric and gas utilities, as well as a group of varied, small industrial borrowers. She is a graduate of Syracuse University, and received an M.B.A. from the University of Connecticut.

Bruce E. Alspach holds a BSEE from Union College in Schenectady, New York. His career spans 20 years at General Electric and BFGoodrich, where he has held executive positions, completed management training programs, and implemented significant strategic and cultural change. He joined Trimble Navigation in 1994.

John J. "Jack" Barry, as the International President of the International Brotherhood of Electrical Workers (IBEW), has maintained the union's tradition of organizing, collective bargaining, and effective advocacy on behalf of the membership. He has also fostered new initiatives in education, human services, innovative organizing techniques, and communications. A second generation electrical worker, Barry is proud of the fact that the IBEW has worked with organized electrical contractors to create some of the finest training and development programs in the world. Barry has served on the boards of many labor, educational, and community bodies.

John R. Childress is President and Chief Executive Officer of Senn-Delaney Leadership Consulting Group, Inc., and has held his current position since 1978, when he and Dr. Larry Senn, chairman, co-founded Senn-Delaney Leadership. With more than 20 years experience in management consulting and leadership development, Childress personally coaches CEOs and management teams of "Fortune 1000" companies throughout the world.

Michele Darling is Executive Vice President of Human Resources for the Canadian Imperial Bank of Commerce (CIBC), one of the largest financial institutions in North America. She joined CIBC in November 1990 as Vice President, Human Resources, Corporate Bank. She was appointed Executive Vice President in 1991. Before joining CIBC, she held a number of senior positions within major Canadian companies, including Consumers Gas, General Foods, and The Oshawa Group. Darling graduated with a B.A. Honors from the University of Sydney, Australia, and earned her masters in Education from the University of Toronto.

William E. Davis became Niagara Mohawk's fifth Chairman and Chief Executive Officer in May 1993. He became the company's Vice Chairman in November 1992, and was named Senior Vice President of Corporate Planning in April 1992. He joined Niagara Mohawk as Vice President of Corporate Planning in 1990. Before joining Niagara Mohawk, Davis was Executive Deputy Commissioner of the New York State Energy Office from 1984-1990. He has served on several civic boards. Davis received a bachelor of science degree from the U.S. Naval Academy in 1964 and a master of science degree from George Washington University, Washington, D.C. in 1971.

Kenneth P. De Meuse, Ph.D., is Associate Professor of Management at the University of Wisconsin-Eau Claire. Previously, he was on the faculties of Iowa State University and the University of Nebraska. For the past decade, De Meuse had been investigating the "human side" of corporate restructuring and downsizing. More than 100 universities and 150 corporations have contracted him regarding his research in this area. He has appeared on Cable

News Network, Associated Press Radio, and National Public Radio and has been featured in *The Wall Street Journal, Industry Week, Across the Board, Business Week, U.S. News & World Report, The Washington Post,* and *USA Today* for his expertise on the impact corporate transitions have on employees. He has published numerous articles on employee attitudes and organizational behavior in several leading professional journals. De Meuse received his doctorate in Industrial/Organizational Psychology from the College of Business at the University of Tennessee.

Mark DeMichele is President and Chief Executive Officer of Arizona Public Service. (APS), an electric utility serving all or part of 11 of Arizona's 15 counties. In 1993, APS was awarded its industry's highest honor, The Edison Award, an annual, national award for a utility's significant contribution to the growth and development of the industry. Before moving to Arizona, DeMichele was a Vice President of the Niagara-Mohawk Power Corp. Besides his duties at APS, DiMichele is Chairman of the Edison Electric Institute CEO task force on global climate change and serves as Director for the National Environmental Education & Training Foundation, Inc. He is a 1955 graduate of Syracuse University.

Jean M. Dickson is a Senior Training Consultant in the Organization Development Department at Boston Edison Company, Boston, Massachusetts. The department provides training and development, organization development interventions, staffing, and compensation functions for the company. She works as an internal consultant to the Nuclear Organization and has facilitated other teamwork throughout the organization. Before joining Boston Edison, Dickson was employed by Dunn and Bradstreet Software Services, Inc., where she was a Project Leader and Training Consultant. Dickson received an M.Ed. from Lesley College, Cambridge, MA, where she was awarded a Commonwealth Fellowship. She graduated cum laude from the University of Maine with a B.S. degree in Psychology and Art.

Joe Doyle, Vice President, Senior Consultant for Senn-Delaney Leadership Consulting Group, specializes in energy services and manufacturing industries. He is an expert in using cultural transformation to assist companies in adjusting to major shifts in industry structure. Before joining Senn-Delaney, Doyle was in the Nuclear Regulatory Affairs Department of Southern California Edison. He received his B.S. in Nuclear Engineering from Arizona State University and an M.B.A. from the University of California, Irvine.

William G. Gang, a Principal at Tim D. Martin & Associates, has more than twenty years of professional experience in the electric utility industry. Before going into management consulting, Gang held key positions at ABB Combustion and General Electric. At Tim D. Martin & Associates, he specializes in strategic analysis, competitive planning, and cost reduction. A West Point graduate, Gang also holds an M.S. in Nuclear Engineering from Massachusetts Institute of Technology and an M.B.A. in Finance from Fairleigh Dickinson University.

J. Kimball Hansen has worked in corporate communications for the last 16 years. Among his employers have been Utah Power & Light Co. in Salt Lake City, Arizona Public Service in Phoenix, and Underwood, Jordan & Associates, a public relations firm in New York City. He graduated with a bachelor's degree in Public Relations and Organizational Communication from Brigham Young University in 1979. In 1990, he earned a master's degree in Mass Communication from the Walter Cronkite School of Journalism and Telecommunications at Arizona State University.

Scott A. Jacobson is Director of Strategic Change Management with Arizona Public Service (APS) in Phoenix, Arizona. He is charged with preparing APS and its employees for the new competitive era that utilities are facing. Jacobson has also served as Director of Corporate Relations for APS, heading APS' media relations, community outreach efforts, and advertising. He has worked for APS since 1985, and before joining APS he worked for 10 years in the publishing industry as a writer and an employee of Bantam Books and Dell Publishing. Jacobson is heavily involved in community activities and is known as a strong advocate of the arts throughout Arizona, having once served as Chairman of the Phoenix Arts Commission.

June T. Johnston is a Regional Manager at Decker Communications, Inc. in Los Angeles, California. She has 16 years of experience in marketing, sales, and sales management in the high technology and communications industries. Johnson graduated from the University of Colorado in 1978. Decker Communications, Inc., founded by Bert Decker, communications expert and best selling author of, *You've Got to be Believed to be Heard,* is a national communications consulting company headquartered in San Francisco, California.

Carolyn Kenady, a Consultant in Towers Perrin's Los Angeles office, specializes in the design and implementation of employee pay programs. Since joining Towers Perrin's compensation unit, she has worked on projects in compensation strategy, job evaluation, and incentive design. Kenady has served clients in aerospace, financial services, utilities, the service industry, and general industry in the design of employee pay programs. She also has conducted survey design and analysis for PG&E and SCEcorp. Before joining Towers Perrin, Kenady consulted to a number of not-for-profit organizations on salary, strategic, and organizational issues. Kenady has a B.A. magna cum laude from Yale University and an M.A. in Public Policy Studies from the University of Chicago. She is a member of the American Compensation Association.

Cynthia Larson-Schwartz, with Decker Communications, Inc., has 15 years of experience in the high technology and communications industries in sales, management, employee development, and strategic planning. Decker Communications, Inc., founded by Bert Decker, communications expert and best selling author of, *You've Got to be Believed to be Heard,* is a national communications consulting company headquartered in San Francisco, California.

James R. Leva was elected President and Chief Executive Officer of General Public Utilities Corporation (GPU) in January 1992. GPU is one of the 20 largest investor-owned utilities in the nation. Leva also is Chairman of GPU Nuclear Corporation and Chairman and Chief Executive Officer of all other major GPU subsidiaries.

Before joining GPU, Leva was President and Chief Operating Officer of Jersey Central Power & Light Company and President of Pennsylvania Electric Company. A graduate, magna cum laude, with a bachelor of science degree in Electrical Engineering, Leva completed post graduate and special utility courses in labor relations and executive management. He obtained his juris doctorate in 1980 and was admitted to the New Jersey Bar the same year.

Robert B. Marshall is founder and Principal of the Marshall Group, Inc. (MGI), a firm that specializes in major organizational change, headquartered in Scottsdale, Arizona. Before founding MGI in 1989, Marshall was Executive Vice President of Drake Beam Morin, Inc., where he directed the consulting resources to serve major corporate clients undergoing extensive organizational change. Marshall holds an M.B.A. from New York University and a B.S. degree in Marine Engineering from the State University of New York Maritime College.

Jack McGourty is a Principal and Vice President of Assessment Alternatives Inc., a management consulting firm located in Florham Park, New Jersey. He consults with senior management of major corporations on such areas as organizational development, team effectiveness, and new pay systems. Before holding this position, he was President and Chief Operating Officer of a medium-sized retail corporation. McGourty is an Adjunct Professor at the Department of Management and Engineering Management at Stevens Institute of Technology. He is a Senior Research Associate of Stevens Alliance of Technology Management. He is also the founder of the Team Research and Education Center (TREC). TREC provides companies with up-to-date information on innovative team practices through applied research and educational programs.

Dr. Cherry McPherson specializes in strategic planning and change management on both organizational and individual levels. McPherson has more than 20 years experience as a manager, consultant, trainer, and professor in the fields of education and organization development. Her management experience extends from front line supervision to administrative director in a number of industries, including retailing, utilities, health care, and education. She has served on the faculties of Ohio State University and the University of Georgia. McPherson has a doctorate in Education from the University of Georgia and is a graduate of the University Associates Human Resource Development Intern Program. She has published numerous articles on education and training. McPherson's current emphasis is developing integrative capacities within individuals and their organizations, including individual strategic planning, concentration skills, and integrated thinking skills.

Jim Ondrus is Senior Vice President, Partner and head of the energy services practice at Senn-Delaney Leadership Consulting Group, Inc. Ondrus provides a unique blend of executive coaching, consulting, strategic implementation, and expert facilitation skills to each client engagement. Ondrus has more than 16 years of corporate consulting experience, including eight years with Senn-Delaney Leadership. He graduated from the University of Akron, where he was awarded a graduate assistantship while working on a masters degree and was also selected to Omicron Delta Kappa, and the National Men's Leadership Honorary. He currently is an associate member of the American Gas Association and Southern Gas Association.

Joseph F. Paquette, Jr. is Chairman and Chief Executive Officer (CEO) of PECO Energy Company. He rejoined PECO Energy in March 1988 as President and Chief Operating Officer, and in April 1988 was elected Chairman and CEO. Paquette previously was employed by PECO Energy for 30 years. Paquette earned a bachelor's degree in Civil Engineering from Yale University in 1956. He completed various courses in finance, accounting, and economics at Temple University's Evening Graduate School. He serves on numerous professional and civic boards.

Mark J. Pastin, Ph.D., is President of the Council of Ethical Organizations and Senior Vice President of Strategic Management Systems. He has advised major corporations and government bodies worldwide since 1973. His book, *The Hard Problems of Management; Gaining the Ethics Edge* (1986, 1994) has been a best seller in the United States, Australia, and Brazil and is under current release in Japan. Pastin has served as advisor to both houses of Congress (House and Senate Ethics Committees) and to state, federal, and local legislatures and agencies in the U.S. and overseas. Pastin received his B.A. (summa cum laude) from the University of Pittsburgh and his Ph.D. from Harvard University (Lewis Award). He serves on several corporate and non-profit boards, and is recognized in *Who's Who in America, Who's Who in Finance and Industry,* and *Who's Who in the World.*

James R. Pearl is the Manager, Employee/Union Relations for the Louisville Gas and Electric Company, a subsidiary of LG&E Energy Corp. He has been with LG&E for 24 years, serving in corporate labor relations since 1981. Pearl serves on several community and professional boards and lectures at the University of Louisville business school. He is active with both the Edison Electric Institute and the American Gas Association labor relations committees. Pearl has a bachelor's degree in Political Science and a master's degree in Labor Relations from the University of Louisville.

Dr. Jo-Anne Pitera is Principal Consultant, Organizational Effectiveness and Staffing with The Southern Company in Atlanta, Georgia. The Southern Company is the parent of one of the nation's largest investor-owned electric utility groups. Pitera is the former Director of Corporate Education and Training at Florida Power & Light Company (FPL). Pitera joined FPL in 1991 from the consulting field. Under her leadership, FPL was nationally recognized for the "Promotion of Excellence in Organizations" through productivity, leadership, and empowerment by Clemson University. Pitera has more than 20 years experience as a trainer, presenter, and consultant. She is a licensed psychologist and received her doctorate from the Florida Institute of Technology and is a member of the American Psychological Association. She earned her master's degree in Counseling Psychology from Nova University, after graduating summa cum laude from the University of Lowell in Massachusetts.

Richard R. Reilly, Ph.D., is the President of Assessment Alternatives, Inc., a management consulting firm located in Florham Park,

New Jersey. Reilly has been a consultant to numerous public utilities, and is a widely published author in such areas as performance measurement and assessment. Previously, he was on the staff of AT&T, where he conducted research and helped to design compensation systems for both management and non-management jobs. Reilly is also a professor of management at Stevens Institute of Technology, where he heads the doctoral program in Industrial/Organizational Psychology.

Shirley Richard has held her current position with Arizona Public Service (APS) as Executive Vice President, Customer Service, Marketing, and Corporate Relations since 1989. She was APS' first female officer when she joined the company in 1984 as Vice President of Corporate Relations and Marketing. Today, she ranks among the top five women utility executives in the country. Before joining APS, Richard worked for the Adolph Coors Co. as Director of Corporate Communications and Director of Legislative Affairs. She is a Certified Public Accountant, and in that capacity, worked as a Manager for Price Waterhouse before joining Coors. In 1993, Richard became the first female to be elected Chairman of the Phoenix Chamber of Commerce. She is also active in utility and marketing organizations nationwide.

Donna Welch-Johnson is a Principal with CSC Consulting in their Philadelphia/Wayne office, where she is affiliated with their Utility Practice Group. She has several years of management consulting experience working both within and consulting to the electric utility industry in areas concerning strategic planning, business and process re-engineering, and wholesale power issues. Prior to CSC Consulting, Welch-Johnson worked with Public Service Electric & Gas, and Theodore Barry & Associates management consultants. She holds advanced degrees from the University of Pennsylvania.

Judy A. Zanotti is Vice President, Human Resources with Public Service Company of New Mexico. Before joining that organization in 1990, Zanotti served as Vice President, Human Resources and Staff Services with the Gas Company of New Mexico. She earned an M.A. in Special Education, with a specialization in learning disabilities and parent counseling, from the University of New Mexico and earned a B.S. degree in Business Education, with a minor in Government, from the University of New Mexico. Zanotti has served on numerous professional and civic boards. Among the awards she has received are the Mortar Board Lobo Award (1990), the UNM Student Service Award (1990), and the YWCA "Women on the Move" Award (1988).